YO-AFJ-224

The Name of Action

The Name of Action:
Critical Essays

John Fraser

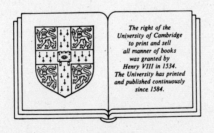

The right of the
University of Cambridge
to print and sell
all manner of books
was granted by
Henry VIII in 1534.
The University has printed
and published continuously
since 1584.

CAMBRIDGE UNIVERSITY PRESS

Cambridge

London   New York   New Rochelle

Melbourne   Sydney

Published by the Press Syndicate of the University of Cambridge
The Pitt Building, Trumpington Street, Cambridge CB2 1RP
32 East 57th Street, New York, NY 10022, USA
296 Beaconsfield Parade, Middle Park, Melbourne 3206, Australia

First published 1984

Printed in Great Britain by
Redwood Burn Limited
Trowbridge, Wiltshire

Library of Congress catalogue card number: 84–9624

British Library cataloguing in publication data
Fraser, John, *1928–*
The name of action.
1. English Literature – History and criticism
I. Title
820.9   PR401
ISBN 0 521 25876 6 hard covers
ISBN 0 521 27745 0 paperback

To Michael Black

And enterprises of great pitch and moment
With this regard their currents turn awry
And lose the name of action.

Hamlet, III, i, 86–8

Contents

Preface

These essays, which were assembled at the invitation of the publishers, were written between 1956 and 1973 and include most of my literary criticism. Some of them are virtually unchanged, in others I have done what I could to make the prose read more smoothly. However, I have not tried to bring any of them up to date or to rethink them with the wisdom, if that is what it is, of hindsight. For one thing, I still very largely agree with what I said at the time. And for another, when I wrote them I was at work on problems to which I did not have any neat answers, so that to attempt to redo, say, the discussion of *The Story of O* in the light of the subsequent sexual revolutions would be to sacrifice an important part of what that article is about, namely trying to find my bearings as a critic in what was then an uncharted region.

Putting the essays together has been a happy occasion for me, not only because some of them, such as the one on *Huckleberry Finn*, may now have a better chance at visibility, but also because of their relationship to my two previous books. *Violence in the Arts* (1974) and *America and the Patterns of Chivalry* (1982) had their beginnings in the essays, and the three books form a triptych. In all of them I was writing as someone who grew up in England but moved to America in the early fifties, and was trying to come to terms with conflicting 'English' and 'American' attitudes towards self-affirmation and social order. And the books complement each other in both substance and technique. In the essays I went deeper into the intricacies of individual works, some of them great ones, than I would do later, and what I learned by doing so emboldened me to move beyond the borders of literature. In one magical summer in the mid-sixties, passed in the French village described in the final essay, I wrote not only the essays on *The Tempest* and *Huckleberry Finn* but the one on Eugène Atget and also a very long essay that I subsequently expanded into *Violence in the Arts*. And after that book was done I went on, without at first realizing what I was getting myself into, to the large-scale cultural and historical explorations of

America and the Patterns of Chivalry, a book which is as much about the nature of sane peace as it is about the appeals of combat. I mention these things because I believe that the study and teaching of literature are important and that literary, social, and political concerns form a natural continuum. The essays are all self-sufficient discussions of their respective subjects, but there is a logic to their sequence and the book is more than a miscellany.

The provenance of the essays is as follows: 'Prospero's Book', *Critical Review* (1968); 'Dust and Dreams', *ELH* (1965); 'In Defence of Culture', *Oxford Review* (1967); '*Othello* and Honour', *Critical Review* (1965); 'The Name of Action', *Nineteenth-Century Fiction* (1965); 'Crime and Forgiveness', *Criticism* (1967); 'Rereading *The Death Ship*', *Southern Review* (1973); 'A Dangerous Book?', *Western Humanities Review* (1966); ''Yvor Winters', *Centennial Review* (1970); 'Mr Frye and Evaluation', *Cambridge Quarterly* (1967); 'Theories and Practices', *Review of English Literature* (1967); 'Atget and the City', *Cambridge Quarterly* (1968); 'Reflections on the Organic Community', *Human World* (1974). 'George Sturt's Apprenticeship' is a conflation of an article of that name in the *Review of English Literature* (1964) and 'Sturt and Class', *English Studies in Africa* (1967). The long Afternote on *The Turn of the Screw* was abstracted from '*The Turn of the Screw* Again', *Midwest Quarterly* (1966). 'Swift and the Decay of Letters' (1956) has not been published before. I wish to thank the journals concerned for permission to reprint the material that appeared in their pages and for having published it in the first place.

I would also like to express my gratitude to the following: to Michael Black of the Cambridge University Press, without whom these books would not exist and who made excellent suggestions about what to put in this one; to my colleague John Baxter, who likewise read more of my prose than anyone should have to and gave valued advice and encouragement; to P. R. Marsh and Maureen Leach of the Cambridge University Press for their considerateness during the production process; and to my wife Carol, who for years has wanted me to get out a book of essays, and who is a presence in these pages. I am in the debt, too, of three institutions that allowed me freedom to pursue questions that interested me, the first two as a student, the third as a teacher – Balliol College,

Oxford, in the late forties, the English Department of the University of Minnesota in the fifties, and my own Department, which has put up with me for almost a quarter of a century.

                                                            John Fraser

Dalhousie University,
Halifax, Nova Scotia

Introduction

> ... this eternal looking beyond appearances for the 'real', on the part of people who have never even been conscious of appearances.
>
> F. Scott Fitzgerald[1]

To speak of a philosophical dimension to these essays may seem presumptuous, given their almost embarrassing innocence of metacritical display. Apart from the remarks about Mr Frye, little or no formal theorizing goes on in them, and I have avoided professional jargons. Moreover, to suggest that I was in possession of any 'system' when I wrote them would be very misleading. I proceeded, as I still do, in an *ad hoc* fashion. I was trying to get things clearer for myself, and each of the works and topics discussed, with its nimbus of critical discourse and ideologies, presented its own kind of challenge, its own zones of puzzlement, of sensed but at times elusive significance. However, by the end of the series something had evidently been worked out, for I was able to stop doing literary criticism, at least of this kind, and go on to other things. So I will risk a few generalizations about what I was up to in the essays, with the recognition that I would not necessarily have put things at the time as I put them now.

Most of the essays were written while I was trying to find my bearings as a teacher after obtaining my doctorate at the University of Minnesota in 1961; and as readers of Frank Lentricchia's *After the New Criticism* will know, those were problematic years for literary criticism, particularly in North America. Actually, I am not sure that I altogether understand what is intended by the term New Criticism in some of the recent accounts of that period. After all, critics like Yvor Winters and F. R. Leavis were as productive during the forties and fifties as were ones like Cleanth Brooks, and to speak as Lantricchia and others do as if, dialectically, criticism *tout court* had arrived at certain impasses, or entangled itself in various nets of its own devising, seems to me simply untrue. But of course, as

Gerald Graff's *Poetic Discourse and Critical Dogma* reminds us,
certain opinions, amounting to an orthodoxy, were a good deal reiterated; and there were certain pressures and presences in those
years that I myself can recall finding particularly bothersome.

In one of Sergio Aragones's cartoons in *Mad Magazine*, a convict
in the obligatory striped uniform is enthusiastically burrowing his
way to freedom. What he doesn't know, and what the reader of
course does, is that the end of his impressive tunnel is now below sea
level and that only a few more inches of protective rock remain
between him and the water.[2] It is a nice paradigm (in more exalted
circles we see the same kind of thing in *Paradise Lost* when God and
the Son have a good smile together over Satan's unawareness of the
real game rules of the universe), and during the later fifties and early
sixties irony was an insistent presence in American criticism and
teaching. The neophyte looked at a seemingly obvious text and
ventured one or two obvious comments ('Well, I guess she's just
trying to be polite to him'). The initiate ('But what does the cup of
tea *symbolize*, Janey?') then demolished the obvious account and
replaced it with a very different one, thereby getting one-up on the
student. And the ironical revelation of error and misperception
became part of the substance of literature itself. Characters in fiction
were mistaken about their own motives and radically misperceived
the situations in which they found themselves. Readers continually
fell into pits dug for them by authors. The ostensibly earnest
comment was intended humorously; the seeming awkwardness was
actually very skilful; and behind every authorial mask there was a
very different face that only the critic had discerned. The tradition of
irony is of course still with us. Indeed, only last year I came upon a
writer in the *Village Voice* speaking of a current *de haut en bas* disposition to view 'the entire history of Western thought as a complex
evasion',[3] which sounds like intellectual one-upmanship with a
vengeance.

The disdain for appearances during my apprentice years was obviously partly a continuation of the New England allegorical
tradition: human feelings and doings – falling in or out of love,
fighting a war, and so on – did not become truly charged with
meaning and value until they had been translated into terms of
hidden but momentous patterns. And it also had analogies with the
seizing of the high ground by Marxists and Freudians which I had
experienced in my argumentative adolescence, and which involved

allegorizing the utterances of one's adversaries and explaining to
them what their statements 'really' meant, which was generally the
opposite of what they thought they were saying. But that did not
make it any the less bothersome, and it was understandable when
Susan Sontag called her first book of essays *Against Interpretation*,
in protest against the kind of critical thinking in which everything
was always really something else. In fictions like *The Pilgrim's
Progress*, or *Gulliver's Travels*, or Hawthorne's 'The Birthmark',
the tangible world stayed tangible, whatever else might be going on:
castles were castles, birthmarks birthmarks, cups of tea cups of tea.
In allegorical criticism, in contrast, there was a curious destabilizing
and devaluing of that world, an opening-up into a simultaneously
less substantial and more 'real' reality behind the kinaesthetic realities of albino whales sounding, chilly mid-Victorian London
chambers, and the various other things that keep us reading in order
to find out what happens next and which contribute to our sense of
the continuing presentness of the works in which we encounter
them. 'Moby Dick is the mind of God', 'The spectral twin coat
buttons of Marley's ghost are Scrooge's suppressed libido' – in such
statements there was something almost black-magical about the use
of the copula and the primacy assigned by it to the intangible. And
so there was too about some of the related conferring of physicality
on the non-physical that went on and that Theodore Spencer
captured so nicely in the forties in his pseudo-exegesis of 'Thirty
Days Hath September'. February, as he explained with just the right
earnestness,

is 'alone', is cut off from communion with his fellows. The tragic note is
struck the moment 'February' is mentioned. For the initial sound of the
word 'excepting' is 'X', and as that sound strikes the sensibility of the
reader's ear a number of associations subconsciously accumulate. We think
of the spot, the murderous and lonely spot, which 'X' has so frequently
marked; we remember the examinations of our childhood where the wrong
answers were implacably signaled with 'X'; we think of ex-kings and exile,
of lonely crossroads and executions, of the incurable anonymity of those
who cannot sign their names.[4]

Alas, poor X! Alas, poor eccentric criticism!
   These essays too, then, were in some ways essays against interpretation. For me the behaviour of the characters in most of the
works that I discussed did not stand in need of allegorizing in order
to acquire meaning. It had it already; the problem was to describe it

accurately, in the same way that we try to be accurate about the behaviour of people whom we have dealings with or hear about. But
the idea of accuracy here did not entail any aspiration to comprehensiveness or any mysterious intuiting of essences. It seemed plain to
me that by and large we piece fictional characters together, as we do
real ones, from the variegated bits and pieces of information about
them that become available to us, and with the recognition that
there are huge gaps in our knowledge and that errors and perplexities may always be possible. And the fact of that possibility need not
throw us into a state of chronic doubt and scepticism, any more than
it does in daily life. The fact that in a particular situation we may be
unable to decide whether someone is being insulting when she asks a
guest if he would prefer wine or tea – which is to say, to 'interpret'
her words, her tone of voice, her facial expression in a more com-
monsensical but not necessarily simpler sense of the term – does not
mean that no one else could have done so or that we couldn't have
done so ourselves if we had possessed more knowledge. In everyday
life, by and large, we are engaged in trying to make more substantial, rather than transform, what we see and learn about – to refine
upon an initial impression rather than reverse it, or clarify a puzzlement rather than dismiss it as a pseudo-problem – and our
conclusions about what other people feel and think make it clear
that there is a middle ground between the kind of reifying in which
each bit of behaviour is treated as an index to a homogenous inner
state, and the disintegrative free-associating parodied in the passage
by Spencer. To say that we cannot know everything about someone
is not to say that we can know nothing. What we 'know', whether
about a friend, or a fictional character, or the creator of that character, is in a sense what we 'see' – this social gesture, that letter, those
poems – and the things thus seen go on connecting up with each
other in a complicated, loose, and sometimes perplexing fashion,
and can be discussed with other people. I am aware that there are
other and valid ways of reading a work. I am talking about the spirit
in which I myself was reading when I wrote these essays.

All this bore for me on the question of the kinds of knowledge that
could be acquired from a work. I myself had never, at least since
childhood, been afflicted with what Jacques Leenhardt calls 'the
sacred awe we feel in France toward *the* text – an awe cultivated by
our educational system',[5] and I could not perceive the wisdom of
the various demands for surrender to a text that are epitomized

in Georges Poulet's statement in 1970, 'When I read as I ought – that is without mental reservations, without any desire to preserve my independence of judgment, and with the total commitment required of any reader – my comprehending becomes intuitive and any feeling proposed to me is immediately assumed by me.'[6] They struck me, in fact, as being so flagrantly at odds with our dealings with all the other bits of discourse that we encounter daily as to be a recipe for disintegration. And I had no desire to dwell in that curious zone of magic and mystification, with its compulsive dichotomizing ('prose/poetry', etc.)[7] and its talk about non-referentiality and organic unity, wherein literature supposedly exists in sharp separation from all other modes of discourse. It seemed plain enough, furthermore, that once magical boundaries and taboos were disposed of, and along with them the aspiration to locate the meaning of a work in the innermost recesses of its author's mind, works of literature were as capable as ones of history, or political science, or philosophy of furnishing knowledge about the world that we all inhabit and have to make our way in. If it was natural for critics to invoke philosophers at various points, this was because the parallels were mutually reinforcing and not because the literary works stood in need of metaphysical validation. However, while distinguished plays and distinguished works of history or philosophy could illuminate, say, the will to domination or the hunger for order in ways that complemented each other because they were not radically different from each other, the procedures of literature with respect to ideas, especially philosophical and political ones, had their own distinctive features.

In one of his essays from the sixties, Roland Barthes divides criticism into 'academic' criticism – principally investigations of the genesis of works – and 'interpretative' criticism, which is to say criticism engaged in operating on works in terms of one or other of the then dominant ideologies – psychoanalysis, Marxism, Existentialism, phenomenology.[8] It appeared to me, however, that in distinguished literature the abstractions of ideologies were tested out in terms of the concretions of individual experience, rather than vice versa. Literature showed us individuals in action, doing things with consequences for themselves and others. And as Shakespeare above all had demonstrated, it was possible to trace complex connections between philosophical or political convictions and the flesh-and-blood conduct towards others of representative individuals in representative situations. In these respects literature, some of it anyway, paralleled the continuum of 'abstract' intellection and 'concrete' behaviour in the writings of philosophers like Plato, Kierkegaard, Spinoza, and Nietzsche. A regrettable aspect of the hunger of some American academics for metaphysics without ethics — a hunger related, no doubt, to the persisting sense of the creative writer as someone who ventures into the depths and returns with a unique kind of knowledge — is that it separates intellection from the demands of action in which some of the testing-out of ideas occurs.

In contrast to that dissevering, the world dealt with in these essays, and in the works discussed in them, is one in which actions matter a lot. In it people have or seek power over others or resist the claims of others to power over them, the problems they face are given rather than chosen, and the decisions that they make about them can have irreversible consequences, sometimes literally life-or-death ones. But it is not on that account a merely Hobbesian or Sadean battleground of power relationships, and it cannot be collapsed into naturalism. In a theoretical article elsewhere I compared the difference between two conceptions of art to

that between modern scientific investigation and scientific investigation as it was conceived of in the mid-nineteenth century. In the latter, the explorer pushes out into a homogenous and essentially unmysterious universe in which the dignity possible to individual men is oddly diminished. In the former, it is many different kinds of explorations that are made, and the explorations themselves, in so far as they are done intelligently and accurately, help to construct, in a task without foreseeable limits, the human universe that we inhabit.[9]

In that world or universe of individual consciousnesses, a multiplicity of value-systems overlap and furnish people with justifications for their conduct, and the relationships between thought and action are in fact more complex than the model of 'concrete' action and 'abstract' thought suggests. Values exist not only as propositions and prescriptions but as embodiments and enactions, and individuals are drawn forward by images of future bliss or woe derived from their past experiences, including their experiences of fiction, written or spoken. It seems to me a Shakespearian world, it feels like our own, and part of what bothered me about the derealizing and devaluing that I spoke of above was its weakening of what in *East Coker* T. S. Eliot refers to as 'the motive of action'.

In a review-essay on *Deconstruction and Criticism*, Gerald Graff quotes a reference by H. G. Schenk to 'the paradoxical double attitude of a near nihilism coupled with the most fervent yearning for the conquest of nihilism that lies at the very heart of the [Romantic] movement'.[10] If the present essays are in some ways essays against interpretation, they also seem to me in retrospect to have been essays against nihilism. I don't mean that they are innocently affirmative or positive with respect to ideals. On the contrary, a number of them are concerned with the harmful consequences of idealism and with the dangers attendant on our hunger for grace and energy and order; and I was very conscious of how such dangers, when viewed through ironical eyes, may seem to furnish grounds for dismissing all aspirations to a greater fullness of being. I was especially conscious of the characteristically American pattern, on display in writers like Hawthorne and Melville and Hemingway, in which a heroic intensity of aspiration leads to overstrain and collapse and to the invasion of the mind by a vision of blankness and meaninglessness, the vision articulated in Wallace Stevens' 'The Man Whose Pharynx Was Bad', the vision described by that American-influenced author E. M. Forster during the performance of Beethoven's Fifth Symphony in *Howards End*, when all the splendour of life and art seemed to 'boil over and waste to steam and froth ... and a goblin, with increased malignity, walked quietly over the universe from end to end. Panic and emptiness! Panic and emptiness!' But though chaos may always be near for some of us, its triumph did not seem to me inevitable, any more than it did to Forster, who did not endorse the goblin vision.

As I have suggested, a consequence of the craving for a realer-than-real reality behind or beyond the human realities that I have talked about, or of an obsessive questioning of the status of such a reality, is that it leaves so large a middle ground unoccupied and undefended. The recent Franco-American preoccupation with freedom and 'bliss', for example, with its yearning to escape from the everyday claims of consciousness into a region of pain-free sporting, seems fundamentally unsociable in its rejection of bonds, including the bonds of scrupulous dialogue; and its devaluing of social structures and implicit licensing of infantilistic egotism make things easier for the dominators and predators who prosper in a Hobbesian or Sadean world. But a desire for grace and energy and order, and a fondness for images of them, including obviously fictional ones, does not have to draw us away from the world of action or result in what I call at one point a 'stultifying contrasting of Edenic ideals and barren actualities'. If a good deal of watchfulness about power relationships and about the possibility of self-deception is obviously called for, the images of happiness that have traditionally moved people forward into action do not have to be at odds with the realities of the will to power and can be at once social *and* liberative. The mundane can have its heroic aspects, self-affirmation can be more than merely personal, and there can be an agonistic order that is not characterized either by overt domination and submission or by the masked dominativeness of neopastoral niceness and blandness. Likewise, there can be intellectual and artistic relationships in which individuals become more free and more themselves by willingly assimilating some of the ideas and procedures of others.

It is not for me to say how persuasively such possibilities emerge in these essays. I am not sure that I could, anyway, and writing an introduction is a risky enough business as it is. But they are implicit in them and in the sequence in which they are arranged; and they are at the centre of *America and the Patterns of Chivalry*.[11]

I

Prospero's Book:
The Tempest Revisited

In an essay some years ago, Mr Leo Marx very composedly did what a number of other people had probably considered doing but turned away from for fear of seeming gimmicky; he discussed *The Tempest* as, in effect, an American play.[1] There was of course nothing gimmicky about his discussion. He wrote as a student of American culture who was at home among the relevant Elizabethan and Jacobean documents, and he showed convincingly that in *The Tempest* Shakespeare was at work on problems that had been receiving a sharper definition in contemporary writings about the American continent, and that his handling of them looked forward in various ways to their handling by American writers a couple of centuries later. Such a transcending of categories was long overdue. If nineteenth-century American literature is the most challenging body of literature in English since the Renaissance, this is obviously partly because some of the same major questions are explored in both – questions such as the respective demands of selfhood and community, the authority of tradition, the anatomy of evil, the workings and worth of conscience, the claims of action and contemplation, the function of violence, the nature of the 'natural', and the metaphysical basis of moral choices. Anything that can illuminate the resemblances and differences between the two groups of explorations is therefore greatly to be welcomed. Indeed, we have probably reached a point where neither can be studied with full profit without a strong consciousness of the other.

That said, however, I am inclined to wonder whether the importance of Mr Marx's essay may not lie rather in the general kind of pointing that goes on in it than in the detailed analysis that he engages in. Given the almost hypnotically cool charm of *The Tempest*, and the gratifications it so insidiously offers our pastoral yearnings, we must of course be grateful that Mr Marx has reminded us so freshly of the tough intelligence deployed in it on major problems of social organization. The besetting weakness of criticism of the play, where it has not been to succumb to the

magical aspects and pastoralize around those, has been to approximate the play to *The Winter's Tale* and pastoralize around what
seem to be the Christian ones. And to take either of those
approaches, it seems to me, is to miss virtually the whole significance of the play. As Mr Jan Kott has said, 'Like all great
Shakespearian dramas, [*The Tempest*] is a passionate reckoning
with the real world.'[2] Yet Mr Marx's account of that reckoning is a
curiously unsatisfying one, and its limitations emerge more clearly
when we turn to Mr Kott's chapter on the play in *Shakespeare Our
Contemporary*. It is true that nothing Mr Marx says conflicts
directly with Mr Kott's thesis that in *The Tempest* we see 'a wonderful, cruel and dramatic world, which suddenly expose[s] both the
power, and the misery, of man; a world in which nature and history,
royal power, and morality, have for the first time been deprived of
theological meaning'.[3] Furthermore, Mr Marx too places a very
salutary emphasis on the importance of *power* in the play. Yet for all
that, his essay is still not far enough from what Mr Kott dismisses as
the 'romantic and idyllic interpretation of *The Tempest* as a play of
forgiveness and reconciliation with the world'.[4] It is all very well for
Mr Marx to say composedly that 'so far as the play affirms the
pastoral ideal of harmony, it draws upon Shakespeare's sense of an
underlying unity that binds consciousness to the energy and order
manifest in unconscious nature'.[5] A steady and intelligent exercise
of power, however, is dependent on a firm set of beliefs, and *The
Tempest* seems to me to go almost as far as *Moby Dick* or *The
Blithedale Romance* in subverting those 'certain certainties' that
have traditionally sustained most men of good will. It is, in fact,
much more 'American' than Mr Marx allows for.

Yet it is also plain that, for all the brilliance of his commentary,
Mr Kott's dominant concern to 'interpret *The Tempest* as a great
Renaissance *tragedy* of lost illusions' (italics mine)[6] is remarkably at
odds with the tone of what is perhaps the most serenely poised of all
Shakespeare's masterpieces. And in the rest of these pages I shall try
to define more carefully than either Mr Marx or Mr Kott those
features of it that are *potentially* deeply disturbing, and to account
for why they do not in fact disturb us. It seems to me of some consequence that Shakespeare, working in so 'American' an area, was
able to avoid what have the look at times of being unavoidable
pitfalls in it.

Let me indicate some of the main points of my analysis. Because of its artificiality *The Tempest* is the most naturalistic of Shakespeare's plays; because of its marvels it is the least numinous; because of its orderliness it takes us the farthest into a universe without moral order. What are now thought of as old-fashioned critics used to speak of the play, with considerable reason it seems to me, as Shakespeare's farewell to his art. Equally I think that we can reasonably follow Mr Kott and see it as an implicit farewell to, a whole area of what we are now all familiar with as the Elizabethan world-picture. What we are shown in the play is a picture of existence in which traditional values and truths are no longer supported by any demonstrations by the course of events – a picture, in fact, that may fairly be termed existential in contrast to the whole strong idealizing or Platonizing thrust in the English Renaissance. Nevertheless it is being presented without protest and without 'blackness', and the reason, paradoxically, would seem to be that Shakespeare is no longer questing for tokens that there is indeed something in some sense 'out there' which corresponds to the constructions we make and validates them morally. The poise of the play is that of someone who has travelled so far in thought that he has come back once more to the solidities of action. Everything, or almost everything, is where it was before and as important as before – love, justice, compassion, self-control, civic order, a decent humility in the face of Providence, even religious belief – and right action is still largely what it always was, namely the steady use of our intelligence and the deliberate application of our will in the knowledge that these are all that we have and that without them disaster can come. The key to all this is the centrality of Prospero.

Regrettable as was that famous note of T. S. Eliot's about Tiresias, I shall borrow from it and say that what Prospero 'sees' is the substance of the play – and this, paradoxically, because Prospero is the antithesis of an Eliotic or Jamesian central consciousness. His rather prickly separateness from us, as from Miranda, is established in the second scene of the play, and at no subsequent point do we get taken any deeper into the felt and inwardly argued reasonings leading up to his actions. We are shown him manipulating people; we are shown him behaving mercifully; we are shown him finally relinquishing his magic powers to rejoin a society composed of people like those whose representative conduct he has watched in the course of the play, and committing himself once more to a mode of existence whose limitations have likewise been implicitly sketched in the play. His actions, however, are those of someone whose thoughts have already been brought to a high degree of order and who can articulate his plans and decisions with only the most perfunctory appeals to general principles. And these aspects of him are the opposite of the faults that they are sometimes taken as being. If Prospero's long exposition to Miranda wrenches us away from whatever straightforwardly empathetic responses the turmoil aboard the apparently foundering ship has evoked in us, it also wrenches us toward Prospero's own viewpoint. The sudden slackening of normal dramatic tension at the start of the second scene – a slackening coming partly from the revelation that it is Prospero himself who has created the storm, partly from the unusual orderliness of the exposition, which is echoed in the orderliness of the play as a whole, and partly from the very staginess of the scene – is in fact replaced by a different kind of tension. Prospero's power and determination are evinced compellingly enough in the second scene, especially in his dealings with Caliban, for the question of what he will do to the criminals he now has in his grasp to be a real enough one for dramatic purposes. However, the more important question that is raised by his exposition, with its air of assured moral certainty, is how the court party *ought* to be dealt with, and according to what principles. But, as I have said, we are given very little in the way of clear pointers to what is going on in his mind in the course of the play. And hence, especially if we feel that he acts correctly, we are compelled to fill in the interstices and to consider or reconsider the human realities in the play as seen from his uniquely God-like and almost 'authorial' point of view. More precisely, our problem with the play is to come to terms not with agitations but with calms – the relative calm of Prospero's acceptance of the human world that he gazes on, and the more absolute calm of Shakespeare's own gaze in the play.

The world that is unfolded to Prospero's eyes and ours and that Prospero accepts when he relinquishes his magical powers is, as I have said, potentially a highly disquieting one – as disquieting potentially as that which we encounter in *Moby Dick*. The kind of Christianizing English criticism that happily places the stress on forgiveness and reconciliation seems to me to misrepresent it radically, and I find it ironical that even Mr Marx, writing so much as an American, should in the first version of his essay have commented in the same old vein that Prospero's 'aim is reconciliation . . . we move from storm to calm, from discord toward harmony. In the end we are shown the possibility of man's earthly transfiguration.'[7] *The Tempest* isn't *The Eumenides*; it isn't even *As You Like It*. Indeed, it is as unlike *As You Like It* in its 'resolution' as it is possible for a nominal comedy to be, and Mr Kott has a good deal on his side when he says that its ending 'is more disturbing than that of any other Shakespearean drama'.[8] True, Prospero and Alonso are reconciled. True, too, Miranda and Ferdinand are going to be married and appear to have an excellent chance of finding happiness together – not that they were exactly estranged from each other to begin with. But what stands out most prominently at the close of the play is the undiminished *irreconcilabilities*. Antonio and Sebastian remain what they have been throughout, so in essentials do Stephano and Trinculo, so does Caliban.[9] And there has been none of the implicit validating of traditional moral values that goes on in almost all the previous plays.

That Shakespeare's plays have so frequently been taken as bearing encouraging witness to a natural moral order is understandable enough. In the great comedies and in the run of the histories from *Richard II* to *Henry V*, the noble aria-like generalizations about love and honour and mercy and justice and order are largely supported by the observed events. They are not the only kinds of generalizations, and the support is not always wholly convincing (as witness the formalizing that brings *As You Like It* to a happy close after the sombreness implicit in the first couple of acts). But after all the necessary cognizance has been taken of dialectical interplays, the fact remains that the journeys in the comedies *do* end in lovers meeting, even if sometimes with the assistance of sleight of pen, and that honourable behaviour is displayed movingly in the last act of *Henry IV Part I*, and that a return to the traditional conception of the good kingdom in *Henry V* eliminates the misfortunes that have been caused by departures from it. And when we turn to the major tragedies it is clear that even though such concepts as love and honour and duty are being probed far more deeply, various actions still have virtually inevitable consequences. The consequences now are largely a matter of punishments rather than rewards, but we can still reasonably feel invited to talk about 'essential human nature' (to use Mr L. C. Knights' term) and to believe that the traditional values somehow correspond to a larger order of things, even in *King Lear*. Edgar's conventional Christian moralizings are by no means adequate to the whole run of events in that play, of course; his answer to Gloucester's voiced despair consists of a trick and some dazzling lies, and even in terms of the play he is simple-minded about the consequences of 'lust'. Yet in a sense *King Lear* does indeed demonstrate that 'the gods are just, and of our pleasant vices / Make instruments to plague us'. And it is understandable that Mr Derek Traversi should have been moved to declare that

All through the tragedies the first consequence of evil has been anarchy and its motive the overthrow of natural 'degree' by the dominating force of passion. 'Degree', in its turn, is associated with the two human institutions, the family and the body politic. These institutions are based, in the widest sense of the word, upon reason and are the foundation of a civilized, moral way of living; and it is only when passion in the individual overcomes reason and aims at the destruction of these institutions that evil enters society.[10]

In *The Tempest*, in contrast, violations of traditional patterns of order are not presented to us as entailing any necessary consequences at all. Where 'passion' is concerned, it is true that Prospero's desire to impress upon the young lovers the need for observing due forms appears to derive as much from an awareness of the heartbreak that can occur when they are disregarded (as with Dido and Aeneas) as from a sense of moral beauties that are made possible by a formalized relationship of sex to society and to larger moral systems. But there is not only no demonstration of disastrous consequences, there are no grounds for thinking that there would have been any for Miranda and Ferdinand had they consummated their love in the nearest cave. And where far more serious violations are concerned, it is plain that Alonso and Antonio have been doing very nicely since their dethronement and (so far as they know) murder of Prospero, and that Antonio and Sebastian would flourish no less, and be no less free of pangs of conscience, after the projected murder of Alonso. In other words, if there is any lesson to be drawn from the argument of events, it points us in completely the 'wrong' direction. Or rather, it is simply that though there are disrupters, usurpers, and murderers (direct or oblique) who make a mess of things and are more or less miserable, like Brutus or Bolingbroke or Macbeth, there are others – and more convincingly, given the remarkable *ordinariness* of the characters in *The Tempest* – who don't and aren't.

Furthermore, the whole structure of events in the play works against the notion of the 'body politic' that Mr Traversi invokes. That the normal social order has been disrupted by the tempest summoned up at Prospero's command is a commonplace – but I am not at all sure that it *ought* to be. To describe things in terms of a disruption of something pre-existing is to misrepresent significantly what we actually see in the play. What we are shown in the opening scene is simply people on a ship in a storm. True, some of them believe that deference should be paid to them on account of positions that they have enjoyed hitherto; but what *we* are conscious of above everything else is the brilliantly evoked violence of the storm, the overriding existential logic of its claims on the men battling it, and the irrelevance of social distinctions in the face of the imminent and overwhelming disrespect of death. And from then on the emphasis continues to be all on individuals facing a common problem – the island – rather than on people filling pre-existing roles in a social structure and to some extent validating that structure intellectually. In previous plays such validation goes on most of the time. Prince Hal, for instance, is obviously never for a moment away from his role as heir-apparent, even while fluctuating between heir-apparent-in-revolt and heir-apparent-answering-the-call-of-duty; he never becomes simply someone in love or a man worrying because his hair is starting to thin out. Othello, *qua* lover, is still steadily enmeshed in his role as general, both in its practical and in its ideal aspects. Macbeth, Lear, Hamlet – at every point, again, the pre-existing roles exert their pressure and the intensely rendered individual consciousnesses are as real as they are partly because of the intensity with which the roles are responded to. That this was not an inevitable dramatic pattern we have a play like *The Duchess of Malfi* to remind us: the Cardinal there might just as well have been an ordinary nobleman for all the difference his cardinalship makes in the play. And in *The Tempest*, likewise, with the exception of Gonzalo, there is no important correlation between the ways the characters' minds work and the roles that they formerly occupied. Alonso is grieving as a father, not as a king; Antonio may wish for his own ends to have Sebastian become king, but the way in which he argues and Sebastian responds could obtain in a number of social situations; and where Stephano and Trinculo are concerned, the fact that one has been a butler and the other a jester is irrelevant to their murderous plannings; they could, I mean, have as easily been a cook and a scullion, for all the difference it would make to their thought processes. Furthermore, until the final scene the general idea of degree is in abeyance where our awareness of the court group is concerned, partly because of the withholding from the group of even the most minimal opportunity to exercise its common authority against social inferiors, partly because members of the group don't invoke the idea against each other, partly because the key hierarchical figure is so little 'there' for us except as a grief- and guilt-stricken father, and partly because as soon as the plotting begins we realize how vulnerable Alonso is as a man and how totally he is without any numinous protection (such as Duncan's for a short while) against the plotters.

And we are not even in a familiar and reassuring world where the supernatural is concerned. The island may have a good deal of the supernatural about it, but the supernatural elements, where they aren't directly under the control of the very human Prospero, don't connect up with a coherent moral world-picture. Unlike the fairies in *A Midsummer Night's Dream*, who exist for us as essentially 'human' beings whose unusual powers are exerted in and around a normal courtly hierarchical social context for familiar motives, Ariel is a being of pure non-moral energy, and the other spirits take from him whatever tincture of definition they have for us. And apparently so little justice obtains in their world that only the chance intervention of Prospero prevented Ariel from being kept groaning in his tree until the end of time. Furthermore, the supernatural effects on the island work ironically *against* the conventional religious moralizing note struck by Gonzalo. Gonzalo's feelings towards the wonders of the island may be proper and decent in the light of what he himself sees, but we ourselves know what lies behind those wonders, including the organ-notes of Ariel's harpy speech. And given the pervasive clear realism of texture even in Caliban's celebration of the island's music, there would seem to be no space anywhere for the trumpet-tongued angels of Macbeth's universe. Nor do the skies darken or birds and beasts comport themselves ominously because of impending crimes. The island, so tangibly *there*, remains unchanged throughout; and indeed the very notion of natural ominousness comes close to being excluded for us at the outset by our discovery that what looked in the first scene like one of the darkest and most awesome manifestations of non-human forces was in fact under the control of a quite ordinary, even if in some ways very powerful, human being. In a sense, indeed, things don't happen of themselves in the play at all but are *made* to happen, and hence cannot be moralized into any conventional causal pattern.

I suggest, therefore, that *The Tempest* brings out a certain duplicitousness in the notion of reason as invoked by Mr Traversi. Two of the assumptions underlying Mr Traversi's use of the term are evidently that the *truly* reasonable is reasonable because it is in accordance with the natural order of things, and that the naturalness of that order is demonstrated by Shakespeare by means of the causal relationships that I sketched above. Now, that Shakespeare himself was engaged in trying to make such a demonstration in most of the plays before *The Tempest* seems clear enough, and most of the time he succeeded, at least in his own terms. Not only does crime not pay, but most of the criminals themselves pay tribute to the values in terms of which they are condemned. Claudius is an obvious example, so is Othello, so is Macbeth; indeed, the three of them do more to vitalize the traditional Christian notions of guilt and redemption in their soliloquies than do the speeches of those who pull them down. And in the case of the three worst villains of all, the weaknesses in their own natures testify scarcely less strongly to the instability of their own brands of rationality. Iago is clearly a prey to uncontrollable, if disguised, neurotic passions and fears; so are Goneril and Regan; and all three are driven forward by their emotions in ways that blind them to vital aspects of their situations, especially the reactions of the ordinary decent people upon whose continuing good will they are dependent. Yet, soothing as all the consolidating of normal values is, there is one figure in the plays preceding *The Tempest* who remains essentially unrefuted in either of these fashions. Edmund's cheerful and articulate amoralism in *King Lear* isn't effectively undercut by his perfunctory last-minute gesture of repentance, and though it is true that he has bad luck with the particular company he gets into in the play, there seems no reason why he couldn't have had perfectly good luck elsewhere and got along absolutely swimmingly. Mr Traversi has suggested that the fact that

the whole series [of the last plays] forms a close artistic unity is clearly revealed in the pattern discernible in the respective plots of the plays. At the heart of each lies the conception of an organic relationship between breakdown and reconciliation, between the divisions created in the most intimate human bonds by the action of time and passion and the final healing of these divisions.[11]

It seems to me, rather, that what happens in that series is that Shakespeare passes from the organic world of *The Winter's Tale*, in which everyone exists inside and pays homage to a single moral system, to a world in *The Tempest* in which the implications of the possible existence of an Edmund have at last been accepted. We may indeed prefer Prospero's value-system to Antonio's; we may feel that Alonso is perfectly right to be stricken with remorse after Ariel's harpy speech; we may find the Epilogue one of the most moving expressions of traditional religious faith in the whole range of Shakespeare's work. But the ultimate validation is denied to such preferences by the play itself: there would be no way of winning an assent to them, or even an acknowledgment of revealed weaknesses in his own position with respect to them, by the sort of rationalist represented by Antonio. Mr Traversi's 'reason', in other words, has become simply one mode among others of reasoning about existence.

And this is why the relationship between Prospero and Caliban is so important, for in it the notion of justice as a kind of transcendent entity has ceased to apply and what remains is simply a struggle for power. Prospero is a civilized human being with a charming daughter, and the thought of Miranda's being raped by Caliban, like the thought of her being raped and taken over by Stephano after the projected murder of Prospero, is shocking. But to claim that Prospero stands for order in a way that somehow transcends and annihilates the very different claims of Caliban would be simply untrue to what we see. Caliban is outside Prospero's moral system altogether, and though we can perfectly comprehend Prospero's indignation at Caliban's ingratitude for being treated decently at first and taught to talk, we can equally well comprehend Caliban's refusal to play within the rules that Prospero has set up and that so obviously favour Prospero. Why *should* he feel grateful? The island may appear to Mr Marx to have been a 'howling desert' before Prospero's arrival, but it was Caliban's island and it suited him very well. The basic fact is that there has been a struggle for power in which one of the two contenders on the lonely island has come out on top because of his superior intelligence; and even though it is with a seasoning of moral judgements that Prospero has the punitive torments administered to Caliban, it is still a ruthless exercise of the will that we witness in the great exchange in the second scene and not a valid refutation of Caliban's position.

What I am leading up to, of course, is that the relationship between Prospero and Caliban is characteristic of what obtains in the play as a whole. It is a play, in other words, in which we are acutely conscious of thrusting individualities striving after power, and for the first time in Shakespeare the low-life characters are as potentially sinister and dangerous as the socially superior ones. But for his magic powers, I mean, Prospero would be every bit as dead at the hands of Stephano and Trinculo as Alonso would be at the hands of Antonio and Sebastian. The normal social machinery, with all its implicit validations of the idea of order, has gone. There is an island and there are beings on it, and power is willy-nilly going to go to the strongest. If there is any one thing that events can be taken as saying unambiguously in the play, it is that; and the fact seems to me to carry over by implication to the so much more solid social order that the group came from and will be returning to. Prospero formerly ignored the first necessity for a ruler and failed to keep order, and when Antonio and Alonso reached after his power the heavens didn't flash out their wrath in his defence; Prospero on the island, having ineluctably to retain control or perish, retains control; Prospero after his return to Milan will presumably be keeping a pretty shrewd eye turned on Antonio, without any illusions as to the latter's attitude any more than as to Caliban's. As Mr Kott puts it,

Prospero's narrative [in the second scene] is a description of a struggle for power, of violence and conspiracy. But it applies not only to the dukedom of Milan. The same theme [is] repeated in the story of Ariel and Caliban. Shakespeare's theatre is the *Theatrum Mundi*. Violence, as the principle on which the world is based, [is] shown in cosmic terms.[12]

It is not at all a comfortable world.

No demonstration by the nature of events on behalf of a traditional value-system; a forceful display of the ruthlessness with which unpleasant people can go after power, and a reminder of the success that they often achieve; the possibility or even likelihood of there being essentially as many value-systems as there are people, with almost no overlapping at times; an extremely strong intimation that it is not morality but power that is the prime factor in social order: in general, surely, the play might seem to bring us strikingly close to that merely naturalistic universe the vision of which, with its draining of significance from all moral values, constituted the abyss of whose blackness Melville was later so dismayedly conscious. But in fact 'blackness' is one of the last terms that would occur to anyone in connection with so serenely poised a masterpiece, and it is for this that I shall now try to account.

I suggest that a major reason for the play's poise is precisely that the idea of the power struggle and of multiple value-systems is accepted in it. That the view of things that I have just sketched can appear as disturbing as it often does is due substantially to what can be called the reductive fallacy: namely, that trick of the mind by which, other things being equal, the less complex seems to insist that it possesses a greater measure of reality than the more. Ruthless self-seeking is liable to appear more natural, more humanly fundamental, than self-denying co-operation in the interests of ideals; the hunt for short-term gratifications can look more natural than the striving after less easily definable long-term ones; and as ideal after ideal is seemingly shown to be merely a mask for something more primitive, the long slide down continues without any logical stopping-place until, where the American experience in particular is concerned, we are left with the blankly unresponding and irreducible countenance of nature itself. But of course, if I have been reading it correctly, *The Tempest* is of all Shakespeare's plays the one that is freest of any tendency towards reductionism and that most effectively shows up its fallaciousness.

In previous plays we are indeed confronted with characters intellecting in such a way that their assertions about ideals conflict with each other in a potentially reductive fashion. If Falstaff is right about honour, Hotspur would seem to be not only wrong but foolish, and if Edmund is right about the world, then Lear's and Gloucester's outcries against injustice would seem to be, however understandable, those of the philosophically immature. ('Seem', I say; in reality, of course, the dialectics are considerably more complex.) Furthermore, there is an aspect to a number of those plays that subtly reinforces the threat of reductionism. A basic feature of that threat in general is the lurking suspicion that the simpler modes of organization are the more efficient ones, that the battle may indeed be to the simply strong, and that when it isn't this is simply the result of successful moral or philosophical bluffs by the weak. In this respect *Richard II* is usefully paradigmatic. The Bolingbrokes of this world, we may feel at times, are nearer to reality than the Richards; and this feeling seems to me no accident. In *Richard II* we are in a world of mysteries, a world in which it is impossible to arrive at a firm understanding of the precise motives of the main characters, or even to tell at times whether they are speaking the truth or not. Hence Richard's glittering meditations, so obviously self-delusive anyway, take on all the more the air of nets cast at random into a sea of uncertainties, and the conduct of Bolingbroke appears in contrast to have at least the merit of corresponding to the realities of action; he observes how people are behaving and he gets things done. This dichotomy between thinking and doing persists in most of the plays that follow, with too much reflection drawing people away from effective action. The language of events tells against the overly practical men in the long run, but in the short run it is the reflective ones − Richard, Brutus, Hamlet, Gloucester, Malvolio, Macbeth, Jacques − whose inadequacies are immediately apparent to us. And we are all the time in the presence of uncertainties − of unsuccessful attempts to decipher the universe, or the past, or the riddles of other people's hearts − that we partake of along with those who are doing the thinking. Accordingly, faced not only with the observable drawbacks of intellection but with a measure of doubt as to the knowability of things, we are liable to feel all the more threatened by the confident reductiveness of the realists, with their concern for a simple and efficient manipulation of the present, and to be all the more prone to cling to the traditional verities and to welcome what look like confirmations of them.

In *The Tempest*, in contrast, the unthinkable has actually happened. We are now in a wholly naturalistic world where, except for Prospero's motives, everything is known and there are no mysteries. The past is clear; the supernatural, in so far as it isn't directly under Prospero's control, is an affair of morally neutral and unproblematic natural forces; the significant action of the play all takes place in front of us inside a time-scheme in which there are no lacunae; and in general, for the first and last time in Shakespeare, we are given a god's-eye view of events. What we witness, in other words, is a situation in which almost all the vital facts are unequi-vocal, and in which the conduct and thinking of the wanderers on the island can be judged with considerable precision in relation to those facts. Viewed in this way the practical men have no fuller a

measure of reality – that is, no more adequate and efficient a correspondence between their thinking and the actualities of their
situations – than anyone else. Gonzalo may be vulnerable as a social
philosopher to the deflating thrusts of Antonio and Sebastian, but
he is not only more admirable in his attitude towards Alonso's grief
than they are, he is more accurate in his attitude towards the island
and its mysteries. Antonio and Sebastian are in fact wholly mistaken
about their situation, in a way that reminds us that slickly rationalistic minor machiavels can be overreached at their own game by
superior human intelligences unassisted by supernatural means.
And the inefficiency of Stephano and Trinculo speaks for itself,
except for one piquant aspect: there can be little doubt that had they
been able to pull off the murder of Prospero they would very soon
have found themselves not the masters of the island but the slaves of
Caliban, the latter being so obviously more intelligent, more knowl-
edgeable about the island, and more ruthless.

This brings me back to the question of power and values. With an
eye turned once more towards the fiction of the American 'renaissance', I suggest that in *The Tempest* Shakespeare has successfully
handled the problem of the subjectivity of values precisely by being
so objective about human behaviour. The risk run by Melville and
Hawthorne was that in making the characters in their masterworks
– in *Moby Dick* especially, and in *The Scarlet Letter* and *The Blithedale Romance* – either intellectuals, or symbols, or the
representatives of highly articulated systems of thought, a derealizing and devaluing of existence became all too easy once the
metaphysical basis of thought itself was questioned. *The Tempest* in
contrast presents us – in a way that, when one hunts for English pre-
cedents, seems paralleled only by the pilgrims in *The Canterbury
Tales* – with individuals who are all living with equal conviction and
reality in such a way that we can neither pull the more primitive or
wicked characters inside the value-systems of the 'higher' ones nor
feel that the solidity of the latter is diminished thereby. We are
reminded that people will go on being themselves whatever intellectuals choose to think about existence; in other words, that most
people, like the characters in *The Tempest*, are not particularly
introspective or philosophical and that the world that *they* inhabit is
an indestructibly solid one that invites and sustains confident self-
assertion. And we are reminded likewise that the striving for power
is a permanent fact of existence, and that if power isn't wielded by

Prospero, it will be wielded by Antonio or Stephano or Caliban. This brings me to the kind of higher mental organization that we see or can infer in Prospero. The most profitable approach, it seems to me, is by way of his interestingly un-American conduct in the last act.

A major reason for the fascination of Prospero's decision to re-enter so imperfect a human society, and his mercifulness even towards the utterly unrepentant, is that *The Tempest*, to an extent unparalleled in Shakespeare's works and probably in great literature generally, touches upon the 'If I were king' feeling in us. Prospero, that is to say, has not only an unparalleled knowledge of what is going on in others, but also the power to do whatever he wishes on the basis of it. From a utopian point of view he is uniquely and enviably free. Instead of having to accommodate himself to a pre-established society, he can make – indeed to some extent he has made already – his own brave new world. Served as he is by the vast natural powers of Ariel and Ariel's fellow spirits, there would seem to be nothing to prevent his ridding the island of the human blots on it (doing so, moreover, in the name of justice as presented in Ariel's harpy speech) and then allowing Ferdinand and Miranda to people it anew under the aegis of the pastoral vision so lucidly embodied in the masque, with its evocation of the haunting ideal of an ordered and harmonious plenteousness. Yet he turns away from these possibilities – and turns away, significantly, to a mode of existence in which he will have to live once more without the aid of magical knowledge and power and be as prone to error and fumbling and ignorance himself as the other characters have been in their wanderings on the island. What lies behind his decision? The tempting and sophisticated answer, of course, is that the island paradise wouldn't work out because of 'human nature' and that Prospero knows it. But I can see no evidence for this in the play, and the preferable answer appears to me at once simpler and more interesting. As I have said, we mostly have to guess about Prospero's motives, but his earlier statement to Miranda seems unequivocal enough: 'I have done nothing but in care of thee, / Of thee my dear one, thee my daughter.' The ordinary social world may be one in which the pastoral dream can never be realized; it may even be one that invites philosophical commentaries like the cloud-capped towers speech. But with Miranda's famous exclamation of joyful surprise at the entry of the court party it is brought home to us that for her, not herself having had the experiences out of which the dream and the disillusionment have both arisen, this new world will in fact be far richer than any that she could know on the island, and that one person's experiences and truths cannot be imposed on another. Shakespeare, in other words, has successfully avoided both pessimism and optimism because he has avoided 'human nature' altogether. There are simply people and, like Prospero, one works among them pragmatically. Miranda's capacity for growth and happiness is as much a reality as Prospero's own world-weariness.

And I would like to suggest that the same pragmatism is at work in Prospero's forgiveness of Antonio and Sebastian – that in other words we have something more interesting here than a traditional dichotomy between justice and mercy in which only one of the alternative ideals is right. Admittedly there is no way of arriving at certainty about what is going on in the exchange between Prospero and Ariel at the start of Act v about the 'prisoners'. But I find it more in keeping with the tenor of events in the play to see the entire course of the action as the working out of a single design by Prospero than to opt for the familiar gratification of feeling that Prospero too – yes, even the prickly and superhumanly powerful Prospero – becomes changed in the course of the play through the transfiguring power of Mercy (and a hint or two from Ariel) and goes off at the end into a sunset of Christian brotherliness. If the aim of all his manoeuvrings has been to enable Miranda to return to civilization with her prospective husband, it would be odd if he hadn't equally planned to take Alonso as well as Gonzalo back with them. To revenge himself on Miranda's prospective father-in-law, when his having done so could hardly escape becoming known or at least strongly suspected, would hardly be the best sort of engagement present for the two young people. But if Alonso has to go back, then so, logically, do Antonio and Sebastian. To take revenge even on Antonio would be to cast an irremovable shadow of suspicion and mistrust over the future, since to punish him would be to imply that Alonso too merited punishment, and to leave open (at least from Alonso's point of view) the possibility of such a punishment's coming. And even simply revealing to Alonso the plot against him, quite apart from the obvious tensions that would result, would disclose too much of the powers that Prospero had employed in relation to the group's wanderings on the island, and hence would undercut Alonso's grief and repentance by the revelation that they had been touched off by a series of elaborate practical jokes. I am not, of course, trying to convert Prospero into that most detestable of literary phantasms, the emotionless superman (or non-man) who merely puts on masks of irritation or concern or righteous indignation to serve his own canny purposes. Prospero's voiced indignation at the outset seems genuine enough, especially when reinforced by the accusations in the harpy speech and in the speech that Prospero himself makes to the spellbound wanderers just before they awaken. But Prospero has also shown himself acutely alert to how other people's minds work, which is why he can control them so well. And I suggest that he has already decided when the play begins that certain claims and pleasures, including the pleasures of revenge, of 'justice', and even of revealing the full extent of his magnanimity, must be foregone in Miranda's interests. The point cannot be proven, but in any case such an untroubled turning away from the tyranny of absolutes, like the turning away from the relative stasis of the pastoral ideal, would be in keeping with the treatment of ideals throughout the play.

The Tempest sums up and presents in a quintessential form some of the kinds of static perfections for which the mind yearns, and thereby enables us to see them more clearly for what they are. In this sense it is the most critical of Shakespeare's plays and, in a salutary way, the most duplicitous. A hostile reader, put off by the superficially pastoral aspects of it and by the thinness of the characters (relative to what we find in previous plays) that I spoke of earlier, might suggest that we should read *The Tempest* as an allegorical poem rather than as a play in the conventional sense. But that would be to miss the point, I believe. Speaking of the creative process, Nietzsche observed that

what is essential ... is the feeling of increased strength and fullness. Out of this feeling one lends to things, one *forces* them to accept from us, one violates them – this process is called *idealizing*. Let us get rid of a prejudice here: idealizing does not consist, as is commonly held, in subtracting or discounting the petty and inconsequential. What is decisive is rather a tremendous drive to bring out the main features so that the others disappear in the process.[13]

That we don't find in *The Tempest* the high-energy conflicts and characterization of the earlier plays, I have already acknowledged. But Nietzsche's statement seems to me basically true of it all the

same; and if there is any non-dramatic English poetry the play
especially brings to mind, it is that of poets like Jonson, Herbert, and
Marvell rather than of any allegorists. The tone and stance of *The
Tempest* are of a sort that had been all too uncommon during the
Renaissance – the tone and stance, that is to say, of someone
untrapped by the kind of idealizing that Nietzsche objects to, and
hence able to cope with equanimity with any particulars, however
disturbing, and any ideas, however 'advanced', that you might
throw at him. And in *The Tempest* Shakespeare himself indicated a
more profitable route away from the Renaissance than the kind associated especially with Dryden, in which one set of abstractions
was simply replaced by another and less interesting set.

The charm of certain ideals is richly acknowledged in the play, of
course. The absolute self-assurance of absolute justice resounds in
Ariel's harpy speech; the classical pastoral dream in all its grace is
recalled in the prothalamium-like masque for the young couple; the
pure clean beauty of an untarnished new world comes through in
Caliban's accounts of the island; the moral beauty of absolute
power and knowledge used wisely is embodied in Prospero; the
delights of a completely amoral, non-intellectual freedom are epitomized in Ariel; the charms of the kind of freedom from tension
achieved through a philosophical sense of human transience and of
the ultimate insubstantiality of everything are recalled by the incomparable cloud-capped towers speech; and the calm omniscience that
sometimes seems to inhere in the art-activity itself is embodied in the
whole marvellously crafted play. We are indeed tempted to exclaim
with Ferdinand, 'Let me live here ever!' But just as Ferdinand is compelled to leave the magic kingdom of art and return to society, so too
are we; and in a sense the magic vanishes behind us like the masque
that evoked Ferdinand's tribute to 'so rare a wonder'd father and a
wise'. At the end of the play we not only know that the characters,
instead of remaining tranquilly in a world of purer happiness than
we ourselves can ever experience (as happens in the great earlier
comedies), will be returning to a world no better than ours; we also
have the remarkable curtain speech, whose flatness and directness
break the spell of art and whose larger effect is to recall simultaneously the ordinary humanity of Prospero, the ordinary
humanity of the actor playing the part; and even, if we are not afraid
of being considered old-fashioned, the ordinary humanity of the
creator of the whole work. And it is brought home to us, if such a

bringing home is still necessary, how the organ voice of the harpy and the graceful pastoralism of the masque have alike been simply creations of Prospero, how the calm perfections of the island and the cloud-capped towers speech have marked affinities with the death-wish beauties and simplifications of Ariel's 'Full fadom five' song, and how the god-like knowledge and power that Prospero has possessed are unavailable to any human being. In other words, the human condition, with its errors and compromises and imperfections and power-struggles and lack of certainties that Prospero accepts and returns to, *is* the human condition, and it is with an unperturbed acceptance of those facts that intelligence must go about its business.

Yet even if a number of things have been implicitly defined in the course of the play as fictions, they are not thereby dismissed as essentially false and trivial when judged in the clear light of reason, any more than Marvell's garden is less real than what lies outside it or Caliban's island is more real than the emotions that people feel while on it. Just as it is a heartening display of effective intelligence that we have witnessed in Prospero, so too the cumulative effect of *The Tempest* is not a devaluing but a reaffirming of the creative life of the mind. True, we have been reminded that over-indulging in the charms of intellection can sap our power of right action, sometimes disastrously: Prospero's absorption in 'the liberal arts' cost him his dukedom, and his pleasure in his own artistry in the masque scene could have cost him his life had it made him forget 'that foul conspiracy / Of the beast Caliban' for too long. True, too, some of the ways in which the mind can seek to oversimplify reality and escape from human multifariousness have been defined so brilliantly in the course of the play that *The Tempest* is the profoundest critique we have of the pastoral craving that reached its apogee in the poetry of Milton. But if intellection can draw us away from effective living it can also draw us deeper into it, and the masque reminds us of the truths that fictions can yield when rightly used. From one point of view the masque is annihilated by the moving Epilogue; one of the marks of Shakespeare's intelligence was that he saw so clearly that religion is one thing and classical fictions another and that you don't dignify either of them by muddling them up together. From another point of view, however, as Mr Marx's essay reminds us, the masque lucidly sketches important psychological relationships between nature and artifice, emotion and reason, individual appetites and social order, and its messages about human behaviour can be assimilated by its young spectators and affect how they themselves behave.

The same point can be made about *The Tempest* as a whole. The constructions of art, precisely because a Prospero-like apprehension of human relationships is unavailable to us otherwise, can furnish us with indispensable knowledge and wisdoms; and with only a slight figurative wrenching it can be said that the knowledge and wisdoms of Prospero's magic book are those of the play itself. Since I began this discussion by disagreeing to some extent with Mr Marx's stimulating essay, it seems fitting to let him have the last word here:

As the shaping spirit of the play, Prospero directs the movement ... not by renouncing power, but by exercising it to the full. His control is based upon hard work, study, and scholarly self-discipline ... Until the final scene we are kept mindful of Prospero's nagging sense of responsibility, and his devotion to the reasoned uses of power ... Prospero's success, finally, is the result not of submission to nature, but of action – of change that stems from intellect.[14]

Dust and Dreams and *The Great Gatsby*

> No – Gatsby turned out all right in the end; it is what preyed on
> Gatsby, what foul dust floated in the wake of his dreams that
> temporarily closed out my interest in the abortive sorrows and
> short-winded elations of men.[1]

The concept of pleasure is a slippery one and of very little use as an
aesthetic term, but I take it that most of us, when we are speaking
informally, are implying something similar when we call a novel
enjoyable. We mean, among other things, that it is the kind of book
that goes down well when we are tired, or convalescent, or on
vacation; a book, in other words, that makes it easier for us to relax.
In this sense a number of 'serious' American novels, though perhaps
not a large number, have obviously been widely enjoyed, among
them *Huckleberry Finn*, *The Catcher in the Rye*, and *Catch-22*, but
the novel that I am concerned with here, so elegant, so economical,
so effortless-seeming, is in some ways the most seductive. *The Great
Gatsby* not only subverts the claims of the respectable social world
on our allegiance and shows us insufficiencies in conventional
judgement-making; it also intimates that a strenuous commitment
to a long-term course of purposeful action may only be possible if
we are deluded or trapped by inadequate conceptions of the nature
of things, and that there is an inevitable but honourable correlation
between moral perceptivity and social powerlessness. And it does so
with a greater philosophical aplomb than the other novels that I
have mentioned.

   The Great Gatsby is especially concerned with the relationship
between ideals and conduct, and its thesis on this subject, epitomized in the quotation that heads this essay, is approximately as
follows: to have large romantic ideals is almost certainly to be
mistaken, because of the nature of ideals, but to attempt to do
without them is to live emptily and to thwart a permanent human
craving; hence almost any large romantic ideals, however mistaken,
deserve to be viewed respectfully. In *Heart of Darkness*, to which
the novel is obviously indebted, this notion is raised as a possibility,

but it is confined to the status of a possibility only, since if Kurtz is manifestly superior to the Manager and the ivory-hunting 'pilgrims', he is just as manifestly inferior to Marlow. He is evil, grotesque, and even in his own terms a failure; and in Marlow we are shown convincingly the consciousness of someone who, while aware of a good many of the things that Kurtz is aware of, can yet live admirably and up to a point satisfyingly in terms of a very different set of values. In *The Great Gatsby* this kind of balance is missing; as Arthur Mizener observes, the limitation of the novel 'is the limitation of Fitzgerald's own nearly complete commitment to Gatsby's romantic attitude'.[2] Accordingly, while the novel ostensibly militates in favour of ideals, by doing so only on the grounds that they make life more interesting it undermines their claim to be taken seriously as guides to long-term planning and moral commitment; and the only course that really remains open to the unillusioned but sensitive person is a stylish and detached perceptivity. In the following pages I shall try to account for the air of solidity given to what seems to me an untenable thesis, and to point to certain artistic defects entailed in the attempt to substantiate it.

That the novel is at least as much about Nick Carraway as about Gatsby is rightly a commonplace, but there is an important aspect of Nick's consciousness that has so far been neglected. When we seek to explain the extraordinary period weightiness of so slim a book, it becomes necessary, I think, to consider the functioning in it of a particular set of ideals as apprehended by Nick, namely those promulgated through the entertainment media. 'It was like skimming hastily through a dozen magazines', Nick remarks of the Rich-Suffering-Young-hero persona that Gatsby proffers for his inspection during their ride into Manhattan together, and he could have said with equal truth that the whole Gatsby–Daisy relationship was like that, or like sitting through a dozen popular movies, or listening to a lot of popular songs. And when, after mentioning that in 1922 movie stars live in the West Fifties overlooking Central Park, he goes on to speak of the little girls out in the park singing like crickets of the Sheik of Araby, we are reminded of all the other heroes who are entering their consciousness through the movies and to whose splendid remembered images they will later try to approximate the males with whom they have sentimental dealings. We are in a world – very much a twentieth-century, media-permeated urban world – where the boundaries between life and art, stereotypes and private individualities, have lost their definiteness and in which the question of when some of the characters are being truly 'themselves' becomes almost impossible to answer. If Gatsby is trying to adjust himself to a stereotype, Nick is as familiar with that stereotype as he is; and if when Klipspringer plays for Gatsby and Daisy in the darkened music-room we recognize the appropriateness of the songs to the evening mood, and the roles that others like them have had in the evolving consciousnesses of the two lovers, it is Nick himself who has felt their appropriateness and mentally ('In the meantime, / In between time—') provided the lyrics. Nick's consciousness in these respects is one that most of us have probably duplicated to varying degrees in our own growing-up; it is far closer to most of ours, certainly, than those of Hemingway's rural-oriented Midwesterners, which is no doubt one reason why Hemingway's novels are coming to seem more and more period while *The Great Gatsby* remains, paradoxically, so glowingly modern. Accordingly, the more normal that Gatsby's consciousness and conduct appear in relation to Nick, the more normal they are likely to appear to us; and the tendency of the whole novel is in fact to normalize them.

There is an anecdote, probably apocryphal, of Proust's having been discovered one day sitting on the floor with the proofs of his masterpiece spread around him and exclaiming about his characters, with an air of dismayed discovery, 'But they're *all* like that!' In *The Great Gatsby*, similarly, examples of a single pattern of conduct proliferate: the pretensions of Gatsby are echoed by most of the other characters, including the Buchanans, the former owner of Gatsby's house, the haughty negro trio in their chauffeur-driven limousine, the whole crew at the brilliantly rendered party at Myrtle Wilson's apartment, and a lot of the figures who came to soak up Gatsby's bootleg booze. All are attempting with an unsuccess apparent to Nick's ironic gaze, to conform to 'platonic conceptions' of themselves for which they are obviously unfitted. And the effect of this is the reverse of what it is apparently intended to be. True, we are left in no doubt about the discrepancies between Gatsby's conceptions of himself, of Daisy, and of their future together, and the actualities; and the incongruities here are plainly meant to be underlined by those observable in the other characters, just as the pretensions of Pip are underlined by the pretensions of most of the

other characters in *Great Expectations*, with which *The Great Gatsby* has marked affinities. But in Fitzgerald's novel such under-linings serve in a deeper way to excuse or at least to invite a softening of judgement on the conduct of the protagonist, since they suggest that it arises out of proclivities deeply rooted in human nature. And there is a further and more important respect in which such a softening is invited. Nick himself, I suggest, is presented throughout as being fully alive only to the extent that his own way of looking at things resembles Gatsby's.

Nick's constant romantic self-projection, his own large sense of glamorous possibilities, his ability even while noting the tawdriness of an actuality to understand the glamour that it could possess for an outsider – these are so obvious and so spelled out as to need no commenting on. What I wish to emphasize instead is how when Nick strikes out for himself in an opposite direction from Gatsby's, especially in the crucial matter of sex, he seems positively to be leaving the natural behind.

Nick responds to things in general in a variety of ways, of course. It is a single consciousness in which the city makes wild promises, and a lawn runs and jumps and drifts up the side of a house, and moonlight solidifies and floats on water while the notes of a banjo liquify and drip nearby, and 'our eyes lifted over the rose-beds and the hot lawn and the weedy refuse of the dog-days alongshore' to 'the blue cool limit of the sky'. But in those responses as I have just presented them a spectrum is discernible, one ranging from energies and dialogue to a largely non-metamorphosing relationship with discrete objects; and if the relationship between Gatsby and Daisy belongs near the former end of the spectrum, Nick's relationship with the 'clean, hard, limited', boy-like figure of Jordan Baker belongs towards the latter. In the unillusioned and passion-free re-lationship that Nick has chosen, we see another manifestation of that yearning for a clean and changeless simplicity, a non-human aesthetic purity, that is evident in his grateful response to the ocean's cleanness and to other clean things. But to seek for changelessness of this sort, we are reminded, is to expose ourselves to disappointment when dealing with most things and with all people; sweat breaks out repulsively on the upper lip of the girl back home, Jordan Baker turns away contemptuously, 'foul dust' floats in Gatsby's wake, and, having no special dream that he is trying to realize himself, Nick becomes increasingly conscious of time not as the bringer of fruitions but only as the destroyer of beauty and security. It seems hardly too much to say that in this one novel Fitzgerald's vision has encompassed Hemingway's and placed it more firmly than Hemingway himself was ever able to do.

But more is at issue than Nick's consciousness as I have tried to define it so far. His general conduct, his whole philosophical stance towards existence and especially towards the conduct of others, is involved too, and it is here that the normative pressures at work in the book – and their defects – are most apparent. A highly important component of the pervasive relaxing charm of *The Great Gatsby*, after all, is the general pleasurableness of engaging ourselves with the presented experiences in Nick's fashion. How far the Herr Issyvoo of Christopher Isherwood's Berlin fictions is indebted as a concept to Nick Carraway can only be a matter for speculation; and if there is indeed indebtedness, there has also been vulgarization. But it is easy to see how vulgarization is invited, just as it is easy to see how Fitzgerald himself has vulgarized certain aspects of Marlow: it is very flattering to become everybody's friend and confidant, to be led into exotic encounters, to make amidst the multiplying errors of others no false moves oneself that elicit criticism, and to know that one is always being alert – alert photographically or poetically or morally, and frequently all three at once. There is something to be said, too, for maintaining an unillusioned quiescence in a period in which to act with great vigour may indeed be to act wrongly. But quiescence is only meritorious up to a point, and I think that that point is passed in *The Great Gatsby*. For all his agreeableness, Nick is someone in whom the moralizing process has become largely a matter of observation unrelated to intervention (he does not even visit Tom and Daisy after the killing of Myrtle Wilson), and the quasi-Conradian coolness of his opening reference to the 'abortive sorrows and short-winded elations of men' has been arrived at a good deal too lightly. To borrow from W. M. Frohock's discussion of Fitzgerald himself, the distinctive poise revealed in his narration of the events 'has to do less with morals than with manners'.[3]

But of course the prime question is not how limited Nick appears in comparison with Gatsby, but how normative Gatsby deserves to seem to *us*. Mr Mizener's reaction here is representative enough for my purposes. 'In contrast to the corruption which underlies Daisy's world', he assures us, 'Gatsby's essential incorruptibility is heroic. Because of the skilful construction to *The Great Gatsby* the eloquence and invention with which Fitzgerald gradually reveals this heroism are given a concentration and therefore a power he was never able to achieve again. The art of the book is nearly perfect.'[4] I suggest that, on the contrary, the rhetoric of the book may be nearly perfect but the art most certainly isn't, and this because Gatsby's 'essential incorruptibility' is not heroic but incredible.

To recall that Gatsby is a professional criminal on a large scale is not naive or coarse; and one of the most interesting aspects of the book's rhetoric is the extraordinarily skilful sleight of hand with which Fitzgerald has avoided coming to terms with the fact of this criminality in the interests of sustaining his opening disjunction between the pure figure of the dreaming Gatsby and the 'foul dust' that stirred in his wake. To pick up a term that I used above, a good deal of metamorphosing goes on in the novel, with lawns leaping, and gasoline pumps glowing in the summer darkness like exotic flora, and the boundaries between the human and the non-human, the natural and the man-made, becoming strangely indeterminate in Nick's heightened perception of things. It is a world of surprises, of things escaping from pigeonholes, so that at the outset even the First World War and 'that slender and riotous island which extends itself due east of New York' elude their customary labels. And Gatsby's professional milieu is similarly converted for us into an oddly harmless – almost an innocent – kind of fantasy world. The splendid brief telephone conversation between Gatsby and one of his lieutenants is an obvious example ('I said a *small* town... He must know what a small town is... Well, he's no use to us if Detroit is his idea of a small town...'). But it is Meyer Wolfsheim, of course, who is the prime representative denizen of the underworld in a novel that relies so heavily on representative scenes and figures; and rhetorically the discrepancy between Wolfsheim's comic, sentimental, little-Jewish-businessman appearance and the abstract idea of the Man Who Fixed the World's Series is masterly. So too is Wolfsheim's anecdote of the gangland shooting of Rosy Rosenthal, in which the murdered man's almost dream-like dissociation from his body's vulnerability – his transporting of himself to the restaurant door as a kind of object, as it were, that can subsequently be transported back to resume contact with the waiting coffee-cup – is another example of the dissociating and the conversion of bodies into *things*, by heat or fatigue or alcohol, that goes on throughout the novel. And the transmogrification of the underworld by such means is a contributory element in that slightly nightmarish dissolution of certainties and values that is so important a part of Nick's experience of the East. Yet sleight of hand still seems the appropriate term where its function in the larger argument of the novel is concerned.

In terms of plotting, of course, there is no necessity for Gatsby's being a criminal at all, but it is obvious enough why Fitzgerald made him one. Hovering behind the novel, as I said, is *Heart of Darkness*, with Gatsby standing in relation to Nick and the 'society' characters as Kurtz stands to Marlow and the Manager's gang. And given the emptiness, unawareness, or corruption of the ostensibly respectable, the claims to respect of the single-minded and extravagant risk-taker dominated by ideals increases considerably in force for the judicious onlooker. The crucial difference between the two works, however, is that Conrad has permitted all the elements in the equation to emerge, whereas Fitzgerald has not. Kurtz's power to make not only the young Russian but Marlow 'see things – things' is not allowed to be dissociated from the severed heads on the posts and the general horrors of King Leopold's *domaine privé*. Gatsby, on the other hand, exists for us almost wholly as simply another of Fitzgerald's yearningly aspiring and self-improving Minnesota boys grown up into financial success. As a criminal he is as little present and convincing as Dick Diver in *Tender is the Night* is present and convincing on the Riviera as a psychiatrist; *qua* Good–Bad Guy, indeed, he is almost as stock and sentimentalized a creation as Louis Joseph Vance's Lone Wolf, with whom Fitzgerald was no doubt familiar. And by dodging or metamorphosing the muck and violence of large-scale criminality in the interests of preserving Gatsby's image from contamination, Fitzgerald has also dodged having to consider a crucial aspect of Gatsby's over-idealizing of Daisy and money, namely its connection with the obscured unpleasantnesses of his get-rich-quick career. Admittedly bootlegging in the early twenties, particularly in the East, was less violent than it became later. But given that this is a 'serious' novel, the unqualified sympathy extended by some critics to Gatsby and his ambitions is still curious. 'Mr Heathcliff and I are such a suitable pair to divide the desolation between us. A capital fellow!' – the initial enthusings of Lockwood in *Wuthering Heights* come irresistibly to mind when Marius Bewley, for example, informs us of Gatsby's 'goodness and faith in life, his compelling desire to realize all the possibilities of existence, his belief that we can have an Earthly Paradise populated by Buchanans'.[5]

And yet it is evident all the same what is at stake in Gatsby and why it is so difficult to be hard on him – difficult, that is, for reasons more complicated than simply that Good–Bad Guys in popular fiction are enjoyable or that we too, when younger, may have engaged in Gatsby-like efforts at self-improvement. In his essay on Fitzgerald, Lionel Trilling remarks with his customary urbanity that 'Gatsby is said by some to be not quite credible, but the question of any literal credibility he may or may not have becomes trivial before the large significance he implies. For Gatsby, divided between power and dream, comes inevitably to stand for America itself.'[6] As a piece of arguing this is puzzling, of course, since it is hard to see how anything can have a very meaningful 'large significance' of this order unless it has a firmly credible smaller one first. Whatever Moby Dick epitomizes for his pursuers and for us, he couldn't do it if he were not in the first place a very convincingly formidable old albino sperm whale. Yet Gatsby is indeed very American in the reconciliations that Fitzgerald attempts by means of him. In American terms, it is Nick Carraway's consciousness at the start of the novel, as he looks back at an over-and-done-with experience, that invites uneasiness. It is the consciousness of someone who has seen to the end of a road, has been defeated, and has withdrawn, and whose detachment, when viewed in the light of traditional American patterns and values, is decidedly un-American. '[H]e must have felt that he had lost the old warm world, paid a high price for living too long with a single dream. He must have looked up at an unfamiliar sky through frightening leaves ... A new world, material without being real ...' – Nick's analysis of Gatsby's diminished consciousness after the destruction of his illusions about Daisy is disturbingly relevant to Nick's consciousness too; disturbingly, I mean, in view of the lurking implication in the novel, which Fitzgerald himself must have glimpsed before he wrote the novel, that the latter may be the psychological end to which all the idealistic energies of the American experiment have been leading. But by dividing Gatsby's power from the evil concomitants of that power, and thereby emphasizing the heroism of his dreams, Fitzgerald has been able to maintain Gatsby as a figure counterpoising Nick's, a figure in which a more traditional American pattern of consciousness can still be celebrated, with its 'heightened sensitivity to the promises of life', its 'extraordinary gift of hope', its 'romantic readiness'. And in Nick's sympathetic contemplation of those qualities the actual desolation of his own position can escape being brought into disconcerting focus. The celebration is not quite as traditional as it looks, however, and the conclusion of the novel seems to me to involve metamorphosing the American past so as to suggest that the discrepancies between it and the revealed present are not as accusingly great as they might seem.

The famous four last paragraphs of the novel pluck at the heartstrings, and they are obviously cherished items in many of our mental scrapbooks. To animadvert on them is rather like being nasty about Garbo or Dietrich; they are among the 'beauties' of American prose. But surely they are largely incantation, and surely it is not obtuse to insist on the link between Beauty and Truth affirmed by the poet to whom Fitzgerald himself was so indebted? In those paragraphs we are not waking from a waking dream but going yet deeper into one; and it is not 'the' American dream but a peculiarly twentieth-century, urban, sentimentalizing one. Presumably none of us knows what Dutch sailors in the early seventeenth century were thinking as they eyed the approaching shores of Long Island, but it seems highly improbable that they lapsed into a picturesque trance of 'aesthetic contemplation'. And the gazelle-like leap by which Fitzgerald in the next sentence makes them the representatives of man in general reminds us of how much tougher the early American settlers as a whole were, with their gallimaufry of private and communal ambitions, than is implied in his evocation of that 'old, unknown world' in terms of siren-like whisperings and a soothing feminine breast. So too, for that matter, were those pioneers who were still heroically pursuing their dreams across the Great Plains more than two centuries after this 'last time in history' when man was faced with 'something commensurate to his capacity for wonder'. In other words, far from exalting the multifarious ambitions that have gone into the making of America, Fitzgerald has diminished them to something almost Hollywood in the attempt to raise Gatsby to heroic stature and make the errors in his particular brand of idealizing seem historically inevitable. And by ignoring the role of clear and admirable ideals in the collective American experience he has further diminished their role in individual lives. 'So we beat on, boats against the current, borne back ceaselessly into the past.' Tell that, one is tempted to retort, to William Bradford, or

Thomas Jefferson, or Lincoln. Tell it, for that matter (to invoke a novel that demonstrates what the effective use of the aspiring intelligence feels like) to Tolstoy's Levin. Admittedly American fiction since Cooper has not been notable for the presence of such figures, but that would seem to point not to the nature of man but to an insufficiency in the way in which ideals have often operated in the American consciousness.

In Defence of Culture:
Huckleberry Finn

> There was a power of style about her. It *amounted* to something being a raftsman on such a craft as that.[1]

'There are few other books', Lionel Trilling has rightly observed about *Huckleberry Finn*, 'which we can know so young and love so long'.[2] Such books, however, are liable to be dangerous for critics. As Leslie Fiedler has said about something similar, they 'shape us from childhood; we have no sense of first discovering them or having been once without them'.[3] When a critic cannot shake himself free enough of his childhood responses, he is in some peril of writing, like C. S. Lewis on *Paradise Lost*, as if the work he is discussing were virtually a piece of reporting; and if in addition he assumes that anything that still feels so intensely meaningful to him must somehow be meaningful in a completely adult way, the work is indeed in for trouble. *Huckleberry Finn* appears to have been the victim of both of these very comprehensible tricks of the mind. Mr Trilling himself for instance, has pulled off the remarkable feat of writing about it without ever letting on that it is funny. Mr Fiedler has acknowledged that 'this thoroughly horrifying book, whose morality is rejection and whose ambiance is terror, is a funny book, at last somehow a child's book after all; and the desperate story it tells is felt as joyous, an innocent experience'[4] – but his emphasis is all on the horror and the moral complexities. And when one considers the commentaries of such critics as Henry Nash Smith, Kenneth S. Lynn, Tony Tanner, and Leo Marx, it is hard not to feel momentarily sympathetic towards mavericks like William Van O'Connor and Martin Green who have argued impatiently that the novel simply isn't a great one at all. It *is* a great one, of course – 'one of the world's great books and one of the central documents of American culture',[5] as Mr Trilling has said. But it seems to me a very different book from the one that almost everyone has described in recent years.

What can be called the official account of *Huckleberry Finn* goes more or less as follows. The novel is a poignant celebration of an innocence, a natural decency and simplicity, that has since become culturally impossible and that even in the novel is being constantly threatened by human beastliness and 'civilized' constrictions and distortions. Civilization appears in the novel as two forms – the narrow, blinkered, conscience-instilling, and ego-suppressing pieties of small-town rural America, and the grandiose, ego-inflating, and delusive European romanticism that manifests itself humorously in Tom Sawyer's bookish and pedantic imitatings and far from humorously in the Southern chivalric code responsible for such atrocities as the Grangerford–Shepherdson butcheries and the gunning-down of the unarmed Boggs in the Arkansas village street. And the limitations of these patterns of civilization are shown up under the clear-sighted gaze of a boy, especially with regard to the iniquitousness of the slavery on which Southern culture rests and which the upholders of 'Christian' standards maintain in a perfect conviction of its naturalness. In this account the novel is a realistic one involving the interpenetration of two unambiguous realities – on the one hand the consciousness of an unusually but not impossibly inventive and sensitive fourteen year old; on the other the life of the Mississippi and its inhabitants presented with a vividness that yields up more and more rewards the more knowledge of that life we bring to the novel. It is an account that has been enriched as attention has extended from the riparian civilization (as in Bernard DeVoto), via the River (as in T. S. Eliot), to Huck himself as a moral figure and a richly symbolic refugee from civilization, and it has the merit of making the book appear a distinguished one in intelligible modern terms. The only thing amiss with it is that, like Jim's interesting interpretation of his 'dream' while lost in the fog, it isn't true.

    To begin with, Huck himself as a creation is a great deal closer to Lemuel Gulliver than to, say, Emma Woodhouse, of whom in Mr Trilling's account he appears as a kind of freckle-faced poor relation. His voice from chapter to chapter is wonderfully persuasive, one of the most charming and fascinating first-person voices in fiction, and it describes a good many episodes with the effortless vividness that characterizes Gulliver's account of his first awakening in Lilliput and that we find elsewhere in American fiction only in the greatest sea passages of *Moby Dick* and in a handful of other works. But just as Gulliver cannot be assembled into a coherent character who steadily develops as one extraordinary experience follows another, and who is now, as he recalls them, consistently the product of that development, so Huck cannot be assembled in that way either. To be sure, the fluctuations in his sophistication, moral perceptivity, and command of language aren't as great as Gulliver's, but they are there, and to attempt to put together the Hucks of the St Petersburg chapters, of most of the raft portions, of the Wilks episode, and of the Phelps' plantation section is to wind up with an even more Frankensteinian creation than is necessary if the unfortunate heroine of *The Turn of the Screw* is to be made to fit with the madness-and-no-ghosts theory about that tale. Yet when Martin Green objects impatiently (and somewhat excessively) that 'The only constant, connecting reality is the writer. Not Huck himself. Huck sinks to being a mere recorder quite often, and occasionally disappears',[6] we realize that of course this doesn't matter. And the fact that it doesn't matter, and that the weaknesses of the Wilks and Phelps sections (like those of Book Three of *Gulliver*) are not offensive in the way that the authorial manipulating of Satan in *Paradise Lost* is offensive, is a pointer to the kinds of significance that we can legitimately find in the novel where Huck is concerned.

The reason why the inconsistencies in Satan are deplorable while those in Gulliver are beside the point is that a good deal is made to depend on the cumulative development of the former, whereas with Gulliver (except in Book Four) it is always upon the *local* response to this or that novelty and its demands that our eyes are meant to be focused. Gulliver's own consciousness at every point, I mean, is filled very largely with the present rather than with a desire to fit together what he sees and further a dominant purpose of his own. *Local* reflections and generalizations occur, of course. But the pride-of-Lemuel-Gulliver kind of relating of them to each other seems to me possible only by postulating, in a curiously old-fashioned way, a whole network of unconscious relationships that are simply not there on display in the vivid immediacies of the text itself. And the same is true of the 'Good Huck, *Noble* Huck!' moralizings of Mr Trilling and the 'Alas, Poor Huck!' empathizings of Mr Fiedler. It is not *that* kind of significance that Huck can sustain, except momentarily, and in that sense Twain's warning in his prefatory notice is very much to the point. Moreover, a good deal more is involved here than merely that the tone of the narrative is so unworried, casual, and good-humoured, so implicitly the tone of someone who has come through unscathed and who is not even giving the reader any hints of the 'Little did I know!' variety along the way. A concern with the novel's 'blackness' or sombreness results, it seems to me, from splitting off the life of the Mississippi from the manner in which Huck experiences it, and just as Huck's character is not a naturalistic one, neither is that experience. On the contrary, it is a romantic one, in ways that are both cruder and more complex than has hitherto been allowed for. When Mr Fiedler wonders how the book can 'be at once so terrible and so comfortable to read',[7] I think we can answer him easily enough.

The charm and comedy of the opening account of Tom Sawyer's gang consists substantially in this, I take it: that Twain has so beautifully captured the boyhood craving, as against the imposed orderliness and security of one's community, for adventure, violence, triumphant self-assertion, and a general reaching after the heroic – yet always with the comfortable certainty that nothing that one does in one's play is in fact dangerous or irrevocable, and that one can always re-emerge from it at any time to find things as they were before and oneself as approved of as ever. The essential irony is conveyed when Huck recalls how 'I got into my old rags, and my sugar-hogshead again, and was free and satisfied. But Tom Sawyer, he hunted me up and said he was going to start a band of robbers, and I might join if I would go back to the widow and be respectable.' And if the boys are in imagination transcending the limitations of their particular society, it is in the name of society – the larger society of Tom's 'European' readings – that they are doing so. I shall be taking up later the question of Huck's relation to 'Europe'. At the moment I want to point out how reading the book – at whatever age – can gratify very much the same kinds of desires that moved Tom and his cohorts. 'The spirit of adventure in boyhood' may not be the 'central theme' of *Huckleberry Finn* as John Erskine claims,[8] but it is as much a feature of the book as it is of *Treasure Island*.

Mr Fiedler has suggested that, as a hero, Huck, unlike Tom, is not adventurous at all but timid; but if this is so it is merely in the technical sense that he doesn't seek out dangers or enjoy taking risks. Compared, say, with Dickens' Pip or Oliver Twist or David Copperfield, his is a superbly unintimidated and resilient consciousness that gives way to despair only once, and then momentarily; and when we hold in mind the childhood novels of Dickens, or even, for that matter, Twain's own *The Prince and the Pauper*, we see how *soothing* an adventure story his saga really is. The landscape through which he passes may be one in which violences occur, but the perpetrators of them are singularly unintimidating in his accounts of them. The killers overheard on the wreck talk at a level of brutality and credibility scarcely above that of villains in a boys' serial. The Grangerford and Shepherdson families perpetrate violences upon each other, but the individuals whom we are shown are handsome, gracious, and admirable to the point of idealization. The Bricksville lynch-mob may be potentially murderous, but the individuals whom we see are merely contemptible, and no one displays the murderous insensate energy that produced the gouging, nose-and-ear-biting fights of the period. Colonel Sherburn, while gunning down Boggs, is a dignified figure who, like the Shepherdsons, presents no threat to Huck himself. And the one seeming exception to my generalization about the villains is not an exception at all. The shock of Pap's first appearance in Huck's bedroom is memorable, but Huck remarks that 'right after, I see I warn't scared of him worth bothering about', and, except for the night of the delirium tremens, being with him is a good deal more pleasurable than not. Pap isn't Fagan or Bill Sykes or Tom Canty's father, he isn't even Long John Silver or Blind Pew. Though repulsive, he isn't purposefully malevolent; most of his actions that are described are amusing; Huck, as I have said, is quite unintimidated by him; and he is the worst figure that Huck encounters who constitutes a personal threat. Thereafter when potential human antagonists are met head on by Huck they not only are overcome almost immediately but for the most part disclose unexpected and reassuring benevolences; and if the river itself furnishes its memorable shocks ('Raf'? Day ain' no raf' no mo', she done broke loose en gone! – en here we is!'), they are soon enough taken care of and are far outweighed by the river's large generosity and benevolence.

In sum, Huck's progress through the ostensible dangers of the trip downstream is very largely that of the superboy of Tom Sawyer's imaginings. He is someone to whom adventures happen in an abundance to gratify any boy's romantic cravings, and who invariably says and does the right things to propitiate the natural and human dragons that menace him along the way. And in the end it is revealed that in relation to the one seemingly irresolvable problem, the fact of Jim's slavehood, he has been safe from real social disapproval all along – and, for that matter, not only safe but rich too. It is hardly

surprising that Tom Sawyer at the Phelps' plantation was getting
all set to imitate Huck and 'have adventures plumb to the mouth
of the river'. Nor does that exhaust the soothing aspects of the
book.

That Huck's voyage should be so almost universally pleasurable
for readers points us towards a fundamental duplicity in Twain's
handling of its central moral issue, the question of slavery. Those
American librarians who banned the book were quite right in one
respect: Huck is indeed throughout most of the book free of the
nagging claims of the puritan ethic, the steady pressures of long-
term plans, commitments, and decision-making. A prime reason for
this, however, is that slaves and slavery are so presented in the book
that they are not in fact issues at all. The great set pieces with Jim
and the claims of conscience are what they have been so widely
admired as being, of course. But they *are* set pieces, and not
common factors, at least if I am right in contending that Huck's is
not a single consciousness but a succession of units of consciousness
more or less loosely related to each other by family resemblances.
And if Huck's consciousness (or family of consciousnesses) is bliss-
fully free elsewhere of the tensions that normally come when
someone is violating a key taboo of his society, this is only possible
because slavery itself has been so romanticized in most of the novel
that the novel comes very close to being a validation of the conventional Southern image of it. For Huck (who even temporarily gets
his own at the Grangerfords) the niggers are simply there as normal,
contented, and amusingly naive and gullible parts of the landscape
(e.g., 'there was nigger boys in every tree, and bucks and wenches
looking over every fence; and as soon as the mob would get nearly to
them they would break and skaddle back out of reach'). And it isn't
merely that, as Carson Gibb puts it, 'Huck's attitude towards
niggers is standard – the attitude of the rich and the poor, of the
prim and the disreputable, even of the niggers themselves.'[9] The
plain fact is that Huck and we are not shown anything, apart from
the two or three exchanges with Jim, to make his own attitude
appear questionable. We not only hear of no instances of physical
cruelty towards the slaves by their owners, but the actual owners
whom we observe are kindly people behaving in a normal, decent,
master-to-servant fashion in their personal exchanges with them, a
fashion thoroughly consistent with the conversation between
Joanna Wilks and Huck:

'How is servants treated in England? Do they treat 'em better'n we treat our niggers?'

'*No!* A servant ain't nobody there. They treat them worse than dogs.'

'Don't they give 'em holidays, the way we do, Christmas and New Year's week, and Fourth of July?'

'Oh, just listen!... Why ... they never see a holiday from year's end to year's end; never go to the circus, nor to theatre, nor nigger shows, nor nowheres.'

'Nor church?'

'Nor church.'

Of the two episodes in which *mental* pain is inflicted during the course of the action, the sale of Jim by Miss Watson is done from need, and reluctantly, while that by the King and Duke at the Wilks' household is done by scoundrels and generally deplored, with the girls and the niggers 'hanging around each other's necks' in paroxysms of tears. And replete with horrors though the phrase 'selling down the river' may actually have been, Jim at the Phelps' plantation is to all appearances so little perturbed by the prospect as to put up with the extravagances of Tom and Huck without any anxiety about the mounting risk of discovery and of the closing off for ever of his chance for freedom. When he remarks, '"I never knowed b'fo', 't was so much bother and trouble to be a prisoner"', there are no indications that this is meant to be read ironically; and in the casual and equally unironical reporting of Miss Watson's re-morseful setting-free of Jim in her will the stress falls, especially when the fact is revealed in the midst of the so very agreeable slave-owning Phelpses, merely on the wrongness of selling a slave down the river, and not on the absurdity and iniquity of one person's 'owning' another in the first place.

I am not, it scarcely needs saying, speaking of slavery as it actually existed, nor am I overlooking Twain's treatment of it in the Huck–Jim exchanges, or his treatment of it elsewhere, especially in *Pudd'nhead Wilson*; and I can understand why Mr Marx, with his eye on the actual institution, should indignantly compare the Phelpses (and presumably, by implication, all the other owners in the novel) to 'those solid German citizens we have heard about in our time who tried to maintain a similar *gemütlich* way of life within virtual earshot of Buchenwald'.[10] But it is plain that in *Pudd'nhead Wilson* Twain was more concerned with using the institution in order to attack the stupidity, cruelty, and moral blindness involved in certain kinds of pigeonholing in general than with redoing *Uncle Tom's Cabin*. And in any case to read one work in the light of another when dealing with such a fantastically uneven writer as Twain is so risky a business that it should probably be left alone altogether. After all, what usable bridge *can* be thrown over the artistic gulf between, say, *Huckleberry Finn* and those ponderous adolescent pessimisms that Twain was indulging himself in, in the year after its publication, in 'The Character of Man'? The facts of *Huckleberry Finn* when viewed in isolation seem to me to be as I have described them, and the reason why slavery is treated so differently in *Pudd'nhead Wilson* and *Huckleberry Finn* is also tolerably plain. In the former Twain's energies are all bent towards attacking civilization. In the latter, whatever Twain may have consciously thought he was up to, they are bent towards celebrating it, in a way that it will take the rest of this discussion to clarify.

That Twain started out to do something answering to the orthodox account of the novel is evident when we contemplate the stacking of the cards that goes on in the St Petersburg section. The narrow-minded restrictions of an old maid, the well-intentioned ineffectualities of her sister, the naive, self-flattering, and justly defeated presumptions of one judge, the chicanery of another, the flamboyant yet pedantic inventings of a bookish boy – it is hardly surprising that when civilization comes at Huck in these forms the darkly numinous and irrational subculture of the slaves is the region most charged with imaginative life, and that when a demonic figure like Pap comes forward, society is powerless to protect Huck against him or counter his appeal. Equally obviously, though, whatever Huck and Jim feel themselves to be doing in relation to civilization as thus presented, the novel confronts both Huck and us with progressively denser and richer manifestations of civilization, and the actual matter of the novel is not an escape from civilization at all but a journey deeper and deeper into it. Even at the outset of the journey downstream Mrs Judith Loftus is a good deal more 'there' as an individual than is the Widow Douglas, just as more of the equipment of everyday civilized living is there in the floating house than we see in the accounts of the Widow's house and Pap's cabin; and where communal activities and mutual aid are concerned, the same can be said of the rural lives and comings and goings evoked by Huck in his various roles and responded to with sympathy or concern by his rural listeners, in contrast to what we see of St Petersburg. With

Huck's arrival in the Grangerford household we are obviously confronted with much more in the way of cultural manifestations than hitherto, and I shall be returning to the episode later. There is, however, relatively a show-case distance to the household, and in saying that I have in mind not only the catalogue-like description of the inanimate objects in which cultural values are embodied, but also the *strangeness* of the Grangerfords for Huck himself, with their story-book beauties and rituals, their incomprehensible savage code, and their scrupulous exclusion of Huck himself from any involvement in the consequences of that code. To put it another way, the ideals that energize and order the household are not experienced by Huck from the inside. With the entry of the King and Duke, however, he is confronted dynamically with a number of 'European' conceptions variously invading, victimizing, stimulating, and being rejected by rural American communities; and I shall be returning to this point too. In the Wilks episode, furthermore, Huck himself is drawn in as a participant and a moral agent, making moral choices and altering the course of events in much the most complexly functioning community that we have seen so far. And finally in the Phelps' plantation section Huck is involved in the full texture of domestic living in a normal household, with its day-to-day demands, relationships with its neighbourhood, and connections with more distant parts of the country. As Henry Nash Smith puts it, 'The Phelps plantation ... from the standpoint of geography eleven hundred miles downstream from St Petersburg, is from the standpoint of Mark Twain's imagination very near the starting-point of Huck's and Jim's journey.'[11] We have been shown more and more of the texture of social living in the course of the novel, and if we were asked to indicate that section of Huck's experience that best conveys the feeling of living in society it is the end of the book and not the beginning that we would have to point to.

I suggest that the fundamental reason for this progression and for its not being a tragic or even a sombre one is that what Twain had given himself up to in the novel was the celebration of precisely the kind of imaginative energy with which he was nominally at war when it manifested itself in 'European' romanticism, and that, whatever his consciously judging mind may have told him, this energy was inseparable in his own creative imagination from the constructions of civilization, especially Southern civilization. Richard Chase has spoken of 'the book's profoundest, more hidden

and most ambivalent exorcism – that of European culture itself'.[12]
The greatness of the book is due in good part to the fact that the
attempted exorcism was not only ambivalent but unsuccessful.

I have spoken already of those aspects of *Huckleberry Finn* that
make it one of the most glamorous of all adventure novels, one that
is all the more glamorous because, like *Robinson Crusoe*, it has such
an air of being *true* – of demonstrating that wonderful adventures
can still happen even though the seemingly indispensable 'Have at
you, knave!' social machinery has gone from the world. And the
Tom Sawyer sections of the novel make it plain that Twain's war
against cloak-and-rapier romanticism was that of someone who had
steeped himself in it when young and could throw himself wholeheartedly into re-creating that youthful experience of it. But more
than re-creations and transpositions are involved. When James M.
Cox points out that 'all of Tom Sawyer's world has been imported
into this novel' and that 'the substitution of Tom's humour for
Huck's vision' in the Phelps' plantation section 'indicates that Mark
Twain, though aware of the two sets of values, could not keep a
proper balance between them because of his fascination with Tom
Sawyer', he is looking in the right direction but not looking far
enough. Had he looked further he would not, I think, have asserted
so confidently that 'There is bitter irony in Huck's assumption of
Tom's name [at the Phelpses] because the values of Tom Sawyer are
so antithetical to the values of Huck Finn... From Mark Twain's
point of view in this novel, Tom Sawyer civilization involves obedi-
ence, imitation, and is directly opposed to a dynamic and creative
frontier imagination.'[13] The truth is surely that just as the novel as a
whole wouldn't have been what it was without the novels of Scott,
Dumas, and Co., so Huck's 'creative frontier imagination' would
not have been what it was, at least in substantial stretches of the
novel, without the educative influence of Tom Sawyer.

When we contemplate the self-satisfied scoring of points off Tom
Sawyer that has been going on, and the related conversion of Huck
into as good a boy as the Widow Douglas could have wished for, it is
hard to resist feeling that the presiding deity in much of the discussion of the novel has been, not the river, but the spirit of Sid
Sawyer. And when the episode of Huck's boarding the wrecked
steamboat is singled out as an Awful Warning against romanticism,[14] more is at issue than merely the respective claims of a certain
kind of prudence and a certain kind of adventurousness. ' "Do you

reckon Tom Sawyer would ever go by this thing?"', Huck asks the reluctant Jim. '"Not for pie, he wouldn't. He'd call it an adventure – that's what he'd call it, and he'd land on that wreck if it was his last act. And wouldn't he throw style into it? – wouldn't he spread himself, for nothing? Why, you'd think it was Christopher C'lumbus discovering Kingdom-Come. I wish Tom Sawyer *was* here."' The key word in that speech is surely 'style', and the conception is an absolutely central one. Tony Tanner, alone of the critics I have read, pounces on it, but only in order to draw attention to 'the perverse folly of Tom's ideal of "style"' and to the fact that 'style' is 'the word which seems to explain the nonsense in Tom's head and the illogicalities and pointless cruelties in society at large'. The essential wrongness of this approach comes out in Mr Tanner's contention that 'Tom – stuffed with style – thinks Huck has nothing to reflect with. But Huck reflects with something bigger than Tom or his society could understand: he reflects with the river, with nature.'[15] It isn't merely that we have Huck's several tributes to Tom on account of his 'style', especially apropos of his escape from Pap's cabin and his manipulating of the Wilks girls in their own interest. ('I felt very good; I judged I had done it pretty neat – I reckoned Tom Sawyer couldn't a done it no neater himself. Of course he would a throwed more style into it, but I couldn't do that very handy, not being brung up to it.') Even if we didn't have those remarks as pointers, the inventiveness that Huck displays most of the time would plainly not have been what it was without the influence of Tom's romance-derived imaginings. It is obvious, for instance, that the escape from Pap's cabin, though undertaken in a wholly practical spirit, would not have assumed so tightly knit and masterly a form – it is eminently 'stylish' in a way recalling the great escapes whose details bubble out of Tom's mind at the Phelps' plantation – if Huck's sense of possibilities hadn't been enlarged through being in Tom's company. The same can be said of the manipulations at the Wilkses. And so too, I think, with the unhesitating deftness, the 'Odysseus-like wit' as Sydney J. Krause has called it,[16] that Huck displays in his various role-playings. It is true that there was a whole 'native' tradition of American inventiveness, but the more we reflect on that epithet the more slippery it becomes, especially if we stick to what is shown in the novel. After all, the 'native' part of Huck's own background consists essentially of Pap and the slaves. The slave consciousness exhibited in the book and to some extent assimilated by

Huck has its own kind of imaginative richness, but it is essentially that of victims or potential victims inhabiting a world of dark forces that they do what they can to propitiate. With Pap, on the other hand – and the contours of his mind receive further illumination in the description of Bricksville – we are confronted with a consciousness owing its peculiarly repulsive force to an almost total *lack* of imaginative vitality. Being free, that is, of any sharp sense of possible consequences and any images of fuller modes of existence against which to judge itself to its own disadvantage, it can pursue its gratifications with animal directness, persistence, and shamelessness. In neither Pap nor the slaves, in other words, do we see anything resembling the kind of 'style' that Huck displays.

Nor do we see it in the indigenous shrewdness displayed by the 'big iron-jawed' doctor at the Wilkses, by Mrs Loftus when she catches Huck out in his female role, and by Huck himself at times, especially with regard claims to nobility of the King and Duke when they first arrive on the raft. And this brings me back to the ambivalence in Twain's attempted 'exorcism' of Europe that Mr Chase spoke of. The shrewdness I have just mentioned is obviously desirable where self-preservation is demanded, but it is essentially uncreative, and its manifestations in the novel consist almost entirely of one person's seeing through the role assumed by another. According to the stock account of the novel, this unillusioned gaze is wholly good, and is being celebrated the most obviously in Huck's relationship to the King and Duke. Not only do the latter, in Kenneth Lynn's words, 'represent, as Pap did, the sordidness, the cynicism, and the anarchic cruelty that are inescapable in the world beyond the pale of Eden';[17] they also richly exemplify the exploitation of American gullibility in the name of Europe, romance, and 'culture'. The facts of the matter, however, seem to me more complex and more interesting.[18] When Mr Fiedler suggests that Huck's compassion for the two rogues when they are tarred and feathered is obliquely pity for himself, the suggestion may be sentimental in its context but it points in the direction of an important truth.

The ease with which the King and Duke in their larger chicaneries take on such roles as those of reformed pirates and members of the English gentry is obvious enough. In their more private existence as we see it on the raft, however, the romantic role-playing continues in a way that suggests that their relationship to the romantic-exotic is

more than the simple one of shrewd-eyed tricksters composedly manipulating a repertoire of masks for money-getting purposes. I am
thinking especially of the Duke here. There is, of course, splendid
comedy in the way in which, having begun the Duke business for
practical purposes, he then becomes trapped by the King inside the
rules of the game that he himself has laid down and inside which the
two of them thereafter play so consistently in front of Huck and Jim.
But I am not the only reader, I imagine, to whom it has occurred that
the language of the Duke's avowal is that of someone who would in
fact very much *like* to be the exiled rightful heir to a dukedom.[19] It is
the sort of mournfully self-dignifying language of exile, I mean, that
permeates too his dealings with the theatrical. There is not only a
wonderful comic disproportion between the claims of those show-
bills and what the audience will actually see. ('"But if Juliet's such a
young gal, Duke, my peeled head and my white whiskers is goin' to
look uncommon odd on her, maybe."') There is also a wild kind of
poetry and even a sort of pathos, in that it is as if for their composer
the idea of Mr Garrick, Mr Kean, and 'the whole strength of the
company', in all its richly anachronistic splendour, were more real
than the actualities of the coming performance, and as if he too were
becoming momentarily one of the heroic servants of 'the histrionic
muse'. His gallimaufry Hamlet soliloquy may be preposterous, but
its melancholy resonances can be heard in the Shakespearian-
theatrical diction of his conversation on other occasions, and even,
to judge from its title, in the poem of his own composing that he
leaves set up in the printing office. And however preposterous his
notion of theatre in general may be, it doesn't seem excessive to see
him as being in part a romantic hero himself because of it – as being,
I mean, in some measure self-consciously estranged from those
around him by his sense of a larger and nobler reality which they
cannot share.

That all four of the white protagonists – Huck and Tom, the King
and the Duke – function in some strikingly similar ways in relation
to 'ordinary' people in the novel is a point that presumably doesn't
need much elaboration by now. With their restlessness, curiosity,
inventiveness, alertness, purposeful role-playings, and manipulations, they are set sharply apart both from the respectable folk of
St Petersburg and the Wilks and Phelps communities and from
drifters and idlers like Pap and the Bricksville whittlers and chewers;
and if I have been reading the novel correctly, the chief factor that

gives their activities their particular shapes is what can roughly be called 'Europe'. It is not, of course, a single clear concept that is shared by all of them. Indeed, in a sense it is not a concept at all. Rather, it is a cluster of heroic images of larger-than-life figures – noble outlaws, great actors, daring prison-breaking aristocrats – whose patterns of conduct have been assimilated into their own lives by way of books or conversations, even though their conscious relationships to those images may at times be cynically exploitative or outright dismissive. And this indebtedness seems to me the reverse of ironical, regardless of what Twain may have thought he was up to about Europe and romanticism. From the point of view of the richer life of the mind and its irrepressible cravings, the novel brilliantly demonstrates how mistaken is the attempt to draw any sharp lines between realism, naturalness, and truth on the one hand and romanticism, artificiality, and (by implication) falsity on the other. Just as the novel is not anti-romantic, so it is not anti-cultural either, and for the same reasons.

To sneer at what Mr Marx has called 'the tawdry nature of the culture of the great valley',[20] especially the 'higher' cultural manifestations, is a temptation to be resisted, it seems to me. We can understand, of course, why V. S. Pritchett should have said that,

As Huck and old Jim drift down the Mississippi from one horrifying little town to the next and hear the voices of men quietly swearing to one another across the water; as they pass the time of day with the scroungers, rogues, murderers, the lonely women, the frothing revivalists, the maundering boatmen and fantastic drunks of the river towns, we see the human wastage that is left in the wake of a great effort of the human will, the hopes frustrated, the idealism which has been whittled down to eccentricity and craft. These people are the price paid for building a new country.[21]

But if such a reaction is understandable – and a similar air of distaste is discernible in several of Twain's *American* critics – it seems to me to result from overlooking not only the generosity but the subtlety of the book, and involves a celebration of gentility under the ostensible guise of celebrating freedom. The river, I suggest, is the great central symbol that it is, not by virtue of being cleaner and nicer than human society, especially frontier society, but because it is the greatest natural manifestation of *energy* in the American landscape – and because the flow of human energies is what the book is hymning. Viewed from England or New England, the villagers and small-townspeople may 'deserve' their exploitation by the representatively predatory Duke and King. Viewed in its actual context, on the other hand, their vulnerability to supposed or actual phrenologists, singing-geography teachers, revivalists, strolling players, European aristocrats, and the rest is a far from contemptible testimony to a craving for a broadening of mental horizons, an arousal and ordering of energies, a general enlargement of being – in sum, for precisely the things which are prerequisites for the establishment of civilization. And the two areas of achieved order that we are shown the most intimately – the Grangerford and Phelps households – are far from contemptible. Mr Marx may feel indignant at the obliviousness of the Phelpses to the inquity of slavery. But the household *is* a thoroughly decent and kindly one, and (*pace* Mr Marx) no intended irony is apparent when Huck learns from Tom that 'Jim told him Uncle Silas come in every day or two to pray with him, and Aunty Sally come in to see if he was comfortable and had plenty to eat, and both of them as kind as they could be.' Sophisticated modern eyes may discern a 'queer mixture of arrogant show and pathetic provincialism' (Richard P. Adams) in the Grangerford household generally and 'a tawdry and faded effort at a high style' (Henry Nash Smith)[22] in its furnishings and decorations. But if we bear in mind the place and the period, the pervasive orderliness, harmoniousness, and general domestic decency are triumphs of civilization over a wilderness, and the lovingly assembled household treasures testify to more important things than bad taste. Twain himself was a great deal more charitable to the Grangerfords than his critics, and we can see why. The true antithesis to this sort of household in the book is not the natural raft but the naturalness of Pap and the Arkansas loafers, in whom form and order and decency have become lost altogether.

Whatever their limitations, moreover, the Grangerfords, like Huck, have been enabled through their own dealings with culture to live with a greater and more purposeful energy, and to impose themselves on existence instead of being its victims. They *choose* their destinies. Alexander Cowie was pointing to a vital truth when he recalled 'the fact, often lost sight of, that Mark Twain was first of all a Southerner';[23] and to see how Twain's admiration for certain virtues comes to a head in his presentation of the quintessential Southern figure of Colonel Sherburn is to understand why the novel should have started slackening off after the Bricksville section.

Were Sherburn's appearance limited to the gunning-down of Boggs, there would be good grounds for the conventional reading of the novel with respect to Southern romanticism. Here, Twain would then appear to be saying, is what it all comes down to when you strip away the rituals and the glamour: cold-blooded pointless murder. But of course that episode is only half the picture, and when we turn to the Colonel's speech to the would-be lynch mob the picture changes. True, the logic of the speech is a trifle dizzying, particularly in view of the intrusively authorial tone, and we are liable to end up feeling that we are disturbingly close here to the law of the jungle. But the important thing is that the speech is that of a man coolly and bravely facing down a dangerous mob, and doing so while casually tossing them the assurance that they would be perfectly within their rights to lynch him. It is the speech of someone utterly sure of where he stands and what he is prepared to do, and in contrast to the mob he too, like the culture of the Grangerfords, is far from contempt-ible. If, therefore, we have seen one stripped-down aspect of the chivalric code in the ruthless killing of Boggs, we are seeing its converse now in the no less ruthless self-exposure of the Colonel without benefit of help from servants, intimations of retribution, or appeals to the chivalric code itself. Mr Smith has interestingly observed that

Sherburn belongs to the series of characters in Mark Twain's later work that have been called 'transcendent' figures. Other examples are Hank Morgan in *A Connecticut Yankee*; Pudd'nhead Wilson; and Satan in *The Mysterious Stranger*. They exhibit certain common traits, more fully developed with the passage of time. They are isolated by their intellectual superiority to the community; they are contemptuous of mankind in gen-eral; and they have more than ordinary power. [24]

The admiration that Twain accords Sherburn may be ambivalent but, if so, the ambivalence lies in Southern culture as he has pre-sented it, and in that presentation the strengths are inseparable from the weaknesses.

It is therefore not surprising that the momentum of *Huckleberry Finn* breaks after the Bricksville section and that the centre of atten-tion shifts away from Huck and the river. It is not even surprising that the treatment of the Phelps' plantation should be so free of irony, especially about slavery. In terms of his essential themes there was nowhere left for Twain to go after Bricksville except back to the world of his childhood. Having affirmed so strongly the seemingly basic Southern values, he could not develop the Huck-and-Jim exchanges into a radical critique of an institution so intricately bound up with those values; and having given so deep an assent to civilization and culture he had nothing intense left with which to oppose even their duller manifestations. There is something fitting about the eventual disappearance even of his ironies about religion, as in Huck's praise of Silas Phelps:

He was the innocentest, best old soul I ever see. But it warn't surprising; because he warn't only just a farmer, he was a preacher, too, and had a little one-horse log church down back of the plantation, which he built it himself at his own expense, for a church and school-house, and never charged nothing for his preaching, and it was worth it, too. There was plenty other farmer-preachers like that, and done the same way, down South.

It is as if Twain's creative intelligence, wiser than the intelligences of most of his critics, had acknowledged the fact that Huck's untutored goodness, like all his other strengths, was itself a cultural creation.[25]

But I wish to end with an even more important way in which the Bricksville section is climactic. Virtually everything of thematic significance in the novel is there in those three brilliant chapters, including as they do the Sherburn episode, the King and Duke's gulling of the townspeople, Huck's rationalistic yet half-admiring short history of 'Henry the Eight', and the closing account by Jim of his unintentional cruelty to his deaf daughter; and in reading a novel that works so much in terms of juxtapositions it is obviously necessary to hold all the thematic aspects in mind at once if we are not to oversimplify it. But if there is one that deserves stressing above all the others, it is surely what finds such brilliant expression in the account of the circus, especially in the following lovely passage.

It was the splendidest sight that ever was, when they all come riding in, two and two, a gentleman and lady, side by side, the men just in their drawers and undershirts, and no shoes nor stirrups, and resting their hands on their thighs, easy and comfortable – there must 'a been twenty of them – and every lady with a lovely complexion, and perfectly beautiful, and looking just like a gang of real sure-enough queens, and dressed in clothes that cost millions of dollars, and just littered with diamonds. It was a powerful fine sight; I never see anything so lovely. And then one by one they got up and stood, and went a-weaving around the ring so gentle and wavy and graceful, the men looking ever so tall and airy and straight, with their heads bobbing and skimming along, away up there under the tent-roof, and every lady's rose-leafy dress flapping soft and silky around her hips, and she looking like the most loveliest parasol.

It is art and life, truth and deception, self-affirmation and social organization, 'American' expertise and 'European' culture all at once – creative human energy and skill displayed all the more unforgettably and meaningfully because of the highly artificial order that they have taken and their dazzling contrast with the 'natural' life of the streets outside. Furthermore, the thrill of the demonstration of unsuspected human possibilities and transfigurations comes in part, as Huck's reactions to the trick rider remind us, from a generous capacity for participating in make-believe and responding to the power of style.

But pretty soon he struggled up astraddle and grabbed the bridle, a-reeling this way and that; and the next minute he sprung up and dropped the bridle and stood! and the horse agoing like a house afire too. He just stood up there, a-sailing around as easy and comfortable as if he warn't ever drunk in his life – and then he begun to pull off his clothes and sling them. He shed them so thick they kind of clogged up the air, and altogether he shed seventeen suits. And then, there he was, slim and handsome, and dressed the gaudiest and prettiest you ever saw, and he lit into that horse with his whip and made him fairly hum – and finally skipped off, and made his bow and danced off to the dressing room, and everybody just a-howling with pleasure and astonishment.

It is in some such terms, I am convinced, that the greatness of *Huckleberry Finn* itself must be defended.

Othello and Honour

From time to time, a certain posture has been noticeable in English criticism. Displayed for our instruction, and desiderated of other critics and teachers, is what is evidently felt to be a warmer, a more generous, a *nobler* response to literature than has sometimes obtained. Instead of arming himself with moral concerns, clenching himself tight, and staring bleakly at a literary work as if it were an examination answer by an unreliable candidate, the right-minded critic, or so one gathers, has modestly sought out works in which a certain richness and openness of feeling is dominant and then zestfully surrendered himself to them. C. S. Lewis was the master practitioner here, of course, but Miss Helen Gardner's British Academy lecture 'The Noble Moor' is one of the more insidious examples of this attitude, and since its status has been enhanced by its inclusion in Mrs Ann Ridler's second World's Classics anthology of Shakespeare criticism, I shall approach *Othello* itself by way of it. Miss Gardner is concerned to save the play from people who have a 'distaste for the heroic', don't care for 'the beautiful idealisms of moral excellence', and hunt for 'some psychological weakness in the hero ... whose discovery will protect [them] from tragic experience by substituting for its pleasures the easier gratifications of moral and intellectual superiority to the sufferer'.[1] I don't doubt that such people exist, though I haven't read anything by them on *Othello*; I am equally sure, however, that the ostensibly more humane and noble-minded approach of Miss Gardner is no less inadequate to the richness of the play.

Though expressed with her customary elegance, Miss Gardner's attitude to Othello is really pretty much a bobby-soxer one: Othello is still marvellously The Hero, still incomparably noble, his death simply sublime; especially 'he is primarily a man of *faith* [my italics], whose faith has witnessed to itself in his deeds';[2] and thus the play, in presenting to us his destruction by Iago, is still able to provide us with the proper dyke-breaking 'tragic experience'. Well, the 'tragic experience' exists, of course, and I shall offer one or two comments on it myself further on. Heroism exists (though not always in the obviously glamorous forms that Miss Gardner, I suspect, prefers). Nobility exists; so does the poignancy of its destruction. The closing pages of Malory, for instance, are some of the most poignant in English literature, and there are similar parts in other works that give fresh life to the old metaphor of plucking at the heartstrings: 'all the nobility of earth', to borrow from Yeats again, seems temporarily there. But precious as this experience is – indeed, partly because it *is* precious – it seems to me undesirable to seek for it, or for the comparable experience of nobility triumphant in a simpler way, in works that offer either something cruder (some of Yeats' poems, for instance) or something more complex. Certainly nobility and poignancy are there in *Othello*. No reputable critic since Rymer, I take it, has denied it; certainly F. R. Leavis didn't. But a good deal else is there too, and to seek to shut it out in the interests of saving nobility and the 'tragic experience' not only makes the play cruder and diminishes Shakespeare's immense intelligence but casts doubt on the value of what is to be saved. When in addition to extolling Othello as 'primarily a man of faith', Miss Gardner assures us that his 'nobility lies in his capacity to worship: to feel wonder and give service', and that 'loyalty is the very principle of his moral being',[3] she seems to me to be inviting the wisecrack that if you have Othello's loyalty you don't need anyone else's treachery.

But for the evidence of Miss Gardner's piece, I would have thought that by now it was a commonplace that in most of his plays, and especially in those of his creative maturity, Shakespeare was engaged, among other things, in testing out the worth of various attitudes to life by setting them in motion in ways that bring out their implications as fully as possible. In the major tragedies the component forcing us towards evaluation is the commission of crimes or of acts so disastrous in their consequences as to deserve being considered criminal. What happens in the later parts of the plays sends us back critically and analytically to what happens earlier – provided, I suppose, that we are as concerned with the Shakespearian experience as with the tragic one. Were Macbeth, for instance, shown getting away with Duncan's murder and settling down to a comfortable reign, as Antonio was able to do in *The Tempest* in a comparable situation, our assessments of the torments of conscience he suffers before committing his crime would presumably be different. Certainly *Shakespeare's* would have been.

Similarly, were *Othello* to end with Act II or to continue in the same vein we could indeed reasonably feel invited to enthuse about Othello's nobility and the worth of the attitudes embodied in him.

But of course there is also much that contrasts sharply with what we find in that first part and in Othello's closing speech, even in Miss Gardner's own terms, and which Miss Gardner, presumably in the interests of preserving the 'tragic experience' unsullied, chooses almost wholly to ignore. Not only is there the appallingness of the murder itself, there is also the increasing ugliness of Othello's conduct leading up to it – his total inability to see Desdemona, once his suspicion has been aroused, as the lovely, loyal, self-sacrificing individual that she is; his ignoble brutality towards her in front of the Venetian emissaries; the greater and more ignoble brutality and cruelty of his treatment of her in the 'brothel' scene; his ignoble passing on to Iago of the duty of repaying Cassio for the latter's 'dishonourable' actions; and the hideousness of his sending Desdemona to her death without the chance to relieve herself by prayer of some of the burden of what he takes to be her sins. For anyone with normal decent feelings, surely, all this is hair-raising conduct, the workings indeed of what Leavis called 'ferocious stupidity, an insane and self-deceiving passion';[4] and a conception of 'moral excellence' that would allow a critic to feel morally superior to someone who was disturbed by such conduct would strike me as very odd. Moreover, the poignancy of the willow-song scene, with its contrast with the feverish machinations of Othello and Iago that frame it, and the passionate moral indignation given voice by Emilia after the murder, suggest that for Shakespeare too the conduct of Othello, some of it, was more shockingly criminal than even that of Macbeth. To murder a noble king is very dreadful, but Duncan isn't brought before us with anything like the beautiful pitiful substantiality of Desdemona. Accordingly, we are compelled to consider, as Shakespeare seems to me to have been considering, the causes of these horrors, which entails an assessment of attitudes embodied in the characters. Given the apparent nobility of Othello at the outset of the play, given the love relationship that Miss Gardner finely characterizes as 'displaying the capacity of the human heart for joy and leaving on the mind an ineffaceable impression of splendour',[5] *how* can such hideous results have come about so rapidly? It is a question that most critics who have dealt seriously with the play have felt driven to ask, in one way or another. My own answer may be more psychological than is fashionable, but as Leavis's superb essay demonstrates, the play lends itself 'uniquely well' to a Bradleyan approach, and any play that can contain the willow-song scene can bear a good deal of character analysis in modern terms. I will add that more historical approaches to the play (Mr Laurence Lerner's, for instance, in 'The Machiavel and the Moor'[6]) have sometimes left me wondering wherein Shakespeare's genius is supposed to be manifesting itself.

When Othello, amid the ruin that he has caused, is confronted by Lodovico's question 'What should be said to thee?' and retorts, 'An honourable murderer, if you will: / For nought did I in hate, but all in honour', it seems an odd answer – that is, either simply untrue, or else raising the gravest doubts about the value of the honour involved. I think that the answer is correct and that the term 'honour' here points to a kind of masculine disposition, a way of conceiving of oneself, that has been brilliantly defined in the course of the play. There is a good deal to be said for it, moreover. It bothered Hamlet enough, certainly, and I think it bothered Shakespeare enough for him to give it full play in *Othello* and explore how far the Hamletian perturbation was justified. Certainly it has had enough vitality to enchant or intimidate males in Western culture for a longish time now. But if it is arguable that the real hero of the play is not so much Othello as the love of Othello and Desdemona as shown in the first two acts, it is also arguable that the villain is, in a sense, not Iago but the male ego-ideal that operates so strongly in both Iago and Othello, and to some extent in Cassio, too, and even in Roderigo. And it is with the workings of this ideal that I shall be concerned in the rest of these pages.

It is important, first of all, to note the narrowing down, the emphasizing of a certain kind of maleness, that Shakespeare has effected by making his three male protagonists professional soldiers in a warring world. From the outset we are in an environment in which men have to make their way by sheer force of personality, unassisted by any of the externally derived or bestowed numinousness that in the other major tragedies is enjoyed by the royal or noble figures. And the idea of 'honour' is thus of unusual importance. A man's authority with his own men and his power to intimidate the enemy both depend to a considerable extent on his reputation. And not only others but he himself must believe that he has displayed certain admirable qualities in the past and will continue to do so in the future, for the more confident he can feel of this, the more he can act with that unhesitating commitment of all his energies in dangerous situations that alone makes possible the fullest military success. Accordingly a premium is put not only on hardihood, courage, extroverted vigour, and decisiveness, but also on a high degree of self-consistency, self-control, and self-sufficiency – on all those qualities that differentiate their possessors sharply from the teeming, unheroic, indistinguishable beasts and cits conjured up by Iago to spur Othello on so devastatingly to being 'a man'. I suggest that in his cherished, pre-marital, 'unhoused free condition' Othello would have listened very tolerantly to Iago's 'Virtue? a fig!' speech, and that when we consider the reactions of the two men to the marriage we can see the same martial disposition persisting destructively in them both.

The causes of Iago's outbreak of frenetic destructiveness seem to me fairly obvious. Obsessed as he is by the ideal of total self-sufficiency, total self-control, and an irresistible quasi-military imposition of his will on his environment, his precarious stance is especially threatened by the idea of heterosexual love, with its continual invitation to the supreme yielding and fusion. (The beast has two backs but it is a single beast.) But the more aloof he holds himself, the more imperative is it, for the sake of his self-esteem, to believe that if he doesn't go around all the time making sexual conquests it isn't because he couldn't if he chose to: the women, in the running account he offers of them, are always out there waiting, lecherously and contemptibly, for the interested male. Accordingly, the possibility that even one woman could passionately and permanently and selflessly love someone else is hardly to be borne. It is clear that Iago has felt lustfully about Desdemona, in a peeping-Tom fashion. It is equally clear that were he ever to condescend to make advances he would be rejected in a way that would make it inescapable that the very qualities that are the framework of his life (and which have made him an emotional cripple) would preclude him forever from serious consideration by her either as a lover or as a man. Thus the growth of the whole marvellous relationship between Desdemona and Othello has been posing an increasingly insupportable threat to Iago's emotional position; and Othello's promotion of Cassio proves the trigger that it does because Cassio, the intermediary during the courtship, is so much the hymner and promoter of chivalrous love. In turning not only towards

Desdemona but towards Cassio, Othello has seemingly turned away from the simpler mode of existence and set of values that he and Iago have shared hitherto, and no mere verbal pulling down of the idea of love and of women's purity can suffice Iago any longer against the living demonstration of them. The implicit devaluing of Iago is presumably especially unendurable because of the seemingly idyllic quality of the life that Othello is now entering on.

As presented during the first two acts, the relationship between Othello and Desdemona appears from the male's point of view to be virtually ideal. Not only is it one of those near-miraculous Beauty-and-the-Beast relationships in which none of those aspects that might seem to make the male innately unlovable discourage one of the loveliest of women from giving her unstinted love; it is also one in which, on the whole, the Beast can remain a Beast. That is to say, the man can go on being fully, vigorously, and uncompromisingly martial, and whatever happens the woman will stay with him, esteem him, love him; his energies are free to continue flowing steadily outwards in officially sanctioned public actions that consort most with his own drives. However, these are only the possi-bilities; in actuality, Othello's marriage has scarcely begun yet, and what we very soon start perceiving are forces that preclude the re-alization of those possibilities. One highly important one has already been hinted at – the importance, for the representative male that Othello is, of feeling *triumphant*. Iago, as we see him, obtains this gratification not only through his manipulation of others but through his sense of successfully resisting all claims that he worry about other people's opinions; Othello, as a soldier, cares a lot about other people's opinions but is confident that what he does is publicly admired and that he is very much the heroic conqueror. And 'love', for Othello, is still largely a matter of conquering: it is the attainment not only of an incomparable woman in the teeth of powerful opposition but also of the heights of human felicity. We could imagine his 'If it were now to die / 'Twere now to be most happy' speech on his arrival in Cyprus being delivered in his pre-marital state at the close of some desperate battle of the gravest importance. And it is significant that in his last speech in the play the image that he summons up to epitomize Desdemona is that of a pearl – something hard, pure, separate, a prize, an evoker of admir-ation, a source of honour for the possessor. The marriage made, however, the conquest is ended and can't be repeated. And the complexities of actual marriage, in contrast to the imagined simple happiness of it, begin to appear.

That Othello's attitude to Desdemona, when viewed as a whole, is not chivalrous scarcely needs saying. Clearly, too, when we consider the principal proponent of the chivalrous tradition in the play, namely Cassio, we see the weakening of its authority for the audience by the demonstration of Cassio's inadequate self-control and relative ineffectuality. Nor should we overlook the near-comic manifestation of the courtly attitude in Roderigo, with his infatuated willingness to do anything to win his mistress and his quasi-suicidal despair when facing failure. None the less, Othello is to some extent in touch with the chivalrous tradition through his relationship with Cassio and through general cultural assimilation; and what actual marriage, as we see it in the early exchanges between him and Desdemona, involves inside that tradition is the obligation to attend to one's lady as an individual, to listen carefully to her requests, and to provide ungrudgingly, within broad limits, whatever she may desire. For Othello, who has been born into a non-chivalrous culture and grown up under circumstances where he has known nothing about sophisticated European women and hasn't learned to read their signals, the strangeness, the *otherness*, of such a woman is bound to be pretty marked once he is brought into such close proximity to her. And Desdemona's disturbing otherness is all the greater because of her very tenderness and submissiveness, so totally at variance with all that Othello himself has lived by. (Even for the audience there is a certain mysteriousness about her as the crisis grows: we are never allowed inside her mind through a soliloquy.) I think, therefore, that an important truth is revealed when, in response to Othello's injunction to her to 'Think on thy sins', Desdemona cries 'They are loves I bear to you' and Othello retorts, 'And for that thou diest'. The experience of being loved can be a good deal more disturbing than that of loving, since it puts so much pressure on a person to respond tenderly and stay continually aware of the other one's individuality.

But Desdemona's individuality is in fact the hardest thing for Othello to hold clearly in mind. Desdemona, before anything else, is A Woman, and what Iago is able to cash in on, by the most perfunctory hints, is the same deep male distrust of women and uneasiness about sex as his own. The poles of the male consciousness in the play are on the one hand the marble hardness of the heavens, the irresistibility of the sea's icy currents, the bright sharpness of swords; on the other, the mingling, merging, and surrendering of the bed. And the male sense of powerlessness before the threatening and mysterious vitality of woman, with her clinging invitation to formlessness and passivity, gets most fully expressed in Othello's passionate

> O curse of marriage,
> That we can call these delicate creatures ours,
> And not their appetites!

and his conviction that

> 'Tis destiny, unshunnable, like death:
> Even then this forked plague is fated to us,
> When we do quicken...

It is to all the deep-rooted male convictions about the desirability and possibility of hardness and separateness and self-respect that Iago is able to appeal so successfully in his reiterated admonitions to Othello to be 'a man'.

I have already drawn attention to some of the disastrous consequences of Othello's being a man in such a way. That Shakespeare himself was concerned with the *representative* quality of Othello's values and instabilities is further suggested by how, as the two males get increasingly estranged from reality during their fevered plottings, the realities not only of particular women in the play but of women's position in general get brought out during the fourth and fifth acts. When Othello, with outraged masculine indignation, adduces the inmates of brothels as the supreme examples of the corruptness of women, the relationship that we have just seen between Cassio and Bianca reminds us that after all it is men – including some who probably think of themselves as worshipping Woman – who bring them their business. (For that matter, Othello's language to Desdemona suggests that in his time he has brought them some himself.) And when Desdemona, in the willow-song scene, is shown in all her mysterious, lovely individuality prepared to accept whatever her husband may decide to do to her and revealing something very like a sense of being guilty by the mere fact of being female, we have in our minds not only the actuality of Othello as he is currently behaving, but also the robust common sense of Emilia about the male fuss over cuckoldry and her splendid peroration (recalling Shylock's on behalf of the Jews) about the deplorable treatment of women by men. These things linger in the mind when the closing scene arrives; they subtly undercut Othello's pretensions to being a dispassionate bringer of justice, remind us of the wicked absurdity of the idea that if honour is to be saved adultery must be punished by death, and point up still further the fear of woman that Othello reveals during the exchange that culminates in Desdemona's murder. Finally, when the obsessive 'honourable' masculine fantasies get exposed by Emilia for what they are, the impassioned voice of outraged and revolting woman becomes one with that of outraged normal humanity confronting ludicrous error and an intolerable crime.

But if my account is broadly true, and if there are elements in Othello's conduct during the last two acts that wouldn't make savage farce a wholly inappropriate term for some of the action, what room is left for the tragic experience? I think there is room enough.

A frequent element in this experience, I take it, is that at the outset of a play we sympathize not so much with a character as with a disposition, a set of values, an image of admirable human possibilities embodied in him or his situation, so that their erosion or destruction in the course of what follows, when done convincingly, perturbs us deeply because of the devaluing of them that seems to be entailed. Thus far I have been emphasizing the defects of the ego-ideal that we encounter in Othello; the worth of it, however, also needs acknowledging. The conception of integrity, of being so self-coherent that there can be a steady outflowing of the psyche resulting in privately satisfying and publicly commendable actions, is an admirable one; and the instances of the loss of such integrity in the course of the play are both poignant because of the feelings of the characters (Saturn's 'I have left / My strong identity, my real self' in *Hyperion* describes them well) and also threatening. With Cassio's fall we experience chiefly the poignancy. When his drunken brawling, seemingly so natural while occurring, is exposed as the silly, dangerous, and disgraceful thing that it is when described objectively by Iago and judged objectively by Othello in his capacity as General, Cassio's self-reproaches seem painfully justified; there are indeed steps that we can take that suddenly and permanently cut us off from the roles that we have chosen and from our expectations for the future. However, the idea of honourable integrity itself gets strengthened at this point by the seeming demonstration in Othello of what Cassio has lapsed from. With Othello's own far greater fall, however, the whole ideal seems to go to pieces: the very aspiring towards it seemingly precludes its being attained. And yet at the moment of greatest ruin, with Desdemona dead and Othello revealed to himself as having behaved like a fool and a scoundrel, a reaffirmation begins, as Othello starts to re-establish a relationship with his past self that isolates what was quintessentially admirable in it.

The speech beginning 'Behold, I have a weapon' is crucial here not only because it displays his awakening to the totality of his estrangement – an awakening arising brilliantly out of his momentarily feeling in the old way, his sword once more in hand – but also because of his confrontation of his own possible damnation. Miss Gardner's judgement that 'damnation and salvation are outside the field of reference' of the play[7] I find incomprehensible. The play reverberates with reminders of Christian beliefs and feelings, and does so above all in the language of Othello himself, whose mounting preoccupation in the fourth and fifth acts with the possible damnation of Desdemona and the importance of the state of mind in which she dies scarcely seems necessary to point out in these pages. In suggesting, then, that in the lines beginning 'Whip me, ye devils' we have merely 'an intolerably intensified form of the common "I could kick myself"',[8] Leavis surely comes surprisingly close to missing the point. What in fact we see in these flesh-tingling lines is Othello not only developing his acknowledgement that 'When we shall meet at compt, / This look of thine will hurl my soul from heaven, / And fiends will snatch at it', but also relinquishing utterly all claims to mercy; and the depth of his commitment is testified to by his abrupt relinquishment, authenticated by the blazing contrast between this passage and the hitherto characteristic 'Pontic Sea' one, of all future claims to the dignity and inviolability that till now he has striven so powerfully to maintain.

It seems plain to me, therefore, that the elements in Othello's final speech that can not unfairly be described as 'cheering himself up' are not of major importance when the speech is considered in its context, and that its total effect is indeed, as Leavis asserts, 'tragic and grand'. It is the speech, that is to say, not of someone trying to arrive at a position but of someone who is already there. Othello has already judged his crime with the same kind of firmness with which earlier he judged that of the brawling Cassio, and has condemned himself past hope of recall, with the blow that he is about to strike, to an incomparably greater banishment. The torments that, by his own account, he can expect to endure – and only a handful of minutes have gone by since he cried out of Desdemona, 'She's like a liar gone to burning hell!' and protested of himself, 'O, I were damned beneath all depth in hell / But that I did proceed upon just ground / To this extremity' – those torments will be immeasurably more awful than those that his co-conspirator will be facing at the hands of merely human torturers. If, then, Othello hasn't arrived at any intellectual self-scrutiny and condemnation of his mental processes, he has certainly condemned his conduct unequivocally enough – and he dies heroically. To judge a man a hero is not to judge him impeccable or wise or even likeable. None of Shakespeare's tragic heroes, it seems to me, displays much wisdom when dying. But it is precisely because they do die, as they have lived, as imperfect and struggling human beings that we experience that sense of liberation, of a bursting of the dykes, when a certain kind of splendour emerging suddenly out of the most unlikely circumstances reminds us anew of the heroic potentialities in people.

And there is a little more that needs to be said about the effect of the play as a whole. I have suggested that in a sense the real hero of the play is the idea of a particular kind of romantic-love relationship that is evoked before our eyes so powerfully in the first two acts, and that the villain is a certain kind of male ego-ideal; and I have discussed the play largely in terms of the exposure of errors. But to perceive errors in a person or in an idea is by no means necessarily to remain coldly detached. Admittedly we should never discount the possibility of someone's having himself so transcended a certain kind of conflict that he does remain detached – and rightly so: no one, I imagine, would wish to argue that a Spinoza *ought* to bring himself to feel like Macbeth. But for most of us the images of love, as of honour, in *Othello* still have great power. The strangeness and otherness of men and women for each other is a fact of most human experience, and a yearning for miracles, especially the miracle of the seemingly perfect love that is displayed in the first two acts, is very hard to get rid of. The play shows the unwisdom of such a yearning and of the absolutism in which 'honour' and 'love', 'triumph' and 'failure', are like countries whose borders we either stand wholly within or wholly without. It demonstrates that for people to be governed by such rigid ideals and to sit in judgement with such total certainty on each other and on themselves as they do throughout the play is to take too much upon themselves and to reveal too narrow an understanding of the possibilities of human nature. But they are not complacent demonstrations, and Shakespeare himself continued struggling with these issues until he won through to the resolutions in *A Winter's Tale*, *Cymbeline*, and *The Tempest*. It seems to me that most of us participate anew in the conflicts ourselves when experiencing the play. I also believe, however, that it is desirable that we should not only have important experiences, tragic or otherwise, in our dealings with literature, but should be able to learn from them, and my quarrel with Miss Gardner's approach is that it seems to make this impossible.

The Name of Action:
Nelly Dean and *Wuthering Heights*

'It was no concern of mine, either to advise or complain and I
always refused to meddle'.

Zillah on young Catherine[1]

It was inevitable, no doubt, that sooner or later Nelly Dean should
have been discovered to be the villain of *Wuthering Heights*.[2] With
her attempted guardianships, the uncertain limits of her duty and
authority, and her 'little note of neatness, firmness and courage'[3] in
the midst of abnegated responsibilities, destructive eroticism,
ruthless manipulativeness, and grave threats to the innocent, her
situation strikingly resembles that of the governess in *The Turn of
the Screw*; and the critical animosity towards James's unfortunate
heroine has of course been intense. That animosity seems to me
disturbing, and it would be even more disturbing if attacking Nelly
Dean were to become fashionable. Both James and Emily Brontë
present us with individuals who are trapped, partly for economic
reasons, partly by their sympathies and moral inclinations, in situations in which they are confronted by various kinds of
destructiveness and must act resolutely against them; and the
attacks that I have mentioned seem to me symptomatic of a too-
common sentimentality about wickedness and an unwillingness to
acknowledge that sooner or later judgement and action can become
imperative.[4]

As *Wuthering Heights* reminds us, it is easy enough to be tolerant
of other people, particularly more-or-less romantic ones, so long as
we feel in no danger from them ourselves, like Lockwood gazing
benignly on Heathcliff at the outset of the narrative, or Isabella
before she elopes with him. As Heathcliff remarks sardonically of
the latter, 'No brutality disgusted her – I suppose, she has an innate
admiration of it, if only her precious person were secure from
injury.' And naturally enough, when that security and her romantic
illusions are shattered, it is Isabella who turns the most violently
against him, the accents of a bitter sincerity informing her voiced

hunger for vengeance, her 'Is Mr Heathcliff a man? If so, is he mad? And if not, is he a devil?', her flat 'He's not a human being.' When characters in this novel misjudge other people, as all of them do at various times, they are liable to suffer more or less acutely as a result, in ways that make sentimentality a dangerous luxury. And with respect to the necessity for judging well, Nelly Dean is as enmeshed as any of them in what goes on. She is dependent on the good will of her successive employers, answerable to their commands, bound up in their fates, and potentially the victim of violences herself (Heathcliff punches her, Hindley drunkenly holds a loaded pistol to her mouth); and it is to her that the other protagonists keep presenting themselves for judgement, sympathy, and help.

Obviously Nelly judges wrongly at times. Large zones of feeling in Cathy and Heathcliff are simply closed to her, and when we consider her religious commonplaces, her distrust of the mysterious, her dislike of pride (especially feminine pride), and her scepticism about the possibility of earthly happiness, we can see why she should have been felt to be on the side of repression, in contrast to the passionate self-affirmation of the two doomed lovers. But I suggest that predominantly she judges correctly and that the general set of her mind is a good deal closer to the author's than might be supposed. In an extraordinary manifestation of genius, Emily Brontë was able to do three things that rarely occur together. She gave vivid life to the atrocious cruelties that people are capable of, without either transposing them into melodrama or plunging into Isabella's kind of metaphysical questionings about human nature; she accorded an equal reality to various sympathetic aspects of their perpetrators, including ways in which they too were victims, without lapsing into a *tout comprendre* permissiveness; and she took cognizance of the defects and errors of the weak without edging towards a Nietzschean or Sadean celebration of the strong. I think that we see something of this breadth of vision in Nelly too, and her relative ordinariness in other ways makes all the more interesting the fineness with which she comports herself amid moral perplexities.

To begin with, Nelly's behaviour can partly be defined by considering what it isn't – the extremes to which she doesn't go. On the one hand, she isn't afflicted by the kind of over-identification in which we see, virtually, through someone else's eyes, suffer helplessly along with them, and cannot find the mental leverage with which

to alter their attitudes or, when the authority of disinterestedness is
called for, the attitudes of others towards them; and such identifying
is invited particularly strongly by Heathcliff's justifiably embittered
broodings during his wretched boyhood, Cathy's tempests of feeling
later about Heathcliff and the emotionally inadequate Edgar,
Isabella's post-marital loathing of Heathcliff, and young
Catherine's charming quasi-maternal yearnings after Linton. On
the other hand, she does not succumb to any of the modes of excessive disengagement that the novel displays for us, such as the shallow
and flippant aestheticizing of Lockwood, the callous 'realism' of
Zillah with her 'I always refused to meddle', and Isabella's kind of
dehumanizing. Nor does she display the dehumanizing pseudo-
understanding with which we classify someone as a case and
consign them into the hands of 'experts', or the impotence that
comes from having made so many or such serious mistakes ourselves that we no longer dare trust our own judgement, or the more
insidious kind that results from a chronic uneasiness about the
purity of our motives. (The salutary undermining of self-
righteousness by novelists like Hawthorne, James, and E. M. Forster
has had some less salutary side-effects.)

And something else is absent from how Nelly responds to people.
When dehumanizing occurs, it is generally accompanied by the
belief that we know what the 'real' self of the other person is like,
either because some aspect of his conduct (for Isabella, Heathcliff's
abominable cruelty to her) has so thrust itself upon our notice that
all the others fade into insignificance, or because we flatter ourselves
that we discern the main relationships inside his psyche, as if contemplating a map or diagram. The belief that we can grasp what
people really 'are' is fostered, of course, by the extensive chartings of
them in fiction, biographies, psychological case-histories, and so on;
and the extent to which we hold it is closely allied to how we go
about judging people morally. In *Pride and Prejudice*, for example,
the characters predominantly judge one another by taking note of
various actions and inferring from them a constellation of dispositions that will remain the same for the rest of the other person's
life; and actions are responded to as much for what they reveal
about this self as for their effects on others. The assurance with
which Jane Austen herself sums up some of the characters ('She was
a woman of mean understanding, little information, and uncertain
temper'), the predictability of most of them, the fairly narrow range

of development in the ones that do change, the fact that the latter, in changing, are becoming more stable, the public availability of a good deal of true information about all of them (especially about the Wickham–Darcy relationship), and the way in which Elizabeth Bennett attains to ever fuller and clearer knowledge of Darcy, all tend to validate this approach. In *Wuthering Heights*, in contrast, the characters come to us piecemeal and often surprisingly, as they do to the two main narrators, and without any comprehensive assessment of them by the author, the absence of any yardstick for measuring 'success' or 'failure' being especially noteworthy. I suggest that Nelly Dean, similarly, does not seek to define and judge the 'real' selves of those around her and that this makes it easier for her to respond justly to their actions, since it considerably increases her mental flexibility.

That flexibility is assisted, furthermore, by her religious faith. A very different thing from the self-aggrandizing fundamentalism of Joseph, it seems to consist chiefly of a feeling that God will administer justice eventually and that it is therefore presumptuous for people to sit in judgement upon one another. The feeling is most noticeable when she reproves others for wanting revenge, but it also contributes to her almost total abstention from comprehensive assessments of what other people are, as distinct from how they behave, and from attempts to forecast their futures. And because she doesn't construct rigid mental images of those around her and over-commit herself to them, she can change her attitudes to people as those people change. Her half-contempt for Edgar as a child and youth turns into respect for the husband who behaves on the whole with decency and dignity during the various crises of his marriage.[5] Contrariwise, her affection for the young Heathcliff is replaced by a deep distrust of the grown man who comes to menace the peace of the Linton household. And after the springs of Heathcliff's desire for vengeance have broken and he is drawing away into hallucination (or vision) and the embrace of death, he changes for her again and becomes someone who may, as she tells him, have 'lived a selfish, unchristian life' since he was thirteen, but who now needs to be encouraged to eat and sleep more and stop brooding. At no point during even the times of his greatest cruelties is she incapacitated from dealing with him by a choking sense of horror or disgust. And except for a momentary invasion of her weakened mind during a period of great strain, her religious consciousness precludes any massive self-condemnation either. She can acknowledge her mistakes without becoming morbidly undermined by them.

She does not, of course, simply banish the past from her consciousness; but her reactions to others are determined almost entirely by how they are behaving in the present. The one seeming exception, namely her persisting awareness of the melancholy contrast between what 'her' Hareton was like as a child and what he has become since his brutalization by Heathcliff, seems to me not really an exception: Hareton is not injuring others, and the virtues that Nelly recalls can still be glimpsed in him at times and bear on the question of young Catherine's future well-being. For the rest, the relationships in the novel all serve to corroborate Nelly's observation, 'Well, we *must* be for ourselves in the long run; the mild and generous are only more justly selfish than the domineering' – a remark that, in the context of the novel, is neither cynical nor indignant but merely a dispassionate acknowledgement of what Spinoza calls 'the endeavor wherewith everything endeavors to persist in its own being'.[6] That endeavour manifests itself here in an insistent interplay of thrusting individualities. And Nelly's interventions in their affairs are directed towards mitigating some of the more obviously harmful consequences of their actions when those actions force themselves upon her attention, in a spirit in accordance with her own *conatus*.

Most of her interventions during Cathy's childhood are small and *ad hoc* – trying to cheer up a neglected boy on Christmas Eve, encouraging him to take more pride in himself, removing the charges from the shotgun of a homicidal drunkard, standing up to the latter when he dangerously loses control – and after Cathy's death she is principally concerned to protect young Catherine from Heathcliff's machinations. Frequently she is unsuccessful, and at times she is seriously mistaken, such as when she allows herself to be persuaded into letting Catherine resume her acquaintance with Linton. But almost without exception she behaves humanely during the first period, shrewdly during the second, and courageously during both, and no large problems are posed either by how she intervenes or by the alternatives confronting her. Her role during Cathy's courtship and marriage is obviously more complicated, especially when she 'catechizes' her about her feelings for Edgar, informs Edgar of the relationship between Heathcliff, Isabella, and Cathy, and is unsympathetic to Cathy during the hysteria brought on by the confrontation and expulsion of Heathcliff by Edgar. In each of these episodes what she does, whether by speaking or by remaining silent, has more or less disastrous consequences. In each her incomprehension of the complexity of Cathy and Heathcliff's states of mind is glaring. And in each we are strongly conscious of a relationship that seems to transcend normal moral considerations and demand an unusual tolerance from less passionate natures. It appears to me, none the less, that Nelly's interventions are thoroughly defensible.

Two kinds of response seem invited by Cathy's conduct during and immediately before the 'catechism' scene. On the one hand, it is disturbing to be brought into contact with a person who is incapable (except in the special case of Heathcliff) of perceiving the pain she causes others; who believes that she is innately lovable, that when she behaves badly it is outside her control (not part of her 'real' self, as it were), and that if others object it is they who are being unjust; who is convinced that she is entitled to impose her will on anyone whenever she wishes; and who is capable of considerable cruelty when thwarted. On the other hand, the moving revelation of her feelings, and the spontaneity that is her chief charm, work to prevent the hard-headed (i.e., callous and pharisaical) dehumanizing with which it is easy to respond to a less interesting case. Yet what the situation in question illustrates is the irrelevance alike of general condemnation and general tolerance. Cathy has committed herself to affecting the lives of at least two other people, namely Edgar and Heathcliff. She will almost certainly affect them badly, for she thinks of Edgar as a mere tool and is so little aware of how Heathcliff feels about her as to have no inkling of the offensiveness of her proposal to keep him with Edgar's money as a kind of pet. And she has come to Nelly seeking reassurance that what she is up to is correct.

Nelly's conduct during this scene, both in her response to Cathy and when she keeps silent about Heathcliff's having overheard part of the conversation, seems to me scrupulous and right. That Cathy cannot be *told* what to do is plain from her angry refusal to hear any more when Nelly advises her against accepting Edgar's proposal. The 'catechism' that follows makes equally plain to Nelly and to the reader how Cathy feels about Edgar, Heathcliff, and the marriage. And so far as I can see, it serves to put as clearly in front of Cathy as could be done under the circumstances the nature of her own feelings, the proper state of mind in which a person should be embarking on a marriage, and the undesirability of the marriage that she actually intends. Nelly has not sought the exchange of confidences in the first place, nor has she persisted in refusing to be drawn into it; and, once in, she has worked for clarity, neither dishonestly reassuring Cathy that she is right, nor fattening her own self-esteem by ignoring the details of Cathy's feelings and pontificating about her 'wrongness'. Though she herself admits elsewhere to having disliked Cathy – with good reason, I would think – it is hard to see how an avowed friend could have done better by her here, particularly at the age of only twenty-two. As for her keeping silent about Heathcliff's presence and departure, its consequences were large, certainly, but the consequences of her speaking would have been almost certainly as large, and to have spoken would have been a graver piece of gambling with other people's lives. Cathy is obviously determined to marry Edgar, and though a confrontation between her and Heathcliff at this point would have produced a titillating abundance of passionate emotion, she would almost certainly have gone ahead with her disastrous plans, but in a more disturbed state of mind. As it is, when faced with a limited train of consequences which two people have set in motion (and it should be remembered that she has no supernatural insight into Heathcliff's tumultuous feelings at this point), Nelly is not so presumptuous as to replace it with a potentially more violent and certainly more unpredictable train of consequences of her own choosing. Instead, she endeavours to find out more about what Cathy's attitude to Heathcliff is, and only reveals the truth when Heathcliff's absence gives cause for alarm. The whole scene brilliantly demonstrates both the kind of intervention that can reasonably be made in other people's affairs and the ultimate responsibility of people for their own actions – Heathcliff's keeping silent being, after all, as much an action as Cathy's determination upon marriage. Paradoxically, Cathy, with her presumptuous plans, stands for tyranny over others; Nelly, for freedom.

It is against tyranny or would-be tyranny that Nelly stands, too, in her relation to the Cathy–Edgar–Isabella–Heathcliff quadrangle. In a sense, of course, she precipitates the crisis at the Grange by telling Edgar of Heathcliff's intentions towards Isabella. But those intentions are shocking, Heathcliff's disturbing effect on Cathy is plain, and when later Edgar indignantly reproves her for 'meddling' (in a way that brings to mind the exasperating Mrs Pocket in *Great*

Expectations), she puts the alternatives to him concerning both women with unanswerable clarity:

'I knew Mrs Linton's nature to be headstrong and domineering', cried I; 'but I didn't know that you wished to foster her fierce temper! I didn't know that, to humour her, I should wink at Mr Heathcliff. I performed the duty of a faithful servant in telling you, and I have got a faithful servant's wages! Well, it will teach me to be more careful next time. Next time you may gather intelligence for yourself!'

'The next time you bring a tale to me, you shall quit my service, Ellen Dean', he replied.

'You'd rather hear nothing about it, I suppose, then, Mr Linton?' said I. 'Heathcliff has your permission to come a courting to Miss, and to drop in at every opportunity your absence offers, on purpose to poison the mistress against you?'

To have connived at the relationship by remaining silent would have been not only to violate her duty as a servant but, once again, to choose the greater potential violence in a situation, in preference to what might reasonably have been supposed to be the lesser violence of a householder's denying his house to a highly undesirable visitor and causing temporary unhappiness to his wife and sister. And few readers, I assume, would argue that things would have turned out better had the relationship been allowed to continue clandestinely.

But the most consequential thing that Nelly does during this part of the novel, of course, is persuading Edgar to disregard Cathy's anguish after the expulsion of Heathcliff and leave her alone during the three days in which she keeps herself locked in her room. As I said earlier, she turns out to be mistaken. But I do not see that, given the evidence that she has to go on, she decides foolishly, and once again she is standing against tyranny. Quite plainly, Cathy is trying to break Edgar with the weapon of her threatened illness, after having failed to do so in the appalling scene that she contrives between him and Heathcliff in the locked room; and what she is after is permission for Heathcliff to be effectively in command of the household. Nelly is mistaken, certainly, in believing that 'a person who could plan the turning of her fits of passion to account, before-hand, might, by exerting her will, manage to control herself tolerably even while under their influence'. But Cathy's commands to Nelly encourage that belief, and so does the speed with which she abandons her trance-like condition in fury when Nelly advises

Edgar about what is going on. The motive for Nelly's intervention is plain: 'I did not want him to yield, though I could not help being afraid in my heart'; and the choice, as it offers itself, is between the destruction of Edgar and the doubtlessly painful, but by no means certainly disastrous, setting of a limit to Cathy's exorbitant demands.[7] It is highly unlikely, moreover, that an unconditional surrender by Edgar, a humiliating abasement of himself before Cathy and Heathcliff, would have turned out any better for any of them than what actually happened; in all likelihood the unnatural tensions of such a relationship would have been even more devastating. Some readers, I suppose, may feel that the destructive ambitions of egoists should not be thwarted and that a man deserves to be sacrificed because he is not a romantic hero. But this would be simply another instance of the dehumanizing that such readers would indignantly object to when practised on more glamorous figures.

   The world that Emily Brontë presents in the novel is one in which all actions form part of traceable causal chains; in which people's natures are modified by their environments but are basically not modified very much and can sometimes destroy them no matter what choices they and others make; in which there are no unquestionable social and moral norms; in which the consolations of religion (to judge from Heathcliff's confident rejection of Nelly's suggestion about obtaining ministerial comfort) may well be attributable only to an individual's temperament rather than to a perception of actual truths; a world, in fact, in which 'we *must* be for ourselves in the long run'. Yet if in these and other respects it resembles that bleakly deterministic world that science was once popularly supposed to have revealed to us, it is also a densely human one, and not only in the intensity of the characters' emotions. As this novel of multiple narratives reminds us, 'objective' overviews are available only to fiction-writers, and perhaps not even to them. In the process of actual living, as figured by Nelly Dean, people exist for each other as incomplete encounters, unreliable signals, fragmentary reports and recollections, and loose working hypotheses whose inadequacies may at any time be shown up by the sudden staggering gesture or the autobiographical disclosure of unguessed-at passions and perplexities. Choices are none the less inescapable and consequential, and if we choose badly, as the novel amply demonstrates, disaster may result. But it is also possible so to comport ourselves as to diminish the margin of uncertainty, and as the career of Nelly shows, particularly when complemented by the Nelly-Dean-like survival of young Catherine and the emotional rebirth of Hareton, there need be no inevitable tilt towards disaster. Most of us have more complex commitments and concerns than Nelly, obviously. But even so, the world that she confronts so admirably in *Wuthering Heights* looks remarkably like ours – more so, in some respects, than that of almost any other novel in the language.

Crime and Forgiveness:
The Red Badge of Courage in Time of War

War is waged by men; not by beasts, or by gods. It is a peculiarly human activity.

Frederic Manning, *The Middle Parts of Fortune*[1]

To lecture to North American undergraduates on *The Red Badge of Courage* even before the fighting in Vietnam was to have the uneasy sensation of advancing through a moral minefield. It seemed a bit presumptuous to be a well-fed academic ensconced behind a lectern and composedly analysing the mental processes of a youth undergoing the dreadful strains of battle; and over and above the risks of pharisaism, certain ironies suggested themselves about the academic search for patterns in the novel. If so brief a work has invited so much commentary, this is obviously partly because of the extraordinary immediacy with which Crane renders the movements of consciousness. No other classic American novel so brilliantly gives us the impingement of data on the mind, the creative activity of the mind in its dealings with them, the tricks and games and manoeuvres that a normal mind is capable of. And it shows us too – indeed, in some ways it is precisely 'about' – the dangers of premature orderings, including the orderings of mechanical pattern-making and symbolizing; so that to be guilty of them ourselves when reading the novel is more than usually regrettable.

At the same time, however, if the novel celebrates openness it does not license randomness. The battle and its demands are *there,* and though Crane provides uncommonly little analytical guidance to the main changes of direction in Henry's consciousness, there seems to me a strong and convincing emotional logic to them. I propose to talk about that logic and about how Henry comes to terms with the moral complexities of battle and with himself.

That Henry's eventual accommodation to battle conditions is estimable is clearly far from a truism. By now a host of young readers must have learned from Richard Chase's introduction to the

Riverside edition of the novel (he is quoting Charles Child Walcutt) that

Crane 'makes us see Henry Fleming as an emotional puppet controlled by whatever sight he sees at the moment', that when Henry does return to the battle it is not as a valiant adult but 'in a blind rage that turns him into an animal', [and] that if there is 'any one point in the book' it is that 'Henry has never been able to evaluate his conduct'.[2]

And a similar note is struck by other critics in judgements like, 'Henry is unquestionably courageous, but the underlying causes of his deeds are neither noble nor humane', and, 'Although Henry does show courage there is decisive evidence that he is motivated chiefly by animal fierceness and competitive pride'.[3] War is an abomination, Henry adjusts himself wholeheartedly to war, therefore the mental processes involved cannot be creditable ones – thus the unspoken argument runs, intensified presumably by a feeling that improvement ought to entail introspection, increased self-understanding (which is to say, understanding of one's errors), and some kind of abnegation and general withering into truth. Viewed from such an angle, of course, Henry most decidedly doesn't improve. Not only does he continue to delight in the thought of winning glory, he actually *does* win it, and does so, moreover, in flagrant defiance of the customary novelistic decencies. He has allowed his comrades to assume that he was respectably wounded during his absence from them; he has taken advantage of his wounded-hero role and picked on his now tenderly helpful friend Wilson; he has become, in fact, positively *jaunty*. And yet, 'Who should 'scape whipping?' To speak in such terms is to feel their niggling ungenerosity when we stop and consider the boy's age and inexperience, the shocks of battle, the abrasive torments of his wanderings behind the lines, and the fact that the blow he receives from the panicked deserter's rifle butt is just as much a wound as a graze from a bullet would have been. And more is at issue than pharisaism.

To approach Henry in the moralistic fashion that I have sketched is especially ironical in that these are the terms in which he himself was operating up until the time when he rejoined his regiment, and from which, I shall be arguing, he is beneficially liberated. To complain as Mr Walcutt does, apropos of his encounter with the walking wounded, that 'the guilt he feels among these frightfully wounded men ... should be enough to make him realize his brotherhood, his indebtedness, his duty; but his reaction as he watches the retreat swell is to justify his early flight',[4] is to miss the point by a sizeable margin. The novel up to and including that episode has been a brilliant study of psychological disintegration resulting from ethical over-intensity, and Henry's shameful abandonment of the tattered soldier (quite properly it is the thought of *that* that returns briefly to haunt him at the end of the novel) is caused directly by his crippling sense of guilt and his dread of exposure. The consequences of his liberation from those feelings seem to me unquestionably salutary, and to acknowledge them makes it possible to move further into the novel's moral significance.

When Joseph Conrad reworked the basic situation of the novel in *Lord Jim*, he was implicitly indicating that Henry's final stance involves more than merely the attainment of military effectiveness. Henry *is* effective now, of course; he fights instead of running, he fights with great energy, he rallies his panicking comrades and saves them from being overwhelmed. But 'effectiveness' is too narrow a term, even though when fighting is called for the first necessity for a soldier is presumably to fight as well as possible. Henry's change has also been an improvement psychologically, at least if a unified state of consciousness is superior to a fragmented one. After his return to his regiment, he is no longer emotionally estranged from his fellows by the exasperated brooding he engaged in before he panicked. Nor does he suffer now from the paralysing self-estrangement, the inability to settle on a single reading of his situation and conduct and act accordingly, that landed him in his apparently hopeless impasse just before he was engulfed by the fleeing soldiers and received his own 'wound'. And to speak in these terms is also to speak in moral ones. The Henry who sympathetically notices the changes in Wilson, and who feels a healthy indignation on behalf of his unjustly abused regiment and 'a love, a despairing fondness' for its flag, is much closer to other people and in a much better position to act morally than the egoistically brooding youth of the earlier part. Earlier on we were told that 'He had been taught that a man became another thing in a battle. He saw his salvation in such a change.' A man – or at least much more of a whole one – is what Henry has now become; and when Crane writes of his comrades that 'The impetus of enthusiasm was theirs again. They gazed about them with looks of uplifted pride, feeling new trust in the grim, always confident weapons in their hands. And they were men', there is no reason to think that he is speaking ironically. True, Henry hasn't become impeccable – but then, why should he?

If I am right about the improvements, we would appear to be invited to consider rather carefully the causes of Henry's breakdown in the first place, and the nature of the process by which he recovers from it.

To say that in the first engagement of his regiment Henry is basically in trouble because of the Christian pacificism ingrained in him by his mother would be over simple; among other things it wouldn't allow for his tendency to preconceive situations over-rigidly and then be thrown off balance by the discrepancies between preconceptions and actualities (e.g., 'The youth stared. Surely, he thought, this impossible thing was not about to happen. He waited as if he expected the enemy to suddenly stop, apologize and retire bowing. It was all a mistake.'). But it wouldn't be a gross oversimplification, and I shall try to refine upon it. More precisely – given Henry's romantic craving for distinction – the destructive tensions result from the conflict in him between that Christian pacifistic ethic and the kind of neo-pagan ethic pointed to in a well-known and, in its essentials, twice-repeated statement that 'He had long despaired of witnessing a Greeklike struggle. Such would be no more, he had said. Men were better, or more timid. Secular and religious education had effaced the throat-grappling instinct, or else firm finance held in check the passions.' And this is where the equally well-known supernatural imagery is so helpful an index to how the currents of Henry's feelings are flowing. That the forthcoming engagement presents itself to him almost exclusively in terms of an ultimate test of his moral worth is obvious enough; and that he has a sense of the test as taking place under the eyes of *someone* emerges when he lags 'with tragic glances at the sky' and reflects that 'he would die; he would go to some place where he would be understood'. (After he has broken, he notes approvingly that the squirrel at which he tosses a pine-cone doesn't 'stand stolidly baring his furry belly to the missile, and die with an upward glance at the sympathetic heavens'.) Yet the proliferation of the infernal imagery – the comparisons of both sides to serpents, imps, monsters, dragons, and the like – indicates how far from innocent and Greeklike the military scene appears to the deeper reaches of his mind, and testifies to his growing unconscious anxiety about the meritoriousness of the activities that he committed himself to initially with such neo-pagan enthusiasm. He himself is entangled now with those balefully serpentine columns and those figures 'dodging implike around the fires'; and when the fighting begins and he breaks, the fact that at that point the enemy onslaught figures to him in terms of ravening demonic monsters coming inexorably towards him bears witness to an overwhelming upsurge of guilt-feelings. The enemy's persistence is all the more demoralizing because of his feeling that if he is to be tested morally it must be under fair conditions, and that conditions are becoming increasingly unfair. And the failure of battle conditions to conform to his expectations is a further subliminal intimation that the battlefield is the wrong sort of place for him to be and that he was radically in error in his initial neo-pagan commitment to its values (though his conscious sense of the battle as a straightforward moral test isn't affected thereby).

Viewed in this light, Henry's overwhelming sense of guilt after he has broken doesn't call for much explication here. It is obvious enough what is going on when he looks at the unbroken soldiers and 'felt that he was regarding a procession of chosen beings' and that the gap between him and them was 'as great ... as if they had marched with weapons of flame and banners of sunlight'. Similarly, when the tattered soldier questions him,

he was continually casting sidelong glances to see if the man were contemplating the letters of guilt he felt burned into his brow ... His ... companion's chance persistency made him feel that he could not keep his crime concealed in his bosom. It was sure to be brought plain by one of those arrows which cloud the air and are constantly pricking, discovering, proclaiming those things which are willed to be forever hidden. He admitted that he could not defend himself against this agency.

And when we put these and all the other supernatural references together they point unmistakably (despite Crane's canny avoidance of any specific reference to the Christian deity) to Henry's sense of a supernaturally penetrated universe in which crimes are absolutely and inescapably crimes because known inescapably to *someone*, and so are almost certain to be visited by retribution.

What we see Henry becoming liberated from, I suggest, is his disposition to view what he is up to in terms of such a universe and to seek, unavailingly, to justify himself to it. After he rejoins his regiment – and nothing, it should be recalled, has happened to validate his conduct in terms of his earlier set of rules – the supernatural imagery virtually disappears, and with it his conviction of his own worthlessness and the inevitability of his exposure. The nature of the change in him gets spelled out in certain much quoted passages that I shall consolidate into a single one here:

His self-pride was now entirely restored. In the shade of its flourishing growth he stood with braced and self-confident legs, and since nothing could now be discovered he did not shrink from an encounter with the eyes of judges, and allowed no thought of his own to keep him from an attitude of manfulness. He had performed his mistakes in the dark, so he was still a man ... He had been taught that many obligations of a life were easily avoided. The lessons of yesterday had been that retribution was a laggard and blind ... He had been out among the dragons, he said, and he assured himself that they were not so hideous as he had imagined them. Also they were inaccurate; they did not sting with precision. A stout heart often defied, and, defying, escaped ... Yesterday, when he had imagined the universe to be against him, he had hated it, little gods and big gods; today he hated the army of the foe with the same great hatred. He was not going to be badgered of his life, like a kitten chased by boys, he said. It was not well to drive men into final corners; at those moments they could all develop teeth and claws ... He had a gigantic hatred for those who made great difficulties and complications ... He had been to touch the great death, and found that, after all, it was but the great death. He was a man.

If my account thus far is more or less correct, Henry is no longer bothered by the presumed hostility of the 'big gods and little gods' because he has ceased to bother about the gods in any Christian sense at all; and because he has ceased to bother about them, he has ceased to introduce supernatural values into the activities of battle. Hence the act of fighting is no longer some kind of ultimate moral testing of the self (is he one of the elect or not?), and even death becomes simply death and not a stage on the way to further judgement. We are not, so far as I can see, being invited to react with patronizing irony when informed that 'He saw that he was good. He recalled with a thrill of joy the respectful comments of his fellows upon his conduct.' And the fact that we can refrain from doing so testifies to a deeper moral validity in what has been going on.

I have not, of course, been arguing that *The Red Badge of Courage* is valuable because it demonstrates that to be a good soldier one should not be a good Christian. It demonstrates nothing of the sort, for Henry is not a *good* Christian at all. He is something more familiar to most of us, and perhaps more relevant, namely a person in whom religion-induced dispositions persist in a vulgarized

form and without any strong accompanying affirmations and consolations, and who is in a state of muddle, perplexed by impulses
towards a (seemingly) non-moral self-affirmation on the one hand
and a (seemingly) moral self-denial on the other, and by a conflict
between a view of the world as rationally ordered and demanding
reasonableness in return, and a view of it as not ordered at all. By
putting an intellectual, albeit a very inept one, into the situation of
battle where attitudes have more immediate and weighty consequences than they normally do, Crane has clarified the
undesirability of that kind of muddle. He has also, it seems to me,
made it easier to come to terms with war, when one is in it, as a
normal aspect of human existence. By 'normal' I do not mean inevitable. Nor, of course, do I mean commonplace; part of the
brilliance of the novel consists precisely in its continual demonstrations of the immense *strangeness* of battle. But war itself is
treated by Crane, as it is by Homer, and Shakespeare, and Tolstoy,
as a condition in which so many of the deeper problems of existence
are present that, when we are in it, it is no longer something to be set
against 'life', it *is* life; and he has brought out that if a value-system
is to be fully tenable it must somehow be adequate to both peace *and*
war. The same can of course be said of other distinguished presentations of war.[5] But one of the temptations for the 'enlightened'
American consciousness is to plume itself on its moral superiority to
foreign and less idealistic ones, and hence to regard non-protesting
responses to war as merely examples of moral underdevelopment.
Crane, however, has dealt with war in terms that not only include
that kind of consciousness but transcend it; and he has effectively
precluded the concession, 'Well, perhaps as a matter of *expediency* a
temporary transformation of the psyche may be necessary' – a concession whose moral reservations push us right back into the
muddles that Henry is in before he breaks. In terms of the novel
there are not two moralities, a lower and a higher, but one, and it
seems to me intellectually respectable.

That Henry has travelled from one intellectual position to
another without engaging in any ratiocination except of the most
rudimentary kind is of no consequence if the implicit logical progression is sound. I believe that it is and that the novel does not even
oblige us to choose between religion and naturalism. If we are presented with a journey from a certain kind of Christianizing to a
certain kind of naturalism, the naturalism is so rich that it is in fact

compatible with a superior way of being religious, even though the novel is manifestly by someone who is not a Christian himself. And this brings me to the most remarkable intellectual aspect of the book, namely that Crane, in a period in which absolutes were notoriously disintegrating, was able to assist in the process without falling into the 'amoral extremism or ... sheer objectivism or romantic nihilism'[6] that have been imputed to him. In comparison to *The Red Badge, Lord Jim,* for example, is philosophically crude, the product of someone who, no longer able to believe in any supernatural sanctions for values, can only fumble around with the notion that if all value-systems are man-made, all values presumably become equally meaningless when we really reflect on them. Of course the events in *Lord Jim* give the lie to the naive Marlovian pessimisms; it does indeed matter when a shipload of pilgrims are abandoned to a fiery or watery death, or when a community is saved from predators. But in *The Red Badge* the language of events is a good deal clearer and more compelling, and during Henry's wanderings between his flight and his return to his regiment, events speak to him in ways that block his attempts to escape from ethical claims by invalid philosophical moves. It is to these moves that the term 'naturalism' can properly be applied pejoratively.

What I have especially in mind are the episode in the chapel-like glade and the subsequent death of Jim Conklin. In the 'chapel' episode, Henry attempts to shut out the ethical exactions of the battle, and with them the torments of his own failure in it, by reconceiving nature so that peacefulness and self-preservation become the natural order of things and the battle a mere remote aberration incapable of moral claims. But the hideously solid corpse in the glade is an irrefutable witness to the continuing reality of the battle, and the ants busily at work on its face are a reminder that predatoriness is as much a part of the natural as the reassuring self-preservation of the *sympathique* squirrel. They also presumably recall subliminally the battle's scale, because what Henry next attempts is the conversion of it into something that is ethically harmless because vast and inhuman, a mere machine-like activity that he can remain emotionally detached from and assert his superiority to by contemplating it – by positively seeking it out, indeed – as an aesthetic spectacle. This very fin-de-siècle move is countered in its turn by his sudden confrontation not with ant-like distant figures but with the human warmth, decency, and courage of the tattered soldier and the appalling fact of the mortally wounded Jim Conklin. The comforting metaphor of the battle as an 'immense and terrible machine' producing corpses vanishes when juxtaposed not with an anonymous corpse, however shocking and incongruously located, but with a man, and, worse, a known and liked man, going through the awesome and untranslatable act of dying.

It is in this latter scene, with its culmination in the wafer image, that Crane's dissolving of the conventional disjunction between religion and naturalism reaches its climax. There is a piquant irony to the well-known attempt of R.W. Stallman to appropriate the wafer image for conventional Christian purposes. Wafers are flat, and things to which they are pasted are also more or less flat, and psychologically the image simultaneously destroys the numinousness of the sun as an external agent giving life to the earth and converts the bowl of the sky into an opaque surface holding the mind's eye back from penetrating into the space of the heavens. In terms of the deeper currents of Henry's mind, we could hardly be further from that moment earlier when the quasi-patriarchal figure of the mounted general 'beamed upon the earth like a sun' and three times in the space of some twelve lines exclaimed jubilantly 'By heavens!' – and 'the youth cringed as if discovered in a crime. By heavens, they had won after all!' Yet if Henry's fist-shaking protest indicates a rejection of the claims of the universe to being informed with a Presence whose severities must be respected because of its paternal benevolences, it has just been demonstrated that no diminishment of the mysteriousness and numinousness of life need be entailed therein. One of the objections to certain ways of being religious is precisely that they *do* diminish those qualities. In *Paradise Lost*, for instance, it is noteworthy how unmysterious are the presented depths of the heavens and how commonplace their chief occupant, so that it is only in and through the consciousnesses of the two humans that we experience any sense of genuine mysteries and profundities in existence. In *The Red Badge*, similarly, in contrast to the tritely physical supernaturalism of Henry's guilt-ridden imagery, it is the truly marvellous, the sense of immense human lonelinesses and intensities in the face of existence, that gets reaffirmed in the account of the death of Jim Conklin. In a very small compass we have been led from the ostensibly broad – and false – view of human activities, via the presences and pressures of men *en masse* and the greater intimacies of decent fraternal concern, to the impenetrable isolation of the individual confronting the unknown.

In the title of this essay I mentioned forgiveness, and it is concerning that that I shall close. I have spoken of the language of events and how events in the novel speak to Henry judicially. But events can comfort as well as lacerate, forgive as well as condemn. That Henry, apparently in a hopeless impasse after Jim Conklin's death, with every mental escape-route blocked by his own arguings, is able to awake the following day a free man is certainly the strangest thing in the novel; and yet the mechanisms at work are both convincing and heartening. Having witnessed the mind's ability to construct a reality in terms of which it appears condemned beyond all hope of reprieve, we also see the power of life to disown such a construction and relax the death-grip of the past. When Henry is overwhelmed by the fleeing men he is shaken out of his conviction of the fixity of the battle lines and his own uniqueness in running. With the blow from the rifle butt the moral order of things is further loosened: instead of Henry's behaving unjustly to just people in an ostensibly just universe, someone else is now behaving unjustly to *him* – and doing so impersonally too, so that the blow seems to come simply from life itself like a random bullet, instead of like one of those carefully aimed retributive arrows he had been imagining earlier. And in his encounter with the cheerful soldier he sees that it is possible for someone who has deserted like himself to function with unabashed equanimity, good humour, and kindliness. In a profound gesture of benevolence from life, finally, he is skilfully guided through the woods by his new companion in a manner that recalls, albeit in a wholly secular way, the loving figure of the Good Shepherd, and is welcomed back with tender considerateness by his comrades, the latter changed both from what they were earlier and from the implacable judges of his imaginings. And more than an illustration of Paul Tillich's formulation about being accepted because one is unacceptable is involved. In view of the fullness with which he has been exposed to the tempests of existence, Henry in a sense has *earned* his acceptance and his subsequent wholeness and success. When at the end of the book the thought of his abandonment of the tattered soldier returns to haunt him, he 'gradually mustered force to put the sin at a distance. And at last his eyes seemed to open to some new ways.' Quite rightly he is now able to reject the claims on him for a renewed sense of guilt that could be crippling in the same way, if not to the same extent, as the guilt he had felt after his first, and lesser, moral failure. The book, in sum, demonstrates that it is always possible to become 'another thing', and not just in battle.[7]

The Red Badge of Courage does not in the least mitigate the atrociousness of war. Indeed, to re-read it is to feel more thankful than ever that we do not have to go into battle ourselves, and more humblingly uncertain as to what our own conduct would be under conditions like those faced by Henry Fleming. But to insist on the affirmative quality of Crane's treatment of war is not to diminish those facts. Crane has neither exploited war in the interests of nourishing a self-pitying fatalism about the inexorable destruction of the good and beautiful by life, nor indulged in a facile indignation about human brutishness and folly. Like B. Traven in *The Death Ship* – and like almost no other American novelist – he has succeeded in writing with unforgettable vividness about the atrocious in a way that makes it simply a part of life and not an indictment of it, or an indictment of 'man', or any sort of indictment at all. In its psychological richness and its religious openness, *The Red Badge* is not only one of the most remarkable of American novels, it is one whose wisdoms are especially valuable nowadays. In exploring war as a closed situation in which an intellectual cannot escape from the moral claims of events merely by willing it – escape by focusing only on the kinds of events that feed his vanities – Crane has helped to show up the fashionable nihilisms of today as the empty and arid things that they are.[8]

Rereading Traven's *The Death Ship*

'Every great novelist who has not had his due', F. R. Leavis observes of D. H. Lawrence, 'is a power for life wasted.'[1] I don't know whether B. Traven is a great novelist, but he is an extremely interesting one and unquestionably he is a power for life. I have tried once already to do justice to his masterwork, *The Death Ship*.[2] My excuse for returning to it is not simply that I was wrong about it then but that it is a novel that it is very easy to be wrong about, and for interesting reasons. In the past few decades a number of novels which were under-read at first – *Huckleberry Finn*, for example – have been shown to be more complex, more coherently structured, more *crafted* than they appeared initially. But their New Critical *gravitas* has sometimes been bought at the cost of certain distortions. The idea of the well-made novel is still dominant in academic criticism, and when we approach certain works with that as our norm, it can be rather as if we were linguists trying to deal with an American–Indian language in terms of English grammar. We can do certain things with that grammar, but after a while we get stuck; and when that happens, the natural tendency is to ignore those features that won't fit into our discussion. I shall try to offer an account of *The Death Ship* that does justice to its peculiar grammar, and I hope that it may shed some light on problems posed by other novels.

Let me first get an ambiguity out of the way. When I speak of *The Death Ship*, I am referring to the novel of that name that was published by Knopf in 1934 and reissued by Collier in 1962 as a paperback. I am not speaking of Traven's *Das Totenschiff*, which was published in Germany in 1926 and has gone through innumerable reprintings and been translated into over a dozen languages, including British English. I shall treat *The Death Ship* as a separate work and, in effect, an American one. The biographical and textual problems posed by Traven's elusive career are numerous and fascinating, but it has always been plain, to me at any rate, that the prose of *The Death Ship* is so idiosyncratic and at times so brilliant that it couldn't have been the work of a translator. And a former editor at

Knopf, Mr Bernard Smith, has confirmed in the *New York Times Book Review* that the novel is essentially in Traven's own English, tempered by editorial revisions of unduly Germanic constructions. ('There was nothing creative about the work I did', Mr Smith recalls. 'I neither added nor subtracted. I inserted no thought or feeling of my own. In fact, I was eager to retain the special flavor – the frequent awkwardness, the occasional stiltedness, the wavering union of toughness and sentimentality.'[3]) Furthermore, *The Death Ship* is about a quarter longer than *Das Totenschiff*, and it is clear from the numerous additions, especially those in the central section, that Traven not only rewrote but to some extent rethought the book. *The Death Ship*, in sum, seems to me almost as much an American novel in its own right as *Almayer's Folly* is an English novel and *En attendant Godot* a French play.

I

I shall start with what seem to me the three most obvious ways of misreading the book.

The simplest (it is the equivalent of seeing *Huckleberry Finn* as simply an adventure story) is to think of it as a proletarian-protest novel; and doing so is not without justification. True, there is a question as to whether Traven's chief target is capitalism or what he calls at one point 'that soulless beast, the state'. But either way his narrator – an American seaman stranded in Europe a year or two after the First World War without any papers – is a traditional enough victim of society. After vain attempts to obtain fresh papers, and harassment by the police of three countries, and a couple of brief imprisonments in France, he eventually signs on as a coal-drag or stoker's assistant aboard a broken-down gunrunner, the *Yorikke*, which is the only kind of ship that will take him without any questions asked; and just when he is finally becoming reconciled to the appalling conditions aboard her, he is shanghaied onto an outwardly more respectable ship that is almost immediately wrecked for the insurance money. A lot is said and shown about the follies and nastinesses of capitalism and about the generous fellow-feeling that 'simple' workers can display towards each other when they are not mucked around with; and there are numerous parallels between *The Death Ship* and Traven's later novels, especially the series dealing with the exploitation and eventual revolt of Mexican

Indians during the Porfirio Díaz regime. In these respects *The Death Ship* is indeed a proletarian novel – one of the greatest.

At the same time, though, there are obviously more modern elements in it than the term 'proletarian novel' suggests. The treatment of bureaucracy in the first section brings to mind the Kafkaesque absurdities of the McCarran–Walter years that Gian Carlo Menotti dealt with so movingly in his opera *The Consul*. The world of the *Yorikke* in the second section has all-too-disturbing analogies with that of the concentration camps, in both its physical and its psychological aspects.

> Then for the first time we became aware that our language lacks words to express this offence, the demolition of a man. In a moment, with almost prophetic intuition, the reality was revealed to us: we had reached the bottom. It is not possible to sink lower than this: no human condition is more miserable than this, nor could it conceivably be so. Nothing belongs to us any more; they have taken away our clothes, our shoes, even our hair; if we speak, they will not listen to us, and if they listen, they will not understand. They will even take away our name: if we want to keep it, we will have to find in ourselves the strength to do so, to manage somehow so that behind the name something of us, of us as we were, still remains.

This, as it happens, comes from *If This Is a Man* (1959), a translation of Primo Levi's account of a year in Auschwitz,[4] but at a first glance one would swear that it came from *The Death Ship*. And in the final section the sinking of the real death ship, the *Empress of Madagascar* ('elegant dame, silk outside, crabs underneath'[5]) looks suspiciously like a sardonic commentary on European civilization in general. All in all, given the numerous reminders of human unpleasantness, it would be natural enough to take our cue from the title and see the novel as a symbolic presentation of human existence in a very black universe, a universe with obvious parallels to that of Céline's *Death on the Installment Plan*.

But we can be more 'modern' still. Just as in successive rereadings of another symbolically titled novel, *Heart of Darkness*, our attention moves on beyond the 'protest' and 'black' elements to the psychological changes in Marlow, so we can become increasingly interested in the inner development of Traven's virtually anonymous narrator. (His real name, Gerard Gales, is mentioned only once.) Dark as his world may be, he is still very different from Céline's Ferdinand: he is capable of tenderness, compassion, play-

fulness, even love. And there seems to me excuse enough for wishing
to see the book, as I myself saw it earlier, as presenting us not only
with a stripping away from a man of all the aids and comforts of
civilized existence, but also with his discovery of the strength within
himself to survive under his new conditions without becoming bru-
talized. Considerable evidence could be offered in support of such a
reading; a full account along such lines would be a complicated one;
and of the three ways of reading the book that I have sketched, this
seems to me the most interesting. Nevertheless, though we can
indeed come away from *The Death Ship*, as we can from a book like
Levi's, with a renewed sense of heroic possibilities in the human
spirit, all three readings now seem to me wrong.

The Death Ship does not in fact offer us a straightforward
vicarious excursion into regions of suffering and darkness that most
of us have mercifully been spared from in our own lives. It is not a
black novel. Nor is it a novel whose blackness is progressively light-
ened so that we close it with the feeling that major values have been
tested and re-affirmed. Nor is it an indignant and would-be ameliorative social exposé, or a celebration of good proletarians oppressed
by the wicked agents of capitalism. And the reason why it isn't these
things is not just that there are other and lighter elements in it. There
are indeed such elements, and I can conceive of someone's coming to
it these days and, in a still more modern reading, seeing it as a sort of
proto-hippie work. The more we look at the first section, for
example, the cooler the handling of the narrator's stateless wanderings in it appears. None of the officials with whom he has dealings is
unpleasant, his run-ins with the police turn out much better than
could be expected, his imprisonments are painless, his passage down
through Europe is as little injurious to him as Huck Finn's south-
ward journey is to Huck, and his consciousness throughout the
section is an untroubled one – amused, sardonic, impudent, irritable
at times, but not significantly disturbed by anything that happens to
him. In talking about the novel in such terms, however, I am still
misrepresenting it, in the same way that *Huckleberry Finn* is misrep-
resented as the story of a 'real' boy passing through a 'real' social
landscape – an account in which it is treated as essentially a third-
person narrative transposed into first-person terms. A good many
novels are like that, but *Huckleberry Finn* is not, any more than
Gulliver's Travels is; and neither is *The Death Ship*. Its structural
grammar is more complicated.

That *The Death Ship* is very much a 'talked' novel, with the kind
of structural looseness that we encounter in conversation, is obvious
enough; and some of the effects that are achieved thereby can be
described in conventional novelistic terms. In the important first
eight paragraphs of the opening chapter, for example, in which each
narrative statement sets off a train of increasingly general reflections, a number of the generalizations contribute substantially to
our knowledge of the narrator in the past as well as of his attitude
now. And in the middle section of the book, in which a relatively
thin narrative line makes its way between numerous passages of generalization or general description, the looseness is eminently
functional. A number of the *Yorikke*'s features are described so
powerfully that Traven doesn't need to provide detailed accounts of
the narrator's dealings with them on a lot of specific occasions. It
isn't necessary, either, for him to do the characterizing of a number
of members of the crew that such accounts normally entail. And the
Yorikke acquires an expressive reality (things very solid; people,
with one or two exceptions, very shadowy; the sequence of events
not sharply defined) that corresponds to how things impinged on
the fatigued and isolated consciousness of the narrator while on
board her.

Furthermore, there are ways in which the talked aspect of the
book works against the first three readings described above. In a
passage like the following we are not simply standing on the quay
with a sailor who, after spending the night with an Antwerp tart, has
found that his ship has sailed without him, and the gravity of whose
abandonment is described three or four paragraphs previously. We
are listening to a voice talking to us *now*, and it is not an agitated
one:

What's the use worrying about that bucket? Gone. It's all right with me. Go
to the devil. The ship doesn't worry me at all. What worries me is something
different. I haven't got a red cent in my pocket. She told me, I mean that
pretty girl I was with during the night, protecting her against burglars and
kidnappers, well, she told me that her dear mother was sick in the hospital,
and that she had no money to buy medicine and the right food for her, and
that she might die any minute if she didn't get the medicine and the food. I
didn't want to be responsible for the death of her mother. So what could I
do as a regular red-blooded American except give her all the money I had
left over from the gilded house? I have to say this much, though, about that
pretty dame: she was grateful to me for having saved her mother from an

early death. There is nothing in the whole world more satisfying to your heart than making other people happy and always still happier. And to receive the thousand thanks of a pretty girl whose mother you have just saved, that is the very peak of life. Yes, sir.

Nor, more importantly, is there any agitation in the middle section of the novel when we step back and don't allow the vividness to overwhelm us. There are passages of horrifying description, there are passages of telling protest. But there are very few of which we can fairly say that the tone is bitter or outraged, and the overall looseness of presentation is clearly not consistent with a drive to rub the reader's nose as vigorously as possible in the step-by-step awfulness of the narrator's experiences aboard the *Yorikke*. Nor, for that matter, are the numerous lacunae and chronological displacements in that section consistent with a strong interest in the narrator's psychological development.

Yet powerful as the sense of being talked to in it is, *The Death Ship* still does not belong with such talked novels as *The Catcher in the Rye* and *The Floating Opera*, in which, however confused or tentative the narrator may be in his attempts to make sense of what happened to him earlier, he is still a consistent mind existing in the present of the novel and standing in a consistent relationship to the doings of his past self. For one thing, there are too many shifts in the speaking voice. The opening dialogue situation of a slyly ingratiating seaman addressing a bourgeois landsman ('I second mate? No, sir. I was not mate on this can, not even bos'n. I was just a plain sailor') quickly vanishes, just as the Ishmael of the opening chapters of *Moby Dick* vanishes, and in the first chapter there are distinct shifts in the level of intelligence of the narrator, and numerous others later on. The voice in the pretty-girl passage is not the same voice as the one in a passage like:

A hundred and twenty years ago there was a saying: 'Every one of my soldiers carries a marshall's baton in his bag.' Today it is: 'Every one of our employees may become president of our company; look at Mr. Flowerpot, he did it.' I think that all these successful men must have shined boots of another sort than I, and the newspapers they sold must have been different from the papers I carried.

And difficulties arise when we try to pin down what the narrator 'really' thinks about some of the matters that he talks about. Not only are there obvious inconsistencies in his generalizations about communism and nationalism, for example; the inconsistencies are sometimes unresolvable because of that innocent-looking little rhetorical device observable in the pretty-girl passage, the shifting use of the present tense. Nothing important hinges on the question of what the 'real' tenses of the assertions in that passage are. But elsewhere it is sometimes unclear whether particular generalizations give us the narrator's sentiments now, or his reflections in the past, or in some measure both; and even when we think we have pinned some of them down, we can't always be sure whether they are the expression of fully pondered convictions coterminous with Traven's own, or flippant or irritable off-the-cuff comments, or something in between.

Furthermore, these shifts are related to others. A number of the passages of description or narration, especially those dealing with work in the *Yorikke*'s stokehold, are absolutely solid. They would survive any literal questions that we cared to raise about them, and in them the narrator's eye and mind are working perfectly normally and precisely. However, we are by no means always in so well-lit a region. True, there is no serious problem about translating a passage like the following back into less figurative terms:

[The *Yorikke*] couldn't be blamed for her behavior. She had begun to get heavy feet; she was no longer as young and springy as she was when she stood by to guard Cleopatra's banquets for Antony. Were it not for the many thick coats of paint on her hull, she would have frozen to death in the cold ocean, for her blood was no longer as hot as it was five thousand years ago.

But such conversions of reality are nevertheless slightly odd, since they entail not only talking about things as if they were different from what they are, but feeling and even acting towards them differently, as in the pretty-girl passage or in this one from the reminiscences of the narrator's fellow coal-drag, Stanislav, about his life ashore:

'Other times, if you had a bit of good luck, a couple of bags of sugar or green coffee [in a freight-car] would open almost by themselves, and right in front of you. Now, if you happen along at the right moment with an empty knapsack and you hold the knapsack right under the spot where the bags ripped open, then, of course, the goods would drop into your empty knapsack. If you didn't put something under the rippings, then the whole thing would go right to the ground to feed only rats and mice. Well, it surely is not my intention to fatten up rats.'

And at times the relationship to 'reality' is oddly ambiguous in another way. There is no general excursion into unreason in the novel: the narrator frequently tries to make sense of the phenomena in front of him and implicitly invites the reader to do so. The trouble is, however, that his explanations range from absolutely plain and solid ones (e.g., of why the handrail on the stokehold stairway in the *Yorikke* is against the wall rather than on the outside edge of the stairs), through less verifiable but still plausible ones (e.g., of why the *Yorikke*'s skipper isn't on a better ship), through markedly implausible ones (e.g., of the fact that a member of the *Yorikke*'s crew when the narrator first sees the ship is wearing full evening dress), to wholly impossible ones (e.g., of why a particular door on the *Yorikke*, to the so-called 'hold of horrors', is kept locked all the time). And we are likely to find ourselves moving at times into wilder and wilder hypotheses if we want to take the narrator's reports on trust and still remain in 'our' world. When the narrator is imprisoned in France for the second time, for example, the behaviour of the workshop warder is rationally explicable only on one or other of the equally unlikely assumptions that he is feebleminded or that he is a consummate ironist. It is even more unlikely that the skipper of the *Yorikke* is endowed with magical powers, though the episode in which the *Yorikke*, chock-full of arms, is searched by a Spanish gunboat hardly makes sense in any other terms. And if this is a normal novel, then reason fails altogether in the episode at the Antwerp police station when the narrator suddenly feels that the officers there are looking at him as if he were just about to be hanged. Not only does he himself assume for several hours thereafter that this is what is going to happen, but one or two of the officers speak unprompted as if he were right.

Now, in some ways the frequent shifts in the degrees of credibility and rationality in the novel are not puzzling at all. Except for the customs search and the narrator's almost too idyllic months in Spain, we are never in fact seriously perplexed as to how to read any of the passages. *The Death Ship* isn't *Last Year at Marienbad*, I mean. We virtually always know how the particular kind of reality presented in a passage is intended to stand in relation to what can be called, in a shorthand way, reality itself, which is to say that we recognize how the various expressive heightenings and distortions function. Yet when we try fitting all the passages together, there *is* a critical puzzle. The plot of the novel is a sombre one, the narrator

himself frequently stresses the representativeness of the shocking
things described (death ships, stokehold injuries, and the rest), and
there are passages of unequivocal protest about such matters.
Furthermore, there is a marked preoccupation in the book not only
with communication but with miscommunication. In the various
dialogues – with officials ashore, with ships' officers, with Stanislav,
and implicitly at times with the reader – there are numerous demonstrations of how language can be used for deception and
entrapment. There are also numerous comments on misrepresen-
tations in the entertainment media, nationalistic propaganda, and
social myths. And the thrust of the book is often avowedly corrective: the reader, the comfortably-off landsman, is to be shown the
real nature of life at sea for the common sailor. Yet, as I have indicated, in other places we would be forced to conclude, if we wanted
psychological coherence, either that the narrator is lying or fantasising now or that he and others behaved very strangely in the past.
And something else about the novel makes the various loosenesses
that I have been pointing to surprising.

The Death Ship presents us with an uncommonly large number of
instances of flagrant, uncorrected, and unavenged injustice; and as a
subject for fiction injustice normally invites one of two kinds of
treatment. Either there is the partisan one, as in *David Copperfield*,
or *The Way of All Flesh*, or *Where Angels Fear to Tread*, in which
our noses are rubbed in the nastiness of various bits of behaviour so
as to make us feel indignantly that we too might have been the
victims of them and that such behaviour oughtn't to be allowed to
exist. Or else there is the ironical distancing that goes on in novels
like *Candide, Justine, Decline and Fall*, and – up to a point – *Catch-
22*, in which a proliferation of injustices is counterbalanced by the
diminished vulnerability of the hero or heroine, so that we are
spared the pain of empathy and are invited instead to gaze ironically
on human nastiness and folly in general, including intellectual or
social systems that don't correspond with the actualities of human
nature. And either way we expect certain psychological boundaries
and stabilities, especially in first-person, and particularly talked
first-person, novels. After all, what the speaker is now as he tells the
story is itself a reflection upon society. If he is as good as, or better
than, the decent civilized reader, the injuries done to him appear all
the more deplorable; and if he is worse than such a reader is ever
likely to be, society will still be at fault, having helped to make him

what he is. For either of these effects to be achieved, however, the narrator has to be a reasonably coherent character and the experiences that he has undergone have to be reasonably real.

Well, obviously another set of conventions than the naturalistic–mimetic is at work in *The Death Ship*; and some of the shifts that I have described are not particularly bothersome in a play like *The Winter's Tale* or a poem like *Piers Plowman*. But the graver the human actualities that are pointed to in a novel, the more we expect, if not a naturalistic, at least a consistent treatment of them. And the freer a novel is in its manipulation of reality, the more likely it is to seem self-indulgent and escapist when the subject matter is grave – a mere debased post-Symbolist assertion of the superiority of language to unpleasant physical and social realities. Yet there is nothing self-indulgent about *The Death Ship*, and nothing escapist; it is a deeply moving work that moves us precisely because of our sense of its truthfulness to the complexities of experience. And the reasons are simultaneously rhetorical and philosophical.

II

The belief that the speaker of a serious novel must have a unified consciousness and that if there seem to be inconsistencies they must be resolvable in conventional psychological terms, such as character development or mental disturbances, is very natural. Quite aside from literary theorizings, when we ourselves use the word 'I' it points to the completest psychological entity that we know, and when we come upon the same word in a novel we instinctively want to believe that it points to a psychological whole there too. Yet it is plain that there are first-person novels of which this isn't true – works in which we hear a number of voices of varying degrees of sophistication, intelligence, general knowledge, command of language, and what I can only call creativity, all linked together by family likenesses. *Moby Dick* is such a novel; so is *Gulliver's Travels*; so, I believe, is *Huckleberry Finn*; and so is *The Death Ship*. And one of the operative conventions in such works, which we acknowledge when the changes in style are as obvious as they are in *Moby Dick*, is that different stratagems and techniques are being used in different stretches of the book. We can still talk about the tone and characterization in individual stretches, and there may be a good many stretches of which similar accounts can be offered in those terms and which belong naturally together. But there are certain questions that we refrain, or at least ought to refrain, from asking. The fact that Lemuel Gulliver is at times an ingenuous John Bull and at others a polemicist as brilliant as Swift himself in his non-fiction is not something to be explained in terms of 'character', any more than we think of Ishmael as a particular individual sitting at his desk and penning his memoirs of life aboard the *Pequod*, a sort of companion piece to Richard Henry Dana's *Two Years before the Mast*. And when the wrong questions are asked and the wrong con-nections made, as seems to me to have happened with *Huckleberry Finn*, it produces more complications than it solves. The sort of structure that I am pointing to is neither good nor bad in itself, of course. *Portnoy's Complaint* is a very bad novel, and all the worse because of its borrowings from *Death on the Installment Plan*, which also partly belongs with the works I have mentioned here. But *The Death Ship*, like *Gulliver's Travels* and *Huckleberry Finn* and *Moby Dick*, is very good. And in it the different techniques are a means of coping with serious and complex realities, which is why we can pass from stretch to stretch without any jolting.

As I have indicated, the human world pointed to in *The Death Ship* is, when considered objectively, a dark one – a world in which there is a great deal of cupidity, callousness, dishonesty, exploi-tation, and injustice. I suggest that in an important respect the novel resembles not only *Gulliver's Travels* but works like *The Waste Land* and Yeats' 'Meditations in Time of Civil War'. That is to say, a variety of techniques are employed in it for coping with experiences that would be cumulatively intolerable if handled by means of a uniform mode of consciousness. And in *The Death Ship* it doesn't matter whether those techniques are being used in the past or the present. It makes little difference whether we are looking at the narrator in the past attempting to define to himself what the stokehold of the *Yorikke* is like when he first sees it, or at his present efforts to let his audience know what it was like, or at Traven himself writing the description of the stokehold. Either way we are looking at the activity of defining and delimiting the atrocious and thereby achieving some degree of mental control over it. So too with the various kinds of generalizing and problem-solving that go on in the novel and the kinds of control and self-affirmation that *they* permit. So too with the escapes, by means of associational move-ments of the mind, from too prolonged a contemplation of some particularly oppressive reality. So too with the numerous 'conversions' of reality. (The invocations of Roman galleys give the *Yorikke* a nobler identity in terms of which it can be thought of less painfully, while the conversions of the police and other officials render them less unpleasant by diminishing their dignity.) And so too with the freedom taken with respect to the rules of various games. In an exchange like the following, the narrator's refusal to be bound by the laws of logic is part of a refusal to play obligingly in the game in which society has denied him his own identity and his right to work:

> 'And you came on the *George Washington*?'
> 'Yes, sir.'
> 'A rather mysterious ship, your *George Washington*. As far as I know, the *George Washington* has never yet come to Rotterdam.'
> 'That's not my fault, officer. I am not responsible for the ship.'

And a similar insouciance, a similar refusal to be respectably obliging, is apparent in the fact that the novel as a whole is so *hors série*, so little a familiar marketable commodity.

What we have in *The Death Ship*, then, are the workings of a mind that is uncommonly at ease with itself and with the world. It can permit itself a much wider variety of voices and tactics than is customary. And it is unconcerned to present to the reader a conventionally invulnerable countenance, either by being morally better or more sophisticated than the ordinary reader, or by being egregiously worse in ways designed to make him feel guilty. Furthermore, it is not straining to get at what the world 'essentially' is and to organize everything philosophically in relation to that perception. And this openness is all the more striking when we consider how much *The Death Ship* is about injustice. For injustice is one of the hardest things to come to terms with intellectually. When we hear of some particularly shocking instance of it, the peculiar mixture of horror, indignation, and fear that we experience derives in part from the sensed *unreachableness* of the minds of those responsible and their implicit denial of our own value-system. And when injustices are monstrous and numerous enough, the spectre of a wholly relativistic and essentially meaningless world starts raising its head. Hence, I suppose, comes the tendency in popular art to create monsters as the agents of wickedness, as if the fact that ordinary people can commit atrocities in terms of ordinary value-systems is somehow too alarming to contemplate. Hence too, no doubt, the importance of the idea of revenge in the bloodier fairy tales. ('And when she saw her she knew her for Snow-White and could not stir from the place for anger and terror. For they had ready red-hot shoes, in which she had to dance until she fell down dead.'[6]) The possibility of murderous queens living just as happily ever afterwards as gentle princesses would be metaphysically even more alarming. But in *The Death Ship* there are no monsters, no vengeance, and no dread of any metaphysical abyss. Traven can contemplate even such possibilities as the subjective nature of truth and the ultimate flux and flow of all things without any perturbation.

This kind of poise is remarkable by any standards, and it is one that has been especially rare in serious American fiction. American literature has notoriously been haunted by a dread of the abyss and by a corresponding yearning to find a position that will give meaning to everything and validate normal values. And the unevenness of novelists like Melville and Hawthorne, Hemingway, Fitzgerald, and Salinger is obviously partly attributable to the strain entailed in that aspiration. On the one hand there are the manifold intensities of experience clamouring to be rendered as concretely as possible. But on the other, the experiences themselves seem to negate the possibility of there being a philosophical position that can give them a more than merely personal significance. The disparate experiences of such fictional observers as Ishmael, Miles Coverdale, Huck Finn, Quentin Compson, Holden Caulfield, Jack Burden, Nick Carraway, and even George Babbitt all seem to reveal a world in which, on the one hand, the ideals of idealists prove to be delusive and frequently destructive and, on the other, the 'normal' standards of ordinary people are incommensurate with the truths perceived by the perceptive. It is a world, in fact, in which to *be* excessively perceptive and philosophical is to be rendered incapable of sustained, purposeful, and successful action. And in the falling off in the later works of a number of important American novelists it is very much as if, having made a strenuous effort in their earlier years to arrive at *the* truth about things, they had found that the truths thus arrived at made it pointless to continue working with the same creative intensity.

Traven's avoidance of this dilemma seems to me not in the least the result of naiveté. In one respect, indeed, the major American novelist with whom he has most in common in *The Death Ship* is the one to whom the foregoing generalizations most obviously don't

apply, namely Henry James. James's sustained creativity at so high a
level is clearly related to his philosophical sophistication. That is to
say, for him there is no one reality. There are, rather, constellations
of individual and social realities, each of which is so hard to perceive
and assess accurately that the activity of the fiction writer can go on
indefinitely, like that of a homesteader patiently clearing an area in a
wilderness that he can never hope to know in its entirety; and the
activity of perceiving and judging is intrinsically good and self-
justifying. Traven's mind is less fine than James's, of course, but in
The Death Ship he too has created for himself a *modus operandi*
that does not oblige him to strain after an inappropriate comprehensiveness. And he has done so without feeling obliged to choose
between the sometimes over-modest precision of a Hemingway or
the slack loquacity of a Norman Mailer. His use of a variety of
tactics functions as it does for poets like Eliot and Yeats. It enables
him to explore his topics with varying degrees of precision and legitimate imprecision. And unlike Eliot, he writes as if there were no
attitudes that are essentially inappropriate when life is experienced
with some fullness, and as if there were no aspects of it that simply
oughtn't to exist at all. If he can be said to have a naturally sanguine
temperament, as I think he can, he is sanguine in the way that a
Chaucer or a Bach is sanguine. And there are definable reasons for
his ability to tolerate a wide range of perceptions without being
thrown into confusion or wracked by inner conflicts.

III

Let me begin once again with a possible misreading of *The Death
Ship*. When we consider the self-sacrificing comradeship of the
narrator and Stanislav and the various intimations that eternal flux
is the ultimate reality, it may be tempting to feel that the stripping
away from the narrator of so many of the normal aids and appurte-
nances of civilization is fashionably tendentious. That is to say, we
might seem to have in *The Death Ship* the kind of attitude that is
commonly attributed to *Huckleberry Finn:* a dichotomy of 'natural'
– and naturally decent – human nature on the one hand, and on the
other the artificialities of so-called civilization, inhibiting the free
flowing of life. And it is true that we have numerous sardonic reminders in the book of how ideas and ideals, especially the nobler
American ideals, can facilitate exploitation by obscuring incon-

venient realities – of how impressive platitudes about freedom and democracy help to mask the economic nature of wars, and how stereotyped ideas of heroism can deflect attention from the sufferings of the ordinary men who have to do the dirty work. Nevertheless, I think that the novel, like *Huckleberry Finn*, is duplicitous about culture and society. The narrator's astringent criticisms of American myths are balanced by obviously serious celebrations of American ideals (some of the passages about his homesickness for the States are among the most moving in the book), and implicit in his yearning to practise his *métier* of Able-Bodied Seaman is the desire to be a part of a socially useful organization and to submit to the claims of collective ego-ideals. Moreover, 'man's aptness for imitation', as he observes at one point, 'makes slaves *and* heroes' (italics mine), and while his reference to 'a couple of hundred stories in imitation of Cooper's *Last of the Mohicans*' may remind us of Twain's tartness about Cooper and Scott, a remark like the following, in its context, is plainly *not* tart: '[Stanislav's] fear of being made a tailor was greater than the love for his parents, whom in fact he hated profoundly for their attempt to make an honest tailor of one who wanted to detect new straits and unmapped islands in the South Sea.' And the narrator's (and Traven's) own responsiveness to the shaping and structuring appeal of the romantic is also like Twain's. We see it in a passage like the following: 'This was no death ship. May the Lord forgive me for the sin of mistaking the *Yorikke* for a death ship! They were pirates hunted for a year by all the battleships of all nations, buccaneers sunk so low that they had come to the point of looting Chinese vegetable junks.' We see it in a number of the conversions that go on with respect to the *Yorikke*'s age. Most consequentially of all, it is manifest in the conversions of the crew of the *Yorikke* in terms of the gladiators of Imperial Rome. And when we consider the various other literary and historical allusions, and the passages of philosophical speculation, and the occasional Christian terminology, it is plain that there are in fact no cleavages in *The Death Ship* between civilization and the individual, or between solid day-to-day actualities and insubstantial culture. The mind whose workings we are observing in the book is one into which a good deal of culture has entered, and in which the images and patterns thus assimilated are constantly being used to organize experience.

But something further characterizes the narrator's philosophical poise. If I now use the term 'acceptance', I am not of course referring to a belief that somehow or other everything is for the best. What I have in mind, rather, is an attitude towards the terms of battle that is similar to Henry Fleming's in *The Red Badge of Courage* after he rejoins his regiment, and the most striking example of which in *The Death Ship* is the superb *morituri te salutamus* meditation at the end of chapter 26. Not only does the narrator accept with pride his new gladiatorial role aboard the *Yorikke*; the language of the passage implies an acceptance of Caesar's role too, the role of Caesar Augustus Capitalismus. And this is more than just a poetic gesture. Three chapters further on we get a disconcerting non-figurative formulation of the same thing with the question (in the past?, in the present?):

Have I any right to despise the company which runs this ship and which degrades her crew to the lowest kind of treatment in order to keep down expenses and make competition possible? I have no right to hatred. If I had jumped over the railing, nobody could have made me work in this hell. I did not jump, and by not doing it I forsook my prime right to be my own master and my own lord. Since I did not take my fate into my hands, I have no right to refuse to be used as a slave.

This curious tolerance towards adversaries pervades the book. The American consul in Rotterdam, for example, is made so human at the end of the fruitless interview that 'I was almost convinced that that man was right after all.' The captain of the *Yorikke*, despite his criminal indifference to the welfare of his crew, is warmly praised in several places for his aplomb and daring. Most surprising of all, perhaps, the newspaper publisher on vacation who roars with laughter at the narrator's hard-luck story is not in fact presented as the all-American commercial boor that he appears to be at first: his scepticism is made understandable, the handout that he finally gives is unexpectedly generous, and he is humanized still further by the narrator's amused self-projection into his attitude towards his empty-headed, chattering wife. And yet all these figures are agents of the oppressive system that is commented on so astringently in the book and the appalling consequences of which are displayed with such disturbing force. What lies behind this paradox seems to me reasonably plain.

At the outset of the novel, the narrator says of the Antwerp waterfront at dusk that:

It made me so very miserable to look at the offices and buildings along the docks, by now all empty and closed. Office windows after closing hours make the same impression upon me as bleached human bones found in a desolate place in the open sun.... All and everything about the docks and the buildings and the offices looked so utterly hopeless, like a world going to pieces without knowing it.

Stasis, sterility, the absence of opportunities for growth and change – these are obviously fundamental enemies for the narrator, whether in his comfortable but jobless months in Spain, or the trammelled lives of the skippers of luxury liners, or the rigidities of bureaucracies. But the antithesis of stasis in the novel is more than merely variety and flow, and the narrator's alertness to manifestations of energy is more than simply the result of a craving for titillation. As I have said, a good deal of prominence is given to communication in the novel – e.g., the numerous dialogues, the demonstrations in them of the various purposes for which language can be used (information-giving, entertainment, entrapment, self-preservation, and so on), the concern with the media, the alertness to possible misconceptions, the *talked* aspects of the book – and the whole thrust of the novel is towards communication with the intelligent reader. But if the narrator (or Traven) strives for communication as he does, this is a corollary of the fact that things communicate so powerfully with *him*. For example, he becomes lost, irrevocably committed to the *Yorikke*, as soon as the simple question 'Want a job?' is shouted to him from her deck; and a prime reason why he doesn't give up and go over the side after the full awfulness of his position aboard her has become apparent is his sense of how

this fellow-drag of mine, left behind with a double-watch, would make my last trip so unbearable that I could not stay below, and it might happen that I would have to come up again just to say: 'Hey, brother-sailor, I am sorry, please forgive me. Won't you forgive me, so that I may stay below?' Suppose he doesn't? What then?

Even inanimate things speak to him and Stanislav at times, whether a temperamental winch or a pile of stokehold coal or the *Yorikke* herself; and suicide suggests itself to him in terms not of a blank annihilation of being but of going *to* something – to the generous, welcoming sea.

The narrator's world, in other words, is one in which there is no question of needing to break out of one's solitude by seizing hold of things and trying to force meaning into them; for the most part they have it naturally and it only needs uncovering. And throughout the novel we see the same attitudes that enabled Traven to deal so movingly with the Mexican Indians: the same intuitive empathy, the disinterested curiosity, the refusal to be content with merely judging things from the outside (the inconvenience of a hand-rail, the aloofness of a consul, the callousness of a skipper), the concern to get behind their surfaces and see in them the intelligible operations of other minds. But there are obvious limits to the narrator's empathy: in at least a couple of places, when the offences committed are against other people, there is no trace of it and those responsible are treated simply as objects. And when we look for common denominators in his more paradoxical appreciations, it becomes plain that what he is responding to is the same kind of thing that he celebrates in his accounts of the skills required for stokehold work on the *Yorikke*. The skipper of the *Yorikke* may objectively be a servitor of international capitalism at its most cynical and destructive, but he is still a brilliant seaman and gunrunner. The vacationing publisher may be, *qua* publisher, a purveyor of rubbish, but he 'knew all the tricks' for holding his own against panhandlers. The scene in which the narrator is signed on aboard the *Yorikke* may be the record of a disaster for him, but it is informed by a wryly amused admiration for the perfect exploitative skill displayed by the second engineer and the smooth role-playing Jaggers-and-Wemmick relationship between him and the skipper. And at one point the *Yorikke* herself is commended because she 'made carcasses inside, outside, and everywhere. She was a model of a death ship.' What is celebrated in the accounts of stokehold work is the satisfaction of being intensely oneself by means of a full and disciplined release of energies in a meaningful context; and in the general alertness of the narrator elsewhere to skilful problem-solving and role-playing, there is a similar esteem for the sort of individuation that is at once personal and social. In fine, just as there is no dichotomy in the novel between concrete individuals and abstract culture, so there is none in it between life and form. If the antithesis to stasis and sterility is life, it is life that is all the more alive because of its formal individuation.

And there is one final dichotomy that Traven seems to me to have escaped. The ethical stance of the novel involves not only a firm awareness of the difference between apprehending entities from the

outside and from the inside (paradigmatically, the difference
between the *Yorikke* as observed from the quay and as experienced
after the narrator has boarded her). It also involves a rejection of the
belief that in any context only one of the two modes of response can
be correct and that to employ both leads to relativism, scepticism,
and quiescence. The narrator's stance does not in the least inhibit
him from judgement and action, any more than Nelly Dean's awareness of the multifaceted individualities of Heathcliff and Cathy in
Wuthering Heights inhibits her from judging and acting in her own
defence and in defence of others. Nor is it inconsistent with his rad-
icalism either: unpleasant systems are not made any better by the
merits of those who keep them functioning, and his protests against
injustice and exploitation are all the more telling because the
humanity in the name of which he is speaking is a manifold one. And
his esteem for individuality and self-affirmation does not in the least
preclude love, self-sacrifice, and a transcendence of the merely
personal. It is by considering this transcendence that I shall close.

IV

In the brief third section, the fundamental attitudes displayed
throughout the novel and articulated in the following passage
achieve their final balancing:

Through these rags of clouds we could see, for a few seconds, the shining
stars that, in spite of all the uproar, called down upon us the eternal
promise: 'We are the Peace and the Rest!' Yet between these words of
promise we could see another meaning: 'Within the flames of never ceasing
creation and restlessness, there we are enveloped; do not long for us if you
are in want of peace and rest; we cannot give you anything which you do
not find within yourself!'

In certain ways the emphasis upon movement and change intensifies
in this section. The initial impression of placidity given by the
Empress of Madagascar is delusive; the luxuries available to the
narrator and Stanislav after she has become grounded on the reef are
unsatisfying; and the whole idea of a ship's transformation into a
static tower is so incongruous that her final dislodgement comes
almost as a relief. It is fitting that the *Yorikke* now appears to the
narrator a thing of natural and organic beauty, integrity, and
strength: the whole novel is a demonstration of the beauties and

strengths of certain kinds of openness and flexibility. But at the same time – and in the last analysis it may be this that makes it still a revolutionary one – the novel also furnishes no less convincing presentations of the heart-stirring beauty of certain kinds of organic stability and order, especially those involving membership in a just community. And it is these that predominate in the final section. The intensified yearning to belong to something meaningful after all the homeless wanderings – to the America of one's dreams, to the *Yorikke* in apotheosis, to an 'honest and decent ship' – becomes almost too poignant to contemplate with entirely dry eyes; and the closing evocation of the greatest and happiest homecoming that men have been able to imagine seems to me scarcely surpassed elsewhere in fiction except in the accounts of the passing-over of Mr Standfast in *The Pilgrim's Progress* and the death of Mrs Gradgrind in *Hard Times*.

Having opened this essay with one quotation from Leavis, I will conclude it with another, this time about Wordsworth: 'What he had for presentment was a type and a standard of human normality, a way of life; his preoccupation with sanity and spontaneity working at a level and in a spirit that it seems appropriate to call religious.'[7] Such a formulation could well serve as a starting point for an extended discussion of Traven. And I can think of few other twentieth-century novelists of whom the same could be said.

II

A Dangerous Book?:
The Story of O

The Story of O is one of those books which mark the reader –
which do not leave him entirely, or at all, as he was before.

Jean Paulhan

I

In the course of some recent animadversions on 'evaluative' criticism, Mr Northrop Frye remarked, a trifle complacently perhaps,
that 'Ezra Pound, T. S. Eliot, Middleton Murry, F. R. Leavis, are
only a few of the eminent critics who have abused Ellipsis. Ellipsis'
greatness as a poet is unaffected by this: as far as the central fact of
his importance in literature is concerned, these eminent critics might
as well have said nothing at all.'[1] What interests me here is not the
Ellipsis controversy, however, but the revealed ease with which a
quite elementary fact can be lost sight of – namely, the critical
origins of whatever local consensuses about literature the reader
happens to agree with. It is easy to see how this happens, especially
with the 'traditional' academic consensus that Mr Frye is evidently
invoking against the critics he mentions. The notion that there is
authority in numbers is a perennial one; so is the anxiety which R. P.
Blackmur pinpointed a good many years ago with his observation
that 'we have a horror of judgment because we do not know what it
might destroy in our potential selves';[2] and as respectful commentaries on the standard History of Literature authors accumulate, it is
natural to feel, relievedly, that the literary atlas has become settled
for good. Hence, I take it, comes the contemporary revival of the
spirit of gentility, with its demands for tolerance and inoffensiveness
and a desisting from revaluations, under the aegis of theorizers like
Mr Frye. Well, there is something to be said, no doubt, for a state of
security like that of Marlow's auditors in *Heart of Darkness*, with 'a
butcher round one corner, a policeman round another, excellent
appetites, and temperature normal ... from year's end to year's

end'. But to explore beyond the conventional boundaries of literature is to acquire a renewed esteem for the evaluative labours that have made that security possible and to feel the relevance of Andrew Marvell's reminder that 'the same arts that did gain / A power must it maintain'.

These reflections have been prompted by a foray into that last dark continent of literature, the erotic. Physically a particular erotic novel confronts us, let us say, in Galignani's bookshop on the Rue de Rivoli; intellectually, in terms of a professional consensus of any kind, it may simply not be there at all, and we are on our own when examining it in a way that raises sharply the question of the responsibility of our judgements. Among the things we have to consider is the degree of embarrassment we need feel when caught by others reading it, the advisability of putting it physically into the hands of sensitive people we are fond of, the problem of whether or not to bring it later to the attention of our students and of whether or not to write about it, and if so in what way, and the question, too, of how much time it is reasonable to devote to it. Almost all respectable novels already exist intellectually in the sense that they or ones very like them are to be found dealt with in the learned pages of an Ernest A. Baker or his counterparts, so that it is relatively easy to pay attention to a little-known one with an unruffled conscience: it's 'there', and the onus rests to some extent on our readers for not having known of what, as professional scholars, they *ought* to have known. But when we contemplate, say, the bulk of the ninety or more titles of works put out by the Olympia Press in the handsome Traveller's Companion series, we have no survey of any kind to aid us even in the preliminary job of buying some of them, and after that we run the risk, *qua* critics, of appearing not only foolish but nasty-minded. In practice, as it turns out, the primary critical task is generally performed these days by New York publishers and by reviewers for *Time* and *Newsweek*. It is they who give particular works existence and status in the eyes of the academic reader and so relieve us of the burden of seeming to challenge society on behalf of something utterly beyond the pale. Even so, though, we cannot get off lightly. Erotic novels have enough untamed vitality in them to provide that deep personal challenge that is at the heart of all serious reading, and they recall us to the fact that many books are potentially dangerous in the sense of being able to change us in ways that we haven't foreseen and may not want. In this essay I propose to consider the challenge posed by one of the most interesting of all erotic novels, 'Pauline Réage's' *The Story of O*.[3] The *humani nil a me alienum* formula is irritating when used as an incitement to a blanket tolerance. But it is a useful reminder that it may not be altogether desirable to live among walls over which we refuse to look and gulfs into which we dare not gaze.

II

An important source of the authority of some novels and of their assimilated persistence in the mind, is that they offer in convincing detail what are felt to be valuable models of consciousness. It is for this reason that 'mere' thrillers, for instance, can be a good deal more valuable than supposedly more serious works: whatever their limitations, the narrators of novels like Geoffrey Household's *Rogue Male* and Donald Hamilton's *Line of Fire* are functioning with far more alertness, courage, and intelligence than, let us say, the narrator of C. P. Snow's *The Masters*. Now, a prime reason why the great majority of erotic novels are unlikely to be of much interest to most of us, to judge from a representative sampling, is that the invited assimilation cannot take place: the reader is repulsed by the consciousnesses of the participants, which are ghastly, and by the obviously obsessive fantasising of the authors. This straightforward withdrawal and dismissal is not possible with *The Story of O*, however. To be sure, the plot is in some ways a classic one. A well-bred young woman is taken by her current lover, of her own volition though in ignorance of the details of what she will find there, to an unusual kind of gentlemen's club in a château outside Paris, where for several weeks, along with other young ladies, she is subjected to a variety of whippings, sexual entries, and ritualized humiliations by club members. Returning to Paris with her lover, who has been an instigator of her sufferings and with whom she is now more deeply in love than ever, she is passed on by him, again with her own consent, to his half-brother, a cool upper-class Englishman. The new incumbent whips her frequently and has her marked painfully and permanently with symbols of her bondage; and she is very happy. The novel stops abruptly at the end of an episode in which, naked, masked as an owl, and led on a leash, she is a placid spectacle and observer at an otherwise normal open air soirée on the Riviera. The sexual activities throughout, it scarcely needs saying, are very well lighted. Yet neither in the author herself – for though the book is pseudonymous I agree with M. Jean Paulhan in his appended essay that it has all the marks of having been written by a woman – nor in the heroine do we encounter consciousnesses that are grossly fragmented and contemptible. On the contrary, there are certain obvious finenesses in both.

At the outset for a few pages there is admittedly an air of reverie, of the author's feeling her way into her subject, as if she knew the emotional states she wished to describe but were still uncertain as to the precise machinery needed for producing them; and there are implausibilities in the book that I shall comment on. For the most part, though, places, people, and states of consciousness are evoked with a sharpness and gracefulness by no means always attained by the well-reputed authors of more decorous novels. It is a pleasure, for instance, to read the account of the White Russian family in which one found

grandmother, aunt, mother, and even a servant, four women ranging in age between fifty and seventy, painted, yelling, smothered under their black silks and ornaments, sobbing at four in the morning in the cigarette smoke and little red glow of icons, four women in the click and clatter of glasses of tea and the pebbly hissing of a language Jacqueline would have given half her life to forget.

So too with a passage like the following:

The moon, almost full, was high, was bright, shedding great snowy pools of light upon the road, the trees, the houses in the villages the road passed through, and leaving sunk in an India-ink blackness whatever it did not illumine. Night-time, and there were still a few groups of people or individual souls up, standing in doorways. And when this large closed car passed (Sir Stephen had not lowered the convertible top), one could sense curiosity stirring in the shadows. Dogs barked. On the side of the road the headlights lit, the olive-trees resembled silvery clouds drifting a man's height above the earth, the cypresses rose like the vanes of black feathers. There was nothing true nor real in this countryside which night made imaginary, nothing save the odor of sage and lavender. The road climbed and continued to climb, but it was the same warm wind that soughed over the earth. O slipped her cape off her shoulders. Ah, she'd not be seen, there wasn't anyone to see her, there wasn't anyone left.

Moreover, the analysis of states of consciousness and of changes in them is done with considerable subtlety, and though the feelings analysed are principally those of guilt and unworthiness and a growing loss of privacy and of 'ownership' of oneself, it cannot be dodged that the novel – and in this I suspect it may come close to being unique among erotic novels – presents with lyrical intensity states of unalloyed *love*. The following rather long but key passage illustrates these points and others that I shall be making shortly. It deals with the start of the heroine's first meaningful love relationship.

In the space of a week she became acquainted with fear, but with certitude also, with anguish, but also with happiness ... and, deliciously, she became captivated, at her wrists, at her ankles, all over her limbs and far down within her heart's and body's secret recesses feeling tied by bonds subtler, more invisible than the finest hair, stronger than the cables wherewith the Lilliputians made Gulliver prisoner, bonds her lover would tighten or loosen with a glance. She was no longer free? Ah! thank God no, she wasn't any longer free. But she was buoyant, a cloud-dwelling goddess, a swift-swimming fish of the deeps, but deep-dwelling, forever doomed to happiness. Doomed because those powerful ligatures, those hairthin cables whose ends René held in his hand were the only lines by which life-giving energy could reach her. And that was so true that when René slackened his grip upon her – or when she fancied he had – when he seemed faraway, or when he absented himself in what O took for indifference, or when he remained some time without seeing her or answering her letters and when she thought he didn't want to see any more of her or was about to cease loving her, everything came to a halt in her, she languished, she asphyxiated. Green grass turned black, day ceased to be day, the night to be night, turning instead into infernal machines which made light alternate with darkness in order to torture her. Cool water made her nauseous. She felt like a pillar of salt, a statue of ash, bitter, useless and damned, like the salt statues of Gomorrah. For she was guilt-ridden, a sinner. Those who love God and whom God abandons in the darkness of the night, are guilty, they are sinners because they are abandoned. What sins have they committed? They search for them in their memory of the past. She would seek for them in hers. She would find nothing beyond silly little self-indulgences which derived more from her disposition than from anything she had done, vanities, trifling with the desires she'd awakened in other men than René, to whom she paid attention only insofar as the happiness René's love gave her, insofar as she was happy to belong to him, filled her with joy, and, abandoned as she was to him, that abandon made her invulnerable, irresponsible, and all her inconsequential acts ... [sic] but what acts? For she could only reproach herself with thoughts and ephemeral temptations. Be that as it may, one thing was certain: that she was guilty, and that, without wanting to, René was punishing her for a sin he knew nothing of (for it was an entirely inner sin), but which Sir Stephen had detected instantly: her wantonness.

When Jean Paulhan in his eulogy of the novel speaks of its 'decisiveness, its incredible decency and that strong fanatical wind that blows through it without pausing once', one understands what could give rise to a claim so seemingly outrageous. What *The Story of O* thrusts towards us, in fact, is the alarming possibility that here in protagonist and author are consciousnesses that are not only more experienced and sophisticated than our own but finer *morally*. This I judge to be its central challenge, and in the rest of this article I propose to take it up and look more closely at the imputed moral fineness.

III

Two or three years ago there was a piquant anecdote about the novel. Apparently when M. Paulhan was put up for election to the Académie Française, an opponent of M. Paulhan's sent copies of it to all the members, including François Mauriac; and M. Mauriac, after expressing his horror of it ('Even to set the covers of *L' Histoire d'O* ajar is to open the gates of hell'[4]), finally concluded that the graver sin was actually that of the sender of the book, who had so troubled an old man's spirit. Whereupon he voted for Paulhan. We can appreciate something of the peculiarly disconcerting power that the novel could have for a devout religionist, especially a Catholic one with a deep distrust of the flesh. Though the tormentors, as I shall be arguing, aren't in fact up to their thematic roles, it is spelled out that the tortures the heroine undergoes at the institution she enters at the start of the novel are intended primarily to teach her that, in the words of one of her initiators, 'you utterly belong to something which is apart from and outside yourself'; and it is the continuation of this process that is analysed with considerable care after her return to ordinary life. When at one point, for instance, she is disturbed that she is no longer to be allowed to enjoy at least the privacy of her own room,

the essential reason for her anxiety was exactly what it always was: [the] state of being dispossessed of her own self. The only difference was that this dispossession had been brought home by the fact that she no longer had any space all to herself in a place where she had been wont to retreat in order to endure it, nor had she any night left to her, nor, consequently, any dream or any possibility of clandestine existence... Here in all likelihood was the source of the strange security, mixed with fright, to which she felt she was abandoning herself and which she had somehow foreseen without understanding. Henceforth there would be no discontinuity, no gap, no dead time, no remission.

And she is grateful when it comes to pass that 'each wish she surrendered to was her guarantee that another surrender would be required of her, each of his wishes she complied with was for her like some debt whereof she acquitted herself; how strange, that her indebtedness was immense; infinite; strange, perhaps, but it was immense, it was infinite'. Moreover, the reiterations about her willingness in the middle of intolerable situations to accept whatever else may come, out of love for him who has delivered her into them, are convincing, unjust though it seems that awfulness should be repaid so selflessly and lovingly. Most disturbing of all perhaps (at least for a reader less sensitive to certain ironies than M. Mauriac would presumably be), we are compelled to believe in the improvements coming in her because of what she is undergoing – in the possibility that 'however astonishing it were, that from being prostituted her dignity might increase, the crucial point was nonetheless one of dignity. It illumined her as if from within, and one could see her calmness in her bearing, upon her countenance the serenity and imperceptible inner smile one rather guesses at than perceives in the eyes of the recluse.' In sum – and I think the point doesn't need labouring – the book awakens us to the possibility that tranquillity, orderliness, and more complexly admirable states of being can be achieved by routes vastly different from, and in some respects less laborious than, those that the cumulative wisdom of Europe has hitherto demanded that we travel. Is it, however, more than a possibility, and, if it is, how desirable are the states of being of the heroine when examined more closely? It is not, I think, naive to attempt to answer these questions with some care. Erotic literature is the only vigorous body of literature devoted almost entirely to the successful pursuit of happiness, and by considering the rather large claims made in *The Story of O* we can perhaps also deal implicitly with some of the smaller ones of lesser works.

The author, it seems to me, has convincingly presented certain temporary states of mind in which peace and improvement, a general fortifying of the psyche, have resulted from intense experiences involving the abandonment of cogitation, choice, and the observation of conventional limits to which one has oneself assented. It seems to me a good deal less plain, however, that the way in which these states as a whole are arrived at and reinforce each other is credible. In surrendering herself to the organization that she does, the heroine has become one of a strikingly homogeneous group who have relinquished some of the major claims ('yours', 'mine', and so on) and consequent sources of conflict and anxiety that most people cherish. The actual institutions in which the highest degree of homogeneity and self-surrender and the farthest voluntary removal from everyday conditions of existence obtain are, I take it, the conventual and monastic ones, and the resemblances between the heroine's experiences at the château and what I assume to be the situation of the novice in some orders are very marked. It is the author herself, at any rate, who has repeatedly drawn our attention to the heroine's sense of her own unworthiness, her desire to learn submissiveness, the great importance assigned at the château to a multitude of prescriptions about dress and deportment, the relative gravity and impersonality with which infractions are punished, and the happiness the heroine finds in the loss of her freedom and ultimately of her selfhood in the service of something terribly and totally 'other' but deserving to be endlessly submitted to and adored. To point out the obvious, however, the organization that the heroine has committed herself to is a private, secular, upperclass sex club. Could such an organization exist? We can conceive easily enough, I think, of an organization's existing that had some of the features of this one, and with the presentation of the middleaged lesbian purveyor of somewhat unusual cosmetic surgery we are likely to feel particularly strongly that we are getting a glimpse of the inside of one of those circles whose well-to-do and unreportable goings-on get hinted at occasionally in Continental newspapers. Could an organization exactly as described here exist? The answer seems to me clearly no. With so many people and such arresting bodily adornments involved it could scarcely be long in reality before its activities came to the attention of ill-disposed persons in positions of authority; and the kinds of males who could in actuality disport themselves in the described ways would undoubtedly be very much less urbanely and dignifiedly moralistic. With its fancy-dress costumes, its self-conscious rituals, and its obsessive flattery of the male ego, indeed, the whole establishment puts one strongly in mind of the Bunny Clubs and reminds us relevantly of why there couldn't be a successful moralizing erotic novel of this sort set in contemporary America. Either the reader would be too aware of the discrepancy between the conduct described and that of any possible jet-set Americans, or else the more plausible the account was, the more the general repulsiveness of the class involved would insist on obtruding itself. It is significant that the only male character in the novel who is presented at all extensively is an Englishman, and hence presumably less susceptible of tests of credibility by the French reader.

The question deserves dwelling on for a moment, I think, of why a writer of a relatively high level of intelligence and sensibility should have fallen into the particular unrealities and stereotypings that she has. (The Englishman just referred to, for instance, is so typically that pale cold milord who has been in and around erotic literature for over a century that one has to keep reminding oneself that he isn't wearing a top-hat.) Of the literate erotic novels a fairly large proportion, as it happens, seem to involve upper-class figures – Sade's, of course, and *Les Onze Milles Verges, My Secret Life, Souvenirs d'une Princesse Russe, Gamiani*, Nerciat's *Le Diable au Corps*, and so on.[5] The basic reason for this, no doubt, is practicality: it is presumably only in a more or less upper-class milieu that people could have the leisure and privacy in which to pursue their sexual proclivities to the limit, the money to sustain them, and other people to do the tidying up afterwards. We are also presumably up against the related emotional appeal of a certain kind of impermeable self-sufficiency, epitomized conveniently if somewhat vulgarly by the males in *The Story of O*, with their taken-for-granted ease with each other inside a shared and unquestioned code, their total indifference to the possible opinions of outsiders, and their freedom from any accusingly unrealized ego-ideals. And beyond this, where *The Story of O* in particular is concerned, there would appear to lie a residual and debased Catholic mode of conceptualizing existence, in which a sense of the beauties of hierarchies persists in a metaphysically non-hierarchical world and leads the author to take for her material a way of life that both inherently and because it is relatively unfamiliar is especially susceptible of being endowed with the required harmoniousness and elegance. This kind of transmogrifying, it scarcely needs adding, is not confined to erotic literature. It is at its most obvious there, however, and so, in a representatively illuminating way, are its defects. An author engaged in it and in the related creation of humanly impossible patterns of conduct seems to

me to be both yielding to and encouraging a disposition to turn our
eyes away relievedly from the study of human nature in the areas of
fullest and most challenging consciousness (in Shakespeare, for
instance, and Tolstoy, and Kierkegaard) and to suppose that
perhaps, after all, the knowledge and principles that we painfully
acquire there may be only one kind among several and that elsewhere, even though we don't know where or understand how, there
may be other people behaving in very different ways that approximate to our adolescent dreams. Viewed in such a light, of course,
human actuality is liable to appear drab and unsatisfying.

IV

But to approach *The Story of O* as I have been doing, it might be
objected, is to be too literal-minded and to ignore still the full challenge of the states of mind shown in the heroine, and especially the
challenge of her love; Macbeth is Macbeth regardless of the witches
and Banquo's ghost. And though *The Story of O* is written predominantly in a detailed rationalistic manner and lacks the consistent
heightening that would make the analogy valid, the retort still
deserves considering. After all, a writer may know certain states of
consciousness very thoroughly at first hand and be able to render
them precisely, and yet fail to enter adequately, for novelistic
purposes, into the consciousnesses of other people. Well, the novel
really is a novel about love, as I indicated earlier; and, as Paulhan
grasped, it presents in an especially pure form that total surrender to
the loved one to which a great deal of lip-service has been paid in the
literature of romantic love. If one indeed loves someone totally and
wishes to give oneself to him completely, may it not be logical to do
whatever he wishes – to make oneself available to whoever he
wishes to offer one to, for instance, if it will give him pleasure – regardless of how contemptibly one might be judged by others to be
behaving? The book in this and certain other respects is a very
handy apotheosis of romantic-love attitudes. Hence it is worth considering both how fair the author plays in recording the sufferings
and selflessness of her heroine and how valuable the kind of love
celebrated here really is.

The term 'pornography', insofar as it has any usefulness, seems to
me to point not to what is put into a work but to what is left out. It
directs our attention to an area of erotic literature in which we find

sex not only without anxieties about the opinions of others but also without worries about the body – sex without menstruation, conception, pregnancy and children, without premature orgasms and post-coital depression, without smells, without bodily weariness and sickness, without, in fact, the truly physical. Writers of erotic novels are for the most part incapable, so far as my reading goes, of acknowledging that the body is more than a pleasure-giving arrangement of holes and protuberances and that it can sometimes stage unlooked-for and not in the least entertaining revolts against abuses of it. The author of *The Story of O* does not entirely escape such distortions. Though she plays uncommonly fair, on the whole, in allowing that certain activities do indeed have physical consequences – that floggings, for instance, leave welts and even scars – she nevertheless dodges evoking the physical discomfort of such things as sitting down after having been thrashed, healing after having each buttock branded with a letter three inches long and half an inch deep, and wearing in the company of sadists a metal pendant fastened through a hole punched in one of one's labia. Moreover, despite the frequent talk about humiliation, the discomforts inflicted on the heroine are relatively limited and unimaginative, with nothing said about defecation or menstruation and no sexual activities (not even those with the man-servants at the château) involving physically repulsive individuals. Apparently if one is going to be endlessly humiliated it must still be in the right sort of way and by the right kind of people. And that unknown atrocities can be awaited as composedly as they are by the heroine testifies to the fact that the full violence of male sexual passion, the uncontrollable, the unaesthetic aspects of it, are really nowhere shown in the novel. 'Few are the men', observes Paulhan, 'who have not dreamt of possessing a Justine. But as best I know no woman [till Pauline Réage] has so far dreamt of being Justine.' In reality, though, Justine had a vastly more unpleasant time of it. It seems in keeping with the elegancies of the carefully described décors and garments in *The Story of O* that none of the males' energies and imaginings disrupt the gracefulness of the author's prose; and it is probably relevant that the lesbian affairs of the heroine are obviously described from firsthand experience.

But if the heroine's love is less truly tested and hence less noble than it is offered to us as being·– and if it might not have survived at all under the wrong kinds of discomfort – what nevertheless are we to think of it as it is actually shown? The pattern in it, after all, is a common one in certain respects and clearly is fairly deeply engraved in human experience. The tale of the woman separated abruptly from all her normal ways of living, subjected to sexual pain and humiliation, and finding at last that she is happier under her new conditions is to be encountered in a number of novels at various levels of decorousness and competence (e.g., *The Sheik, Sanctuary,* and Villiot's *Woman and Her Master*). The recurrence of this situation stems partly, I take it, from the fact that in an intensified form it presents elements found or anticipated in the experience of a good many women surrendering themselves into unions with physically stronger and still largely unknown beings whose sexual demands upon them may alarmingly exceed their imaginings. And when we contemplate the happy outcome of the fictional version it is clear why men as well as women can take pleasure in it. Already entered upon a career, the man is almost inevitably less free to change in marriage than the woman. It is the latter, choosing him as *her* career, who must allow herself to change more and give up more, and in that respect she is more the victim and the one who must forgive the other for being what he is. I do not know whether or not the pattern of affront/forgiveness/acceptance is better than that of a treaty entered into by equals. But it is certainly a more dramatic one, it seems to me a more common one, and for the man involved there can be a heart-moving beauty in the realization that he is accepted and loved even though (or perhaps, in Paul Tillich's formulation, *because*) he is unacceptable. Nevertheless, when Paulhan suggests that love is 'really' what has been expressed in a particular kind of love poetry, with its figurative talk of slavery and chains, this seems pretty much like extolling cannibalism on the grounds that lovers often say that they'd like to eat each other. Concerning love and the surrendered self, the question must surely be raised as to what constitutes that self that one chooses to surrender, and how far, in certain kinds of surrender, it remains the same. The question also arises of whether, given its consequences for the other person, a particular surrender is in fact truly loving – of whether it entails a deep and sensitive concern for the other one, a concern for his or her best potential self and best interests, which may well differ from what he himself judges them at times to be. And the book also exposes certain other fallacies in the notion of the admirableness of total surrender.

As Paulhan acknowledges, though without reaching after the full implications of the fact, the ending of the book reminds us that the end of a process has been reached: the heroine, naked at the soirée, is now totally exposed, totally subservient, totally content. That the author simply stops at this point seems to testify to her inability or unwillingness to confront the fact that from now on, the drama of being overcome having gone from her life, a state of *ennui* is all too likely to set in for the heroine – or, to be more precise, would be likely to set in were the present relationship to continue. In fact, though, as the author herself seems to take cognizance of in her concluding note ('There exists another ending to the story of O. Seeing herself about to be left by Sir Stephen, she preferred to die. To which he gave his consent'), the interest that the heroine possesses for her two lovers is largely the interest of conquering her. The conquests involved are more complex, of course, than those climaxing the pursuit of Clarissa Harlowe or of the unfortunate Présidente in *Les Liaisons Dangereuses*, and in this respect the novel pushes interestingly beyond the conventional climax of seduction in a way analogous to Tolstoy's continuation beyond the conventional climax of marriage. But it is still submission that is sought, the total surrender of the other. This attained (and the dissatisfaction impelling the first lover to move beyond simple cohabitation, and his progressive losing of interest thereafter, encourage the belief), there would seem to be nothing to keep the second lover interested any longer either. And the fact that by allowing oneself to be made over into the person one's lover says he wants, one ceases to be what he wants at all, seems to me not to point to some deep and terrible paradox about the nature of Love but merely to show up weaknesses in a certain way of loving. A lot of moral authority traditionally accrues to failure, however, and I wish now to consider, penultimately, the question of invited injury and even destruction to which the book draws our attention so insistently.

A rather high proportion of significant erotic novels, as it happens, appear to involve cruelty, and in a good many of the 'cruel' novels, I will hazard, a certain duplicity occurs: whereas ostensibly it is the pleasures of the conquering male that are being celebrated, in fact the emotion communicated the most strongly is that which, it is supposed, is being felt by the subjugated female. This can happen the most strongly sometimes, I suspect, when the female's consciousness isn't described in detail at all, since the reader can then have the sensation of a pleasurably painful warm void into which his own consciousness dissolves. In *The Story of O*, however, there is no such duplicity: the central consciousness is explicitly feminine and the gratifications are spelled out. Yet when we look more carefully at it, what confronts us is that the development in it is one that can be as foreign to and as yearningly sought after by a woman as it is for the yearningly self-projecting male. The state finally attained to by the heroine is one in which all the complex varieties of response called for by a keen awareness of differences between other individuals, their value-systems, and their conceptions of oneself, have become replaced by a single mode of response. She has let herself be reduced to a uniform being for others, a totally available body and spirit – and the uniform response that she makes is to do and be solely what is required of her by them. And when we also consider that by the end of the novel she is primarily, and happily, the property of a man who prefers not to enter her by the normal channel, and that dangling almost irremovably from her pudendum is a metal pendant eight or nine inches long, it becomes increasingly plain that what she has given in to and found security in is not the 'essential' nature of Woman but, in reality, the image of womanhood that has been created by the fevered imaginings of certain men – men who hate the challenging actuality of full womanliness, with its concern with motherhood and responsibility, as much as the heroine does herself.

In other words, the novel is probably the fullest demonstration that we have of that craving for an escape from selfhood (including sexual selfhood), and from the constant making of moral choices, that underlies alike the masochistic and, as represented here by the frigidly tormenting males, the sadistic consciousness. Somewhat piquantly, the lie to the attempt to give metaphysical profundity to these disorders of the sensibility and will is given effectively by M. Paulhan himself when he breaks out, a trifle unexpectedly, into an I'm-just-a-poor-male-looking-on-in-awe celebration of the comprehensiveness of Woman. It is agreeable to imagine the sort of reception he would get from the busy, competent, lively housewife and mother he eulogizes were he to burst into her kitchen or nursery with the exhilarating tidings about the novel that

Here we have it at last: a woman who admits ... exactly what women have always – and never more so than today – forbidden themselves to admit.

Exactly what men have always accusingly said was true about them: that they never cease slavishly to obey their blood and temper; that in them, everything, even their minds, even their souls, is dominated by their sex. That they have got incessantly to be fed, incessantly washed and burdened, incessantly beaten. That they have but one requirement, and that is simply of a good master who takes good care to keep his goodness in check and to be wary of it . . . That, in a word, one must have a whip in hand when one goes to visit them.

While it may well be that suspicions of this kind lurk in the minds of a good many men, it seems plain that what most of them crave at bottom is to be shown that their suspicions are untrue and to have their more exorbitant claims rejected in a way that they themselves can assent to gladly – gladly because reassured that they are not in reality compelled to choose between mindless animality and the tense and fearful loneliness of the whip carrier.

V

There is one last issue that I wish to confront, for it is raised quite strongly by the novel itself and even more by M. Paulhan's defence of it, namely the question of cruelty. As Paulhan's comments remind us, the reactionary with his evocation of a world of passion, wrath, tears, religious intensities, and simple irreversible solutions has an initial emotional advantage over the liberal; and Paulhan himself in his attack on the stock response to the notion of happiness-in-bondage attempts to use this advantage by contrasting the present time, in which an inculcated gentleness towards others 'is compensated for by air-strikes, by deluges of napalm and the explosion of atoms', with those healthier times when violence was more direct and personal – the wife or child whipped, the criminal 'boldly' beheaded in the public square instead of left to 'rot' in prison, and so on. I suspect, however, that if it were to be suggested to M. Paulhan that his enthusiasm for the times of more 'honest' violences might not have been shared by the criminals who were boiled alive or broken on the wheel, or that there are still instances enough of children beaten into insensibility by their parents, he would reply that such instances, of course, are not the right *kind* of violence, not what he had in mind at all. So too, I think, with the French admirers of Sade as poet-of-Love. (So too, for that matter, with the extraordinarily silly remarks about corporal punishment by D. H. Lawrence,[6]

whose fury had anyone taken a stick to *him* can be well imagined.)
And it seems to me that what such enthusiasm for violence and
cruelty often involves is a craving for yet another pastoral change in
the rules, so that we can miraculously live inside a system in which
no violence degrades the doer or the receiver and no just limits are
passed in the violences done. As I indicated earlier, yearnings for
such transmogrifications weaken our sense of human actualities – in
the present case the actuality of suffering – and I think we should
keep an especially wary eye on the apologetics that are indulged in
with respect to cruel erotic novels. Admittedly it is difficult to assess
the degree of commitment with which Paulhan expresses himself in
parts of his essay or to escape feeling that he can allow himself the
luxury of being unpleasant because he takes it for granted that
nothing he advocates runs any serious risk of being practised. It
shouldn't be overlooked, however, that novel and essay appeared
only a year or two before the torturers began work in earnest in
Algiers.

Yet there seem to me all the same to be certain important truths
about cruelty lurking behind pieces like Paulhan's. When Paulhan
announces that the only freedoms we care about are those that we
get at the expense of others, he is no doubt chiefly revealing only a
personal idiosyncrasy. Nevertheless the dictum does remind us of
how the freedom to commit ourselves fully to anything worthwhile
must often be fought for against the encroachments of others, and
that in battles it is necessary to give pain. Moreover, there are plenty
of iniquities around us capable of arousing the passionate intensity
that M. Paulhan seems to yearn to be made to feel (his essay, for all
its overstatements, is curiously flabby), and that positively demand
the inflicting of pain if they are to be attacked effectively. It is
possible, too, to act with full commitment in a way that we antici-
pate and perhaps even hope will cause pain, and yet not dwell upon
the imagined involutions of particular pains or take any general
pleasure in the sufferings of others. Indeed, as a work like Georges
Franju's unforgettable *Les Yeux sans Visage* demonstrates, we can
sometimes be wholly unsparing of people's sensibilities *because* we
abhor cruelty, and can all the more ruthlessly conceive and present
atrocious cruelties to their gaze because, looking into ourselves, we
comprehend the ease with which similar atrocities can actually
come about.

At the outset of this essay I looked askance at the flabby gentility that is far too common in the academic world today. It seems to me that in that world in particular there is need for the kind of intense disinterested utterances that give pain because they are true and whose 'cruelty' is the only thing that may inhibit those attacked from persisting in their follies. Moreover, as the careers of critics like Winters and the Leavises remind us, there are still grave risks for those who speak out with appropriate indignation and precision against the literary activities and value-judgements of contemporaries; and the more the academic world settles into a posture of ostensible tolerance and good temper, the graver those risks will be. The work of such critics seems to me especially valuable, not only because of the particular truths in it, or the untruths that do more to make us arrive at the truth than do the truths of lesser critics, or the general display of high intelligence and integrity, but also because it admonishes us that the intellectual life, properly apprehended, is a calling of great importance in which the inflicting of pain may be a duty and in which a great deal of courage may be needed by those who endeavour to live with full commitment in it. There will always be dangers, even among books.[7]

Yvor Winters: the Perils of Mind

I

'All tributes to merit!' the Duchess of Wellington is reported to have said on her deathbed of the great Duke's trophies. 'There's the value, all pure, no corruption ever suspected even.' To speak of trophies in connection with Yvor Winters may seem ironical, of course. He did, it is true, receive one or two national awards, mostly for his poetry, when he was in his sixties, and a few well-known critics such as Randall Jarrell, R. P. Blackmur, Arthur Mizener, Morton D. Zabel, and Allen Tate had occasionally spoken highly of him earlier. But in bulk even the favourable reviews of his books seemed to add up to the proposition that he was admirably independent and dedicated and that sometimes, when he set aside his theories and gave himself up to a text, he could be brilliant, but that his theories were mistaken, his taste narrow, and his judgements often absurd. As for the hostile commentaries, someone could put together an anthology of remarks from *them* for parallels with which we would look in vain except in discussions of F. R. Leavis. And, unlike Leavis, Winters could not have had the satisfaction of knowing at the end that if his detractors had often been brutal, his admirers were now legion. Nevertheless, with the exception again of Leavis, it is hard to think of any other eminent man of letters in English during the past few decades to whom the remarks quoted above could more fittingly be applied, or who is more deserving of being seen as, in a fairly precise sense of the term, a culture hero. The term has been cheapened a good deal, and a sizeable region of the culture of the last decade or two could be charted by examining the processes by which a term formerly applied to figures like Henry James can now be applied with no sense of incongruity to someone like Andy Warhol. What has been lost, of course, is the notion of *heroism* – the notion that someone is admirable not because he has Made It, but because of qualities like endurance, self-discipline, integrity, and courage that have traditionally invited the epithet 'heroic', whether displayed by a great soldier or by a great man of letters, such as Samuel Johnson. I shall try in this essay to define some of the aspects of Winters' character – or, if that seems too old-fashioned a term, of his way of being a man of letters, more particularly an *academic* man of letters – that make his example especially heartening at present, when there is so observable a distrust, even inside the profession, of the academic life and the academic virtues.

That Winters, from the time when he was the Western editor of *Hound and Horn* in the early thirties, evoked a good deal of hostility is a commonplace. But it is a commonplace whose force, in these professionally liberal times, is likely to diminish rapidly as his stock rises, just as there are no doubt now a lot of young readers who are under the impression that Leavis was always recognized as a major critic. It is natural to want to think well of our profession and to believe that – dedicated as it professedly is to the pursuit of truth – it is one in which truth will always out and virtue always be recognized. After all, are we not all, those of us in literary studies, engaged almost daily in the classroom in celebrating the virtues of the illustrious dead and testifying obliquely to our own collective percipience about them in contrast with the impercipience of their less enlightened contemporaries? And even where controversial contemporaries of our own are concerned, it is insidiously easy to feel that when 'unnumber'd suppliants crowd Preferment's gate', almost any kind of reputation is better than none at all and that the very fact of being controversial entails an implicit recognition of one's importance. It is increasingly easy, then, to miss the force of a remark like that which Winters made in a letter to a colleague of mine in the late fifties apropos of a favourable review of *The Function of Criticism*: 'You don't know how nice it is to be called a great critic instead of a son-of-a-bitch until you have been called the second a few hundred times.'

When Winters was an embattled reviewer in *Hound and Horn*, he was not simply a critic with an unfashionable line and unwelcome tone. He was also an academic and, worse, a graduate student, in what appears to have been a very traditional department; and for a number of years thereafter (he did not achieve a full professorship until he was forty-seven) he was a relatively junior member of that department and of his profession. Admittedly he was not shut out from an academic post at a decent university as Leavis was for eight or nine years. But George R. Stewart's novel *Doctor's Orals* (1939) is horrendously convincing about the tightness of the job market in the Depression years and the corresponding power of established academics over their juniors, and the following cool passage of reminiscence in *The Function of Criticism* makes telling reading:

Of the four gentlemen who have been head of the department of English at Stanford in my time, the second, the late Professor A. G. Kennedy, told me that criticism and scholarship do not mix, that if I wanted to become a serious scholar I should give up criticism. He told me likewise that poetry and scholarship do not mix, and that he had given up writing poetry at the age of twenty-five. And he added that my publications were a disgrace to the department. Fortunately for myself, he was the only one of the four department heads to hold these views, but one was almost enough. And he was far from an exception so far as the profession as a whole was concerned. There were other men like him at Stanford, some in positions of greater power; and there were others like him elsewhere.

For it was not a profitable controversiality that Winters was achieving. He was not, at least for many years, able to operate professionally behind the kind of shield that comes from being known by one's duller colleagues to be esteemed in certain influential circles. He was fair game up to the end in a way that none of the other well-known critics have been, again with the exception of Leavis. The reviews of *Forms of Discovery* are instructive; and it is not paranoia that peeps out in his anecdote in it about his unsuccessful attempt, at the request of a Stanford librarian, to get significant first editions of modern poetry on the open shelves put into a special collection:

On a few subsequent occasions I suggested to the more eminent members of my department the importance of such a collection; but I was given to understand that the materials were unimportant, that I, after all, was scarcely competent to deal with the problem, and that I seemed to be making an effort to magnify my importance in the department.

It is the anecdote of someone who for a sizeable number of years was without pull – without clout.

Furthermore, Winters was not just a critic whose books appeared unprestigiously and got some devastating reviews. He was also – he was primarily – a poet, the author, by the end, of close to three hundred published poems; and, as Howard Kaye observed in an admirable obituary article in the *New Republic* in 1968, he was 'among the most passionate of modern poets'.[1] His commitment to poetry was as total as Hart Crane's or Robert Lowell's; and though his continence in speaking of his own work was almost saintly (he never paraded himself in his criticism as Winters-the-Poet), his estimation of that work appears to have been high, if we can go by such clues as the introduction to his *Early Poems* in 1966. But he never enjoyed any of the dispensations and reassurances that have been increasingly available to poets who have lodged in the academy. He was not a guru at a liberal arts college; he was not a peripatetic Visiting Creator. He earned his Ph.D. at Stanford at a time when Ph.D.s were not earned easily. In the letter that I quoted above he commented that his involvement with *Hound and Horn* delayed his getting his degree by at least two and a half years, a cost that perhaps only those who have likewise involved themselves in professionally unprofitable activities while in a Ph.D. programme can fully appreciate. And for the rest of his working life he was a thoroughly professional academic in a major department. In those circumstances, being the kind of poet that he was must have been especially arduous.

In the twenties, Winters had been acquiring a valuable reputation as a poet; indeed, one reviewer announced in the *Nation* in 1930 that 'Mr. Winters' name is one of the best known in circles where modern poetry and modern criticism are discussed.'[2] From the start of the thirties, he lost that reputation. Actually, in the words of Kaye, 'his subjects and his style were modern in the fullest sense'. (Kaye quotes Lowell as saying, 'He was the kind of conservative who was so original and radical that his poems were never reprinted in the anthologies for almost twenty years.') But, having drastically altered his style by an effort of will and intelligence without parallel in the history of verse in English, he had to live for the next two decades with attacks on his principles, his critical judgements, and his own performance as a poet that reached a pitch in the mid-forties, with the near-simultaneous publication of *The Anatomy of Nonsense* and of the major selection of his poems *The Giant Weapon*, that would have broken almost anyone else. True, when the *Collected Poems* appeared in 1952 a few reviewers, notably Frederick Morgan, Hayden Carruth, and Allen Tate, wrote with almost unreserved enthusiasm about them, and one can unearth the occasional rare complimentary remark earlier (for example, by Arthur Mizener and Morton Dauwen Zabel) about his post-'experimental' work. But it was obviously a starvation diet during the years that mattered, the years of his most intense creative activity. And such a diet does not become enriched retroactively, whatever kudos a man may receive in his sixties. Even by the time he died, the only articles, as distinct from reviews, that had been devoted to his poetry were a brief if good one by Richard M. Elman in the *Commonweal* (1961) and a longer one by Alan Stephens in *Twentieth Century Literature* (1963), to which Winters himself took strong exception in print. (There was also an excellent note by Alvin B. Kernan on the sleeve of a record of Winters reading his own poetry.[3]) And even though a few of his poems had started creeping into anthologies, we would look for them in vain in the overwhelming majority of college texts. Furthermore, where such distinguished students or associates of his as Edgar Bowers, J. V. Cunningham, Alan Stephens, N. Scott Momaday, Helen Pinkerton, Catherine Davis and Janet Lewis were concerned (none of whom, representatively enough, is mentioned in M. L. Rosenthal's *The New Poets*, 1967) it was almost entirely Winters himself who had to do the public insisting on their distinction and, implicitly, on the validation that their work helped to furnish for his own principles – not a very felicitous position to have been in.

II

I am not, I must emphasize, trying to get critical justice done retrospectively. My primary concern is with what it must have been like to be a particular writer under particular circumstances. Winters himself, as I have said, was always marvellously continent in references to his own career, and amply earned the right to cast a cool eye on Pope's 'exasperation [in the "Epistle to Arbuthnot"] with people who [had] exasperated him' and to observe drily, 'They were doubtless exasperating, but so are most people; so is life.' But in a passage like the following we are obviously glimpsing the tip of an iceberg about which some biographer will no doubt sometime tell us a good deal:

A first-rate poet differs from his contemporaries (and I include those who think of themselves as literary contemporaries) not in being eccentric or less human, but in being more central, more human, more intelligent. But the difference in this respect between, let us say, a great poet and most distinguished scholars is very great, and few scholars are distinguished; and the scholar cannot recognize the difference and is scarcely prepared to admit the possibility of the difference, for he regards himself as a professional man of letters. To the scholar in question, the poet is wrong-headed and eccentric, and the scholar will usually tell him so. This is bad manners on the part of the scholar, but the scholar considers it good manners. If the poet, after some years of such experiences, loses his temper occasionally, he is immediately convicted of bad manners. The scholar often hates him (I am not exaggerating), or comes close to hating him; but if the poet returns hatred with hatred (and surely this is understandable), he is labeled as a vicious character, for, after all, he is a member of a very small minority group. The poet may become neurotic under such pressure; there is no comparable pressure on the scholar, and he usually remains normal.

Nevertheless, Winters never took either of the obvious escape routes. He never succumbed to the academy, and he never turned against it.

He remained intensely professional, intensely concerned to bring home to creative writers the importance of historical learning and to show that there is no necessary opposition between academic discipline (as distinct from the erudition-gathering of a Blackmur) and creative work. To quote one of his most memorable formulations:

The damnable fact about most novelists, I suppose, is their simple lack of intelligence: the fact that they seem to consider themselves professional writers and hence justified in being amateur intellectuals. They do not find it necessary, so far as one can judge, to study the other forms of literature, or even forms of the novel other than those they practice; they do not find it necessary to think like mature men and women or to study the history of thought; they do not find it necessary to master the art of prose.

Thirty-odd years ago, when conservative academics were a good deal more powerful and dangerous inside the academy than they are now, he objected to the quarrel 'picked with the philologists and the textual critics', and suggested that 'There is far more need even yet for good textual criticism even of many standard writers than these critics seem to realize, and philology has always been and will always remain a subject of fundamental importance for the student of literature. If more poets had studied philology, the quality of our poetry would probably improve.' Nor was this a self-consciously corrective gesture of the kind that one has come to associate, regretfully, with Lionel Trilling: 'We have gone too far in one direction, now let us go too far in the other.' Fred C. Robinson suggested in one of the few intelligent reviews of *Forms of Discovery* (*Comparative Literature Studies*, 1968) that Winters' own training in philology may have played an important part in shaping his critical principles and procedures. And certainly we can see how strong in his work, criticism and poetry alike, is the sense of languages as publicly inspectable things with publicly accrued meanings and conventions whose claims cannot be dodged merely by willing it. Most creative writers in this century, one sometimes feels, have demanded two passports and the right to juggle them at will. Winters, in contrast, insisted that all that is necessary is a single passport and citizenship in a single kingdom, the kingdom of language; that the life of language and thought, the life of the mind, is all one; and that there can be no slipping across frontiers to arrive at greatness. Which is another way of saying that he stood up for certain strengths in the academic life against the customary intimidating claims on behalf of a supposedly very different mode of being – the creative – with its exhilarations, its daring, its shortcuts to truth and wisdom and profundity.

But if he spoke as an academic, there was nothing academic about him, any more than there was about Samuel Johnson; and I have still not accounted for the sense of Johnsonian weight and strength that he can induce.

It is not, to begin with, any easy matter of principles or ideas, central though some of his theoretical statements would have to be in an extended examination of him as a critic. This is especially obvious when the term 'neo-classicism' starts creeping into discussions of his work. The prefix in that term is almost inescapably pejorative, implying as it does the conscious imitation of forms or procedures without the creative energy and daring that led to their invention in the first place. The strength, the peculiar *gravitas*, of Johnson were things that he *earned* – matters, essentially, not of forms and ideas but of a whole complex value-system and mode of being, to the evolution of which his classical reading, like his Christianity, contributed, but which it does not explain. Part of the drama of reading Boswell's *Life* for the first time is that we can never, however much classical or Christian erudition we bring to the task, predict confidently how Johnson is going to respond to this or that specific question; yet by the end we know that the answers will very largely be found to cohere if we work patiently enough at them. So too with Winters' literary judgements. It is instructive to try anticipating what he has to say in *Forms of Discovery* about such poems as 'The Vanity of Human Wishes' and Marvell's 'Horatian Ode', or to read in advance the complete works of some of the poets we know he has commended (Ben Jonson, for instance, or Edward Taylor) and try to spot the poems we would expect him to praise. We will almost certainly end up with a good many more misses than hits. And if, on the basis of *Forms of Discovery*, we then try predicting what poems we will find assembled in Winters and Kenneth Fields' anthology, *Quest for Reality*, we will probably do even worse. It is understandable, moreover, that there is no 'school of Winters' in criticism. It is tempting, of course, to take over his judgements and tone at times, especially when people whose activities one dislikes are under attack. If one is irritated by the apotheosis of William Carlos Williams into a proto-beat father-figure, for example, it is very pleasant to read the flat statement that 'he was a thorough bore in print except on a few occasions', just as, when exasperated by some particular instance of academic stupidity (for example, Thomas H. Johnson's ruinous punctuating of Emily Dickinson), one can only murmur to oneself, with Winters, that 'scholars find it very difficult to stay in their place'. Furthermore, as has happened in England, it is possible to make a reputation of sorts for oneself by reworking some of his ideas and presenting them without acknowledgement to readers unfamiliar with his writings. But we cannot take over except very temporarily the main thrust of his mind, any more than we can take over Johnson's. Winters himself always maintained in print a sharp division between himself and younger writers who admired him or whom he admired. In *Forms of Discovery*, for example, he is rigorous and discriminating enough, in all conscience, in his remarks about such poets as Bowers, Stephens, and even Cunningham, bringing them no closer to us and according them no more privileges than he did Greville or Emily Dickinson or Bridges. And when we come across the judgement that 'few men possess either the talent or the education to justify their being taken very seriously' as critics of poetry, we can be pretty confident that we ourselves would not have been included among them. Winters' stance and voice are all his own.

III

In what may well have been the most intelligent review of *The Function of Criticism* (*Delta*, Cambridge, 1962), Richard Gooder complained a little oddly of a lack of naturalness in Winters' prose style. The style, which seems to me a great one, was eminently natural to Winters himself, however. It was there from the start (which is not to say that his judgements and ideas did not change), and the voice is the voice of someone who is all of a piece and who is not role-playing. It is the voice of a mind that may be complex but in which there are not the customary over-neat dichotomies – literature and life, thought and creation, discovery and teaching, public and private, and so on – that most of us employ in the ordering of our own disorderly mental economies. For Winters it was *all* life, all difficult, and all intensely serious. ('Most of the world's great poetry', he remarked in *The Function of Criticism*, 'has had to do with serious steps seriously taken, and when the seriousness goes from life, it goes from poetry.') Let me try to clarify these impressionistic remarks.

In his discussion of Frederick Goddard Tuckerman in *Forms of Discovery*, Winters observes that 'Wordsworth, the poet of nature, popularized nature but almost never saw it... Tuckerman very often saw it.' So did Winters himself. In his poetry of the twenties he stood with Williams and the Stevens of *Harmonium* as one of the principal modifiers and extenders of Imagist techniques on the American side of the Atlantic, and in the later poems, as in that magnificent short story 'Brink of Darkness', there is likewise vivid precision of a high order, especially in the handling of natural scenes. Howard Kaye is quite right when he says that 'we should remember that for all his intellectuality, Winters was one of the pre-eminent nature poets of our time'. Indeed, one of the most touching passages in his poetry is the second stanza of the lovely 'On Rereading a Passage from John Muir', in which he speaks wistfully of the imagined 'pristine peace' of being himself an uncomplicated naturalist, 'a gentle figure from a simpler age'. But of course he was much more than a nature poet, even in his numerous poems involving nature. I suggest that, paradoxically, it may well turn out that for all his so-called traditionalism he saw modern America more precisely in his poetry than did any of the experimental and ostensibly more modern poets; saw it in a less literary fashion; gave us scenes and places and activities in such a way that they will remain solid indefinitely when all that remains of most other modern poets is the kind of literary blur that seems to exist only for the footnotes that it needs if it is to be intelligible. Allen Tate seems to me marvellously right when he says that a careful reading of [*Collected Poems*] will dispel the generally held opinion that Winters is 'withdrawn from life'. I have not been able to find in another living American poet as much life *actualized* in language.

There is no other modern American poetry more deeply rooted in a particular American background, more informed by American history, or more sensitive to its natural and human features.[4]

Winters' California – the 'slow Pacific swell', the natural flora, the 'gardens bare and Greek', the weather, the hills, the superhighways and airbases – is 'there' in a way that Williams' Paterson or Crane's Manhattan or even Lowell's Massachusetts are not. It belongs to the world that almost all of us inhabit when we are not drunk or suicidal or engaged, *qua* literary men, in disrupting and fragmenting and transmogrifying our surroundings by means of language, especially figurative language, in the interests of notating intensely agitated states of consciousness. 'At the San Francisco Airport', for example, grasps quintessential modern phenomena in a way that Lowell's 'For the Union Dead' does not. Nor is it merely a matter of relative talents, vastly the more distinguished though Winters' seems to me to be of the two. The difference is of the kind that obtains between, say, Wyatt's 'They Flee from Me' and Donne's 'Twicknam Garden'. Donne's poem probably seems the richer of the two when one is young, but the complexity is that of an erudite, powerful, and idiosyncratic mind deploying a complex rhetoric, and not, as in Wyatt's poem, or in a number of comparable ones by Hardy, or in 'At the San Francisco Airport', the complexity inherent in some of the major episodes of life itself. The epithet 'universal' has been overworked and is in any case imprecise. I would prefer to say that what Winters gives us in his best poems is something that answers more to the common experience of intelligent, sensitive, and educated people, whatever their occupation, than almost anything we find in the other major twentieth-century American poets. That is not in itself a prerequisite of greatness, of course; it does not hold true of Stevens, for example. But it is a very remarkable achievement none the less.

And, to step back for a broader view, it is a quite uncommonly real and common world that we enter in Winters' post-twenties poetry and criticism alike – a world, among other things, where books are physical objects that may or may not be well treated in libraries and are sometimes infuriatingly difficult to get hold of, and where academics have economic power over their juniors, and

where 'the first problem with which the critic of literature is confronted is to find a mode of living which will enable him to develop
his mind, practice his art, and support his family', and where poets
and even critics can fall sick and write less well in consequence, and
where alcoholism and madness and suicide and 'natural' death are
not merely matters that furnish writers with copy but can actually
happen to you and me – a world, in fact, which all too insistently
invites such responses as: 'I wish to point out that all people die, that
human life is filled with tragedy, and that commonly the tragedies
accumulate all but overwhelmingly toward the end. To ignore the
tragic subject is to leave oneself unprepared for the tragic experience; it is likely to lead to disaster and collapse.' No young man,
Hazlitt observed, ever thinks that he is going to die; no academic,
one sometimes feels, ever writes as if students of literature are
mortal and have exhaustible stores of health and energy and time.

This revealed knowledge of 'our' world constitutes an important
part of Winters' authority as a critic – I mean, of the sense he
produces that here is someone who brings to his reading a good deal
of uncommonly precise knowledge of the world and of certain
experiences in it. At its simplest it is a firsthand knowledge of
physical activities that surfaces from time to time in a way that
makes most other critics appear too exclusively men of letters, or, at
least, men who have adopted a genteel convention whereby when
they are discussing letters there are certain areas of their own experience (their graduate students among them) that they do not bring
into such discussions. The surfacing does not happen often – it is not
a mannerism – but when it does it is unforgettable. There is, for
instance, his glossing of Stevens' 'as a calm darkens among water
lights', and his setting of a Hopkins commentator right about the
actuality of a falcon's dive, and his challenging of the description of
a hunted rabbit in Cunningham's 'The Chase', and his casual beautiful reference to 'the tremendous and impersonal quiet of the virgin
American wilderness'. And of course there are the Airedales. A lot of
fun has been made of Winters' references to them, and his own
image would doubtless have been helped had he had the romantic
good sense to breed falcons or Afghans instead. But the amusement
is sentimental and, as Winters might say, foolish, and it was foolish
of F. O. Matthiessen, years ago, to imply that it was unseemly of
Winters to write a serious poem about the loss of an Airedale bitch.
Thom Gunn in one of his better poems has brought out some of

the implications of Winters' being a breeder of those intractable
terriers, and Winters' use of them for analogies is brilliant, both in
his challenge in the Hopkins essay to sentimental muddles about
birds and, in the introduction to *Forms of Discovery*, in his illumination of a particular kind of relationship between particulars and
'universals'. Equally telling, incidentally, is the analogy that he
draws in that introduction from boxing, a craft of which, I believe,
he had some firsthand experience:

The great poet resembles the great boxer in the ring. Joe Louis was trained
by a great scholar, Jack Blackburn. He was taught every move and when to
make it; he was born with the ability to make it instantaneously and with
great precision. His knowledge did not bind him; it set him free – with the
result that he seemed to move by instinct. So with the great poets.

And we are recognizably still in the same world when we come upon
some of the more general observations that contribute to the greatness of *Forms of Discovery* (it seems to me indeed a great book) and
of which the discussion of Jonson's 'To Heaven' furnishes one of the
most memorable examples:

[Jonson], in middle age, does not fear death, as Shakespeare professes to
fear it and as Donne apparently fears it; his temptation is 'weariness of life';
his duty, which he accepts with a semi-suppressed despair, is to overcome
this weariness. There is a recognition of reality here, distinct from a literary
convention (as in Shakespeare) and from a gift for personal drama, or
perhaps melodrama (as in Donne), which is very impressive. Much of the
power of the poem resides in one of the elementary facts of life: the fact that
a middle-aged man of intelligence is often readier to die than to live if he
merely indulges his feelings. Jonson deals with the real problem, not with a
spurious problem.

When he speaks in such terms, we know that Winters knows what
he is talking about, that he does not enjoy what he is saying, that he
is not playing the conventionally dignified game of creative suffering.
    Faced with passages like that, and with the reiterated emphasis
throughout Winters' criticism on clarity, control, discipline, it
would, however, be a serious mistake to start deploying terms like
'stoicism' or even 'classicism' (neo- or otherwise), at least if we
hoped thereby to be able to substitute for an individual mind a
familiar tradition. It is true that in a few of his poems, such as 'To
Edwin V. McKenzie', Winters advances more or less classical

commonplaces – commonplaces the truth of which is nevertheless easy to lose sight of and the reaffirmation of which can be very moving. But the generalizations in a number of others, such as 'On Teaching the Young' or 'A Testament', are far from commonplaces, however classical their form. And in a number of his best poems there are no large controlling generalizations at all and sometimes not even that familiar modern substitute for them, the manipulating of crude dichotomies (the human and the natural, the organic and the mechanical, and so on) in the interests of creating a comfortably ironical stance. 'By the Road to the Air Base' is an obvious example; so is 'A Summer Commentary'; so is the very lovely 'California Oaks', in which it is remarkably hard (in a way appropriate to the facts themselves, I judge) to decide precisely what values to assign to the different modes of behaviour described. Which is not to imply that poems of the latter sort are Winters' best. Some of them are among his best, but so are poems like 'To the Holy Spirit'.

And, to step back again, what we see in Winters' apprehension of nature and of man's relationship to the ostensibly so unequivocal objects with which he is surrounded is something highly individual and wholly modern. It can partly be defined in terms of his thought, especially in the different poems of the twenties, which clearly bear a relationship to a passage like the following from an essay of his in 1929:

The facts of life are at best disheartening: the vision of life which man has little by little constructed (or perhaps one should say stripped bare) is all but crushing... The artist who is actually ignorant of the metaphysical horror of modern thought or who cannot feel it imaginatively ... is of only a limited, a more or less decorative, value.

The kind of mental turmoil observable in poems like 'Prayer beside a Lamp' is presumably part of what Kaye had in mind when he commented that 'the fatal temptation towards ecstatic oblivion, the derangement of the senses, immersion in oceanic feeling, was as real to Winters as it was to Crane or to Rimbaud'. However, it is plain that beyond a certain point we arrive at modes of being or perceiving, related perhaps to the insights derived from his experience of tuberculosis in his early twenties (and none the less valid on that account), that are not really structurable in terms of ideas at all, and one facet of which we get perhaps the clearest view of in 'Brink of Darkness'. And we are never far at any point in Winters' career from a sense of what he called 'the invading chaos, the unmanageable and absorptive continuum, amid which the ethical man, the man of free choice and of usable distinctions, exists'. I presume that he was speaking of himself too when he remarked of Elizabeth Daryush's work that 'underlying many of these poems is an acute sense, often hard to lay a finger on precisely, not only of the impermanence of life, but of its almost ironical precariousness in spite of its beauty, and similarly of the precariousness of personal integrity'.

IV

What is communicated over and over again in Winters' writing is a profound sense of the *created* nature of order and of the intense and steady effort required to maintain it. It is much more than a merely personal struggle not to collapse that is involved; more, I mean, than the kind that writers like Roethke and Lowell have talked about or exhibited and to the seriousness of which Winters himself paid tribute when he remarked of Hopkins that 'whatever the nature of his difficulty, his struggle with it, so far as we may judge, was desperate, and, in spite of its lack of intellectual clarity, little short of heroic'. Nor, obviously, is it mere orderliness in thought and expression that he celebrates, the sort that Leavis nicely characterized as that of 'the stiff suit of style that stands up empty'.[5] Poets like Greville, Wyatt, Bowers, Hardy, and Cunningham, for instance, are, at their greatest, among the most intense in the language; and no one can be in doubt, either, about Winters' respect for the more formally turbulent energies of a Melville, a Rimbaud, a Hart Crane even. The conception of order that emerges from his work may well be best epitomized in the poem 'Before Disaster', with its summatory acknowledgement that 'Nowhere may I turn to flee: / Action is security.' Again and again, what comes across is Winters' sense of the enormous energies at work in distinguished art and in the life of the mind generally. But what also comes across is the emphasis on the need for the issuance of thought in action, shaped action – the making of these or those verses; teaching in this way rather than that; the subduing of figurative or literal tracts of wilderness; unflinching persistence along a deliberately chosen road. And, relatedly, there is his strong consciousness of the public nature of various roles, the public responsibilities that are entailed in them, and the fact that important roles, when properly performed, are not masks behind which the real self hides but activities in which the individual can become most fully human and most completely himself. The poem 'To Edwin V. McKenzie, on his Defense of David Lamson' is especially noteworthy in this respect.

Moreover, the three poems elicited by the Lamson case serve to point us towards another truth. Most readers have probably felt, on first going through them, that they are over-written or at least over-dramatic; that the trial of a man of no public distinction or notoriety or political consequence did not, unlike the Sacco and Vanzetti affair, reasonably invite talk about 'Mankind in the eternal sacrament' or 'Outrage and anarchy in formal mien'. But it is really the business of the Airedales again – a matter of stock responses, I mean. Lamson (the details can be found in *The Case of David Lamson* (1934) by Winters and Frances Theresa Russell and in Winters' own 'More Santa Clara Justice' in the *New Republic* of the same year) was a patently innocent man condemned outrageously to death for the supposed murder of his wife; and what Winters had had the power of mind to see was that where justice and injustice in the courtroom are concerned it is not the scope or colourfulness of the drama that counts but the depth of the implications, and that in a case like Lamson's one was witnessing a significant tremor – significant because perhaps symptomatic – in the rationality that makes possible our civilization and in the collective intelligence and nerve of the academic community of which Lamson was a member. Furthermore, the failures involved were all too easy to understand. It is always insidiously easy for intellectuals *not* to act in unglamorous public situations. And it is especially difficult to summon up the will to act steadily unless we can convince ourselves of the importance of our actions by seeing their relationships to ideas and issues of more or less permanent importance – relationships, that is, in which their dignity is rationally increased, not diminished.

Where civic matters are concerned, Winters himself appears to have had an unusually clear and firm sense of such relationships, so that even the homely features of American constitutional democracy (contra the blandishments of Right and Left) appeared precious because of the kind of victory over force that they represented. He was not naive about democracy. As the essays on Cooper and Frost in particular demonstrate, he was sharply aware of the things that can go wrong with it, and of the fact that there is nothing whatever in human nature that guarantees that things will go right. But he also saw that there was nothing inevitable about their going wrong, either. In response to one of Frost's poetic invitations to drop out, he commented:

The difficulties of effective political action are obvious; the English-speaking peoples have been struggling with the problems of constitutional government for centuries. But if the reality of the difficulties results in our stealing away from them, society will be taken over ... by the efficient scoundrels who are always ready to take over when everyone else abdicates. In a dictatorship by scoundrels, the Frosts and the Thoreaus, the amateur anarchists and village eccentrics, would find life somewhat more difficult than they have found it to date.

The operative word in the passage, of course, is 'if'. And it is highly important, I think, that for all his emphatic use from time to time of the word 'evil', Winters was always able to avoid the easy and seductive dichotomy in which a rational world of ideas is opposed to an irrational world of human beings afflicted irredeemably by something that for a while it was fashionable in intellectual circles to call Original Sin – a dichotomy that invited either a disdainful withdrawal from the political world or a scarcely less disdainful support of authoritarian systems. Donald E. Stanford was quite right to bring the political opinions of the writers concerned into his juxtaposing of Winters, Cunningham, Bridges, and Robinson with Eliot, Hulme, Pound, and Wyndham Lewis (*Southern Review*, 1969). It *is* totalities that are involved. We cannot dissever each writer's conceptions of 'human nature', of the healthy life of the mind, of sound and unsound modes of expression, of the relationships of individuals to each other in society, and of the relationships between potentialities and actualities in the history of Western civilization. And Winters' own conception of those potentialities, I believe, derived not from theories but from a perception of the quality of individual minds. As he himself remarked, again in the essay on Frost:

Life is a process of revision in the interests of greater understanding, and it is by means of this process that men came down from the trees and out of the caves; and although civilization is very far from what it should be, nevertheless mankind has shown a marked improvement over the past ten thousand years. This improvement is the result of the fact that man is a rational animal... The uncaged bear, or the unreflective cave-man, is inferior to Thomas Aquinas and to Richard Hooker, to Dante and to Ben Jonson, and to assert the contrary is merely irresponsible foolishness.

He showed up the actual irrationality (both in its own terms and in its implicit relationship to certain demonstrated potentials for greatness) of a good deal of ostensibly rational philosophizing; and he was able, as in a passage like the following, to see odious behaviour in terms not of a mysterious entity called the human heart but of imprecise perception and defective intelligence:

Stupidity is the result of privation of being; privation is evil; and when a stupid man rises to power he becomes pompous, hypocritical, and dangerous. The phenomenon is a common one: I have seen it a good many times in the academic world, but here [in Charles Churchill's 'Dedication to Warburton'] the evil man is operating on a national scale and becomes a major representative of evil.

Thought in action, ideas created and maintained through action, ideas *producing* action – it is his steady awareness of these relationships that makes Winters' work not only so bracing but, where life in the academy is concerned, so peculiarly heartening. Naive as it may sound to suggest it here, a good many of the follies and wickednesses in the almost uniquely *created* North American world can be traced back to the formulations (subsequently modified, corrupted perhaps, or misunderstood, but in any event disseminated in one form or another and eventually absorbed and acted upon by the 'common man') of particular thinkers. Men like Calvin and Dewey, Rousseau, Freud, and Hobbes are not merely texts to be 'taught', or eddies in a stream of ideas; they and others like them are in a considerable measure the makers of the social and institutional world that we inhabit. It is easy enough to pay lip service to this idea. It is no less easy to write and act as if in the world of thought there is a kind of determinism at work involving so many and such complicated and perhaps in the end even such untraceable interrelationships that the question of the truth or falsity, folly or wisdom, of this or that specific piece of discourse is not really of vital importance, and as if the private lives of intelligent and sensitive readers cannot really be profoundly and lastingly altered by what they read, in ways that may sometimes be literally matters of life and death. Well, Winters diagnosed over and over again the nature of various unsound modes of thought and expression, and charted causal relationships between the forms and formulations of specific writers and their consequences for later writers, most memorably and illuminatingly in the great essay 'The Significance of *The Bridge*, by Hart Crane'. He did more than any other American critic to make the question of truth and the pursuit of truth *matter,* not by the customary recourse to a bogus scientism or a vulgarized Platonism, but by demonstrations of the consequences of error. And he points us towards a related important truth about the problem of influences. When we are dealing with gifted writers, we are dealing with men whose thought-processes differ from those of most people not by virtue of being more visionary but because they are much swifter and more decisive, so that sometimes even a single sentence or a turn of phrase in another man's work may be immediately assimilated and start to work like yeast in ways that many students of literature simply cannot comprehend in terms of their own experience. Hence it is natural for scholars to hunt for supposedly more solid explanations in terms of, say, Freudian psychology or irresistible currents of ideas.

V

No less central in Winters' work is the idea of enrichment, not in the sense of acquiring new and fascinating topics to talk about, but in the sense of alterations, sometimes very subtle ones but cumulative in their effects, occurring in our modes of being and doing. This is most obvious in his discussions of poetry, especially in a formulation like the following:

[T]he nature of the human mind is such that we can enter the [great] poet's mind by way of his poem, if we are willing to make the effort, and share his judgment. In this way we may gain both understanding and strength, for the human mind is so made that it is capable of growth and of growth in part through its own self-directed effort. This is the virtue of poetry; in so far as it is good, and we understand both its goodness and its limitations, it enables us to achieve a more nearly perfect and comprehensive being.

But his emphasis on the process of assimilation – or, to use Kierkegaard's term, appropriation – inside the academy, as defined for instance in his two admirable poems on the scholar W. D. Briggs, seems to me no less convincing. And it is not megalomania that informs the wartime poem 'Defense of Empire'. If it is *not* such matters as 'The perils of immortal mind' that in some real sense inform our concerns as students and teachers of literature, it is hard to see that our occupation is really of major dignity or consequence, at least not in the way pointed to in a remark like the following:

'Alexander of Macedon conquered the known world, but any mark that he has left on later times would be hard to identify. Aristotle, his tutor and his father's servant, remains as one of the fundamental rocks on which our civilization is built.' But of course the dignity and the social consequence *can* be there, even in our own time; we have only to think of Leavis, for example. And it is against the heroic potentialities of the life of the mind, even in the academy, even in English, that the specific failures of intelligence and will that Winters defines and judges appear as serious as they do. It is no small matter that, speaking of the Lamson case, he could record that

Lamson's academic neighbours, for the greater part, and in spite of the notorious corruption of Santa Clara County, are unwilling to lift a hand in his aid or an eye to examine his case, and they are to a surprising degree the dupes and even the organs of gossip. Such indifference is an interesting commentary on the academic discipline.

Back in the late forties, when one or two reviewers commented ironically on Winters' claims on behalf of the university, they were no doubt voicing what numerous other readers felt. The *real* world in those days was clearly the world of politics, of forces and masses, of power. But Winters was right all the same, and not just in the sense that the university is now where much of the power lies. In the world of politics, it has been becoming increasingly apparent how things do, again and again, come down to questions of character, questions of the actual measure of integrity, intelligence, courage, and will that this or that particular public man possesses – and to the capacity of people to assess those qualities accurately and act effectively on their assessments. The truly shocking thing about the Chappaquiddick affair, for example, was not Senator Kennedy's conduct, discreditable as that appears to have been. It was the fact that prior to Chappaquiddick it had become a commonplace that the most powerful nation in the world was ineluctably, by some mysterious kind of determinism, going to be given into the keeping of an almost wholly untested young man of obviously limited intelligence and with a significantly blemished past – and that a good many supposedly well-educated people could apparently see nothing especially fearsome or even significant about that fact and may not do so even now. The reasons for this kind of benumbing of the intellect are numerous, no doubt, but among them is almost certainly the bedazzlement produced during the past decade or two by the increasing prominence on the political scene of men of ostensibly good education – men rather flatteringly like ourselves in fact. The gallus-snappers and Neanderthals are still around, of course, but clearly the educated, the intellectually sophisticated politician is the type of the future. This does not mean that America will necessarily be governed better; it may very well be governed worse. What it *does* mean is that it is high time that American intellectuals gave up the self-flattering dichotomy of the educated man versus the barbarians, and endeavoured to discriminate far more rigorously among the various modes of being that are comprised in a term like 'the educated man', which means in turn becoming a good deal more rigorous in their scrutiny of ideas and modes of thought and utterance.

It is in the university, or nowhere, that meaningful standards can be evolved and maintained. Tedious, exasperating, and contemptible as it so often is in its local manifestations, the academic life as Winters described it and as he lived it is nevertheless one to which it is a privilege to belong, because of the potentialities that inhere in it. I do not know of a better brief definition and defence of the university than the one that is to be found in the 'Post Scripta' to *The Anatomy of Nonsense*:

The university is the intellectual and spiritual center of our world... It offers a concrete embodiment, an institutional representation, of the most important ideals of humanity; of the belief in absolute truth; of the importance, in spite of human fallibility, of the perpetual, though necessarily imperfect, effort to approximate truth; of intellectual freedom and integrity; of the dignity of man... The academic ideals are frequently violated, but they remain as ideals, as standards of judgment, and as the chief cohesive force in our civilization; and the scholar is their professional guardian.[6]

Mr Frye and Evaluation

'Service!'
'But this court's *square*!'
'Are you here to play tennis or do surveying? *Service*!'

One of the main reasons for the heatedness of the Leavis–Snow controversy, I take it, was this kind of deadlock. The anti-Leavisians plainly felt that Sir Charles may have had his faults but that he was a distinguished intellectual and that any correcting of his errors should have been done in the spirit of a debate between fellow professionals engaged in the common pursuit of truth. Dr Leavis, on the other hand, was no less plainly acting on the conviction that Snow as a would-be sage was preposterous, that the deference being accorded him was even more preposterous, and that to go through the motions of arguing *with* him would be to concede precisely the assumptions that needed bringing into general question. This kind of feeling does not usually make for urbanity, not least because of the sense of bafflement often entailed in it, but to seek to deny it utterance[1] seems to me a denial of the ultimate seriousness of the intellectual life; we are not all members of the same club merely because we earn our livings in similar ways or commit our reflections to print, and there are higher goods than decorum. A good many of us, I presume, feel in much the same way about Mr Northrop Frye as a literary theorist as Dr Leavis did about Sir Charles as a cultural one; and I think that we should be making ourselves heard more.

Speaking for myself, I recall somewhat wryly my reactions in the late fifties when I inspected the then little-known *Anatomy of Criticism* in connection with an article on poetic theory. Energy, obviously; a wide-ranging mind, certainly; some interesting observations, true; an interesting *bouillabaisse* of muddles as well; and of course it was fascinating to watch someone coming forward so confidently to set the whole world straight about literature and literary criticism at last. But so far as its main thrust and pretensions were concerned, the book seemed to me essentially an elaborate apologia for a conventional academic taste by someone who was incapable of responding passionately to individual works yet craved to talk about literature on the grandest possible scale, and who had been revising the rules of the game to permit himself to escape from genuine critical confrontations; and accordingly I judged it unlikely to be of any particular consequence. I could hardly have been more wrong in my guess, of course. Mr Frye's reputation, as we all know, has gone up and up and *up*, so that even literary journalists now refer to the *Anatomy*, quite casually, as a critical classic. Well, it still seems reasonable to assume that time will do its job and that Mr Frye's theorizings will be joining those of other would-be panoptic systematizers – Herbert Spencer? Fourier? – in the historical junkyard. Yet some systems not only catch on but stay caught on, and some do more harm than others. And though the continuing vitality of Christian Science needn't fill us with any animus towards the intellectual inadequacies of Mrs Eddy, Mr Frye's inadequacies seem to me a matter for serious concern.

A noteworthy episode in the history of Mr Frye's spreading influence occurred in 1964 when three or four American admirers of his joined forces with Mr Frye at Trinity College, Connecticut, to address a conference of teachers sponsored by the Connecticut State Department of Education. Not only was the scent of victory clearly in the air ('criticism', for instance, 'whether we like it or not, is moving into the spectrum of the sciences – and the sentimental outcries we have all heard are partial proof that this is so';[2] thus Mr Paul Smith, in what seems a rather curious *non sequitur*), but under the sponsorship of a former editor the addresses were then published *en bloc* in *College English* (the principal organ of the National Council of Teachers of English, with a circulation of over 10,000) and thereby brought approvingly to the attention of a lot of academics who had probably hitherto known of Mr Frye only by reputation. Since what interests me is the quality of Mr Frye's intellection once we slow down our reading and start probing in depth, I propose to fasten in the rest of this essay on 'Criticism, Visible and Invisible', Mr Frye's very jaunty and ambitious lead-article contribution to the affair.[3] The article is informed by the same kind of energy as the *Anatomy* (it is a number of cuts above those broadcast Talks to the Kiddies that got into print as *The Educated Imagination*), and it is very useful to have most of Mr Frye's basic principles spelled out in a relatively small compass, since the defence can't be offered that if we will only read on trustingly enough a seemingly hopeless muddle on page three will miraculously get converted into cogency by what happens two hundred pages further on. And furthermore, by looking at this particular article with care we can account with unusual ease for the cordiality with which Mr Frye's messages have been received by so many people. There is a good deal in the article that calls out for comment, as a matter of fact,[4] for its pretensions are so thoroughly matched by its confusions that it really is a sort of classic in its way. It is with Mr Frye's dealings with the question of evaluation that I shall concern myself here, however, since the Don't Rock the Boat campaign against criticism with any emotional depth to it is getting considerably too strong these days. I have tried to make my discussion self-contained, though I assume that the interested reader will wish to check my account against the article itself if the latter hasn't come his way already.

Pieced together, Mr Frye's basic position on evaluation in 'Criticism, Visible and Invisible' is as follows. Literary works are 'not so much things to be studied as powers to be possessed'; and they not only *can* be possessed, they *should* be possessed. Since a critic's task is the '*subjection*' of himself (Mr Frye's italics) to 'the uniqueness of the work' being read, 'every writer must be examined on his own terms', no writer can be judged by 'standards derived from another ... however much "greater"', and 'the attempt to establish grades and hierarchies in literature itself' is 'really an "aesthetic" form of censorship'. In teaching, hardly surprisingly, the most desirable situation is when the teacher can 'skip preliminary stages and clear everything out of the way except understanding', since the goal is to ensure that works 'become possessed by and identified with' the student. None of this is exactly news in twentieth-century criticism, and I shall be returning to that point. At the moment I wish to place the reading of literature in a very different context from that in which, seemingly, it exists for Mr Frye, and I shall begin by appropriating for my own purposes Mr Frye's contention that 'works of literature are not so much things to be studied as powers to be possessed'.

Mr Frye, it is true, does virtually nothing to illuminate what *he* means by that assertion, apart from introducing the analogy of learning to drive a car and attaining to a state of 'unmediated unity' with it; yet it happens that the analogy is a felicitous one for my purposes. Normally when we are learning to drive, the mediating agent at the outset is discourse, and our relationship to that discourse can remind us of certain facts about our relationship to most of the discourse that we encounter. Our pedagogically minded friend says that pressing a certain button will start the engine, and we believe him and press it; he warns that there is a sharp corner coming up, and we believe him and slow down. Here, as elsewhere, our picture of reality and our stance towards it are being constantly modified, mostly in small ways, sometimes in quite large ones, by what we hear or read. Metal protuberances turn into headlight-dimmers and cigarette lighters, blank areas ahead are converted by highway signs into intersections and narrow bridges, and as our friend reminisces about the previous evening the North End of the city suddenly becomes blessed with an excellent Chinese restaurant that we hadn't known of. We live, in other words, in a world of other people discoursing, and we are engaged constantly and inescapably in assessing that discourse with a view to deciding what to do with it and how much of it to take over. If we knew from past experience that our friend's taste in food was terrible, the North End *wouldn't* suddenly possess a restaurant that we might later go out of our way to visit; and if, apropos of driving, he were to tell us cheerily that it was perfectly safe to overtake on blind curves we would probably discriminate against him on that point too, with the aid of the advice of other friends or of the driver's manual, or perhaps even of common sense, which is rather more common where driving than where talking about books is concerned. What I am leading up to is obvious. Initially we do not confront 'literature' and 'non-literature', we confront pieces of discourse; and they all invite us implicitly to take them over whole, just as other people's modes of discourse offer themselves implicitly as norms to which we should consider approximating ourselves.

Now, what I have described in summarizing Mr Frye's general position is a singularly thoroughgoing attempt to place our dealings with literature outside any normal human context; there is to be (seemingly) no comparing, no discriminating, no organizing, no self-defending use of creative intelligence in the face of even the largest claims on us for surrender. By what principles, then, it seems reasonable to start by enquiring, is Mr Frye's posited reader–critic–teacher to proceed when he seeks to determine which particular utterances he is to give the magical name of 'literature' to in the first

place (this love poem but not that memo to a secretary, this historical novel but not that historical study, this entry in a journal but not
that passage in a political speech), and on what rational grounds is
he to determine which of the works within the charmed circle are to
merit more, and which less, of his and other people's attention? We
do, after all, exist in time (a fact that Mr Frye, I rather suspect,
prefers to ignore as far as possible), and our time is limited, and life
is by and large a matter of choices – choosing between restaurants
when we want an evening out; choosing between this book and that
when we haven't time to read both on a trip; choosing between this
syllabus and that when we are paid to present literature to our
fellow citizens and have the power to alter their lives by giving them
low marks in examinations. Personally I have read almost all the
agreeable Australian detective novels of Arthur Upfield, and there is
certainly nothing quite like them, but I doubt that we shall ever see a
course in them made compulsory for graduate students at Toronto.
Well, Mr Frye does have an answer of sorts to the problem of discriminating among works inside the circle, and if the clues to how
we go about drawing the circle in the first place that he offers his
New England teachers seem very largely negative ones (we presumably hunt around for utterances about which we can confidently
make the kinds of preclusive assertions that I have quoted), the
answer logically carries over into that problem too.[5] It is breathtak-
ing in its confusions and fascinating in its implications, and I
propose to consider both rather carefully. What we go by, it would
appear, are 'the traditional valuations', and any attempt to 'redistribute' them is unnecessary, futile, and probably due to the critic's
desire to display himself 'to better advantage'.

   Certain points are almost too easy to be worth making, so I shall
get them out of the way quickly. When we speak of the 'traditional
valuations' of Donne and Marvell, for instance, are we talking
about seventeenth-century ones, or mid-Victorian ones, or the
twentieth-century ones with which we are all familiar, and when
consensuses conflict with each other, by what principle other than
that of accordance with our own preferences do we decide which
ones to honour with the epithet 'traditional'? What, for instance, is
the 'traditional' valuation of Cowper? Again, when Mr Frye tells us
approvingly how

old-fashioned books on English literature which touch on 'lesser' poets such as Skelton and Wyatt in the early sixteenth century [and] maintain an attitude towards them of slightly injured condescension ... had to be superseded by a democratizing of literary experience, not merely to do justice to underrated poets, but to revise the whole attitude to literature in which a poet could be judged by standards derived from another poet, however much 'greater',

it is impossible to see how, in Mr Frye's own terms, this was not in fact one of those very 'revaluations' of 'traditional assessments' that Mr Frye deplores – especially since the relationship between the general change that Mr Frye describes and the critical activities of Eliot, Pound, and others is a matter of common knowledge. Furthermore, since Mr Frye is so keen on the 'contexts' in which literary phenomena occur, it seems pertinent to recall at this point that the critics involved in the 'democratizing' were for the most part not simply deciding magnanimously to admire *more* poets than had been admired by the authors of late-Victorian histories of literature; the great poet, *the* great poet, in whose shadow the kinds of reputations Mr Frye appears to have in mind were stunted was John Milton, and it was very largely the devaluing of Milton (and, relatedly, of certain aspects of the Romantics and the Great Victorians) that made possible the elevation of the others. If Mr Frye wishes to contend that the more poems that are 'liked' by everyone the better, that is his privilege, but he cannot reasonably expect applause when he takes self-aggrandizing advantage of certain arduous revaluations yet sneers at the labours of the revaluers and argues that there was 'no genuinely critical reason' for such revaluations in the first place.

But these, as I indicated, are not matters that need lingering over here. What is more to the point is how Mr Frye uses his notion of 'traditional valuations' to shut out evaluative criticism. The following passage is a key one:

There are two contexts in which a work of literature is potential, an internal context and an external one. Internally, the writer has a potential theme and tries to actualize it in what he writes. Externally, the literary work, actualized in itself, becomes a potential experience for student, critic, or reader. A 'bad' poem or novel is one in which, so the critic feels, a potential literary experience has not been actualized. Such a judgment implies a consensus: the critic speaks for all critics, even if he happens to be wrong. But an actualized work of literature may still fail to become an actualized experience for its reader. The judgment here implies withdrawal from a consensus: however many critics may like this, I don't. The first type of judgment belongs primarily to the critical reaction to contemporary literature, reviewing and the like, where a variety of new authors are struggling to establish their authority. The second type belongs primarily to the tactics of critical pressure groups that attempt to redistribute the traditional valuations of the writers of the past in order to display certain new writers, usually including themselves, to better advantage. There is no genuinely critical reason for 'revaluation'.

It is hard to comment patiently on such a passage, I am afraid; many of us, I assume, would not accept its like from our undergraduates. It is absurd, for instance, to speak as Mr Frye does here in the fourth sentence of what *the* critic feels: a critic who judges a work to be bad may be doing so for any of a number of reasons, the reason that Mr Frye gives being only one of them. It is nonsense to say that a critical judgement implies a consensus and that the critic making it 'speaks for all critics'. True, most of us like to imagine that the assertions we make would be assented to by all intelligent readers if they were to consider matters carefully enough; only a megalomaniac, however, is going to delude himself that this assent will actually come, and only a critic who never reads any other critics will be under the impression that he is their spokesman. These are minor faults, however, in comparison with the sleight of hand that then occurs, namely the shuffle by which the test of whether or not a work is successful, and of whether or not a critic is responding to it adequately, becomes a numerical one.

Where no consensus yet exists, a critic is apparently going about his legitimate business when he decides whether or not there is an 'actualized' literary experience in the work. As soon as some sort of favourable consensus has arisen, however, the presupposition for Mr Frye is that if a critic *now* judges that the work is bad he is simply being imperceptive, and probably conceited to boot. Even in Mr Frye's own terms, which I shall adopt for the moment, this is nonsense. If fifty people on the lookout for actualized literary experiences review a brand-new novel in the same week and most of them conclude that there is such an experience in it, no doubt that will be very gratifying to the author and the publishers, but it is in itself no guarantee that the experience *is* actualized, and it in no way alters the fundamental relationship of a reviewer the following week to the work in question. True, a possibility is now open to him that wasn't open to the others; he can become a historian of literary opinion and record the findings of his precursors. True, again, if he happens to respect the minds of some of those precursors he may suspect in advance that quite probably something *is* actualized in the work. But as to whether it is in fact or not, well, just as each of those precursors was engaged in determining whether it was actualized for *himself*, so too must he be, assuming that he wants to engage himself with the work at all. And so on *ad infinitum*. There is no logical point at which what Mr Frye rather condescendingly calls 'reviewing and the like' ceases and a new set of rules comes into operation. The hundredth critic of a work is not the hundredth identical test-tube in a controlled experiment; an account of a hundred critics' opinions is not a laboratory report, it is simply an account of a hundred pieces of writing by readers who undoubtedly vary widely in intelligence; and the authority of each critic (as judged for the purposes of the kind of rough guidance I mentioned above) is generally something that we can only determine by checking that critic's reactions to other works against our own – which brings us back again, of course, to the individual self confronting the individual work. Yet Mr Frye is apparently perfectly confident that he can tell when the collective authentication has occurred and the traditional and unquestionable valuation been arrived at. If *science* had proceeded in such a fashion, Mr Frye's physician would still be studying Mr Frye's horoscope.

But perhaps, as someone once remarked naughtily about Wagner, Mr Frye isn't really as bad as he sounds. Let me probe a little more carefully, therefore, for what is intended in Mr Frye's notion of 'traditional valuations'. The following statement is the most helpful for this purpose: 'Ezra Pound, T. S. Eliot, Middleton Murry, F. R. Leavis, are only a few of the eminent critics who have abused Milton. Milton's greatness as a poet is unaffected by this: as far as the central fact of his importance in literature is concerned, these eminent critics might as well have said nothing at all.' Were Mr Frye to have made the same kind of assertion about, let us say, Robert Louis Stevenson or George Meredith, its oddness and the strategy in it would have been more blatant. But then we all know that unlike the Stevenson and Meredith mills the Milton ones are still chuffing away at top pressure in the academies. And hence when Mr Frye characteristically slithers from the fine bold phrase 'greatness as a poet' (which presumably means the greatness of Milton's poetry as we appropriate it now when reading it) to the phrase 'the central fact of his importance in literature', we may not immediately feel moved to protest. After all, no critic in his right mind has ever denied the immensity of Milton's influence on English poetry and literary thought; indeed, it was precisely because of the continuing strength of that influence that Mr Frye's 'eminent critics' were moved to write what they did about him. On the other hand, even Mr Frye would hardly deny that for a number of decades that influence has been negligible in the writing of significant poetry and that a major cause of this has been the activities of the critics whom he so casually dismisses. And accordingly it can hardly be escaped that what Mr Frye really has in mind is that the majority of academics (including the very powerful editors of scholarly journals and the Milton specialists who read submitted MSS on Milton for them) have either been unpersuaded by the accounts of Milton given by those critics or else, if temporarily impressed during their salad days, have now repented. These facts, however, leave unconsidered the reactions of the by now fairly considerable number of readers who *have* accepted various findings of those critics and now see Milton as an author of great distinction but with grave flaws that they would probably not have noticed otherwise. In the sense that I have outlined it here, it still makes sense to talk loosely of the traditional (or conservative) view of Milton as opposed to the non-traditional one. But once we approach valuations in this way it becomes apparent that that is what we are involved with – valuations, conflicting valuations, and not unquestionable facts. It is Mr Frye's right to prefer one valuation – or, more exactly, one constellation of accounts – to another. But he can hardly expect us to allow the accidents of the history of academic opinion by themselves to determine what we are going to read and appropriate now, and in what spirit. Furthermore, there are some rather sinister implications in Mr Frye's approach to tradition and evaluation that deserve spelling out.

The first involves the question of truth. Fastening upon an unnamed critic who judged Fielding's *Jonathan Wild* a failure 'because no character in it represented a moral norm', Mr Frye objects to 'the critical procedure involved in the "X is a failure because" formula', and declares roundly that 'no critical principle can possibly follow the "because" which is of any importance at all compared to the fact of *Jonathan Wild*'s position in the history of satire and in eighteenth-century English culture'. To begin with, Mr

Frye's implied reduction of value-judgments (with the aid of a couple more examples) to a simple 'X is Y because Z' is either naive or disingenuous, though as is so often the case with Mr Frye it is hard to decide which. Evaluative commentaries of any worth tend to take the form of 'X is A and B and C and D', and if the string of assertions is made convincingly the summatory assertion 'X is really pretty feeble stuff' or 'X is a masterpiece' can be as superfluous as that no doubt apocryphal mid-Victorian comment at the close of a performance of *Antony and Cleopatra*, 'How different from the home life of our own dear Queen!' But even with a succinct statement taken out of context, the question of its truth or falsity would seem from any reasonable point of view to be paramount. Yvor Winters, for example, has called Henry James 'the greatest master in our literature of the most limited kind of narrative matter combined with the most unsound narrative technique antedating Joyce, Miss Richardson, and Mrs Woolf'.[6] Readers who revere James will presumably say this is rubbish, and if they happen to dislike Winters in general they will no doubt add that this sort of thing is typical of him. Readers who have admired some of Winters' writings but are unfamiliar with the quoted remark may feel that its context is worth looking into, even if they at present greatly admire James too. In either case the first question is whether or not James's work is as Winters claims. Furthermore, if we were to conclude after re-examining that work that Winters was right, our attitude towards James's influence on twentieth-century fiction and criticism would alter too, just as our attitude towards the Nazis in their beer-hall days is modified by our knowledge that they succeeded in gaining power. For Mr Frye, however, all judgements involving 'because' that include the ethical appear to be dismissible as merely symptoms of 'anxieties'. And when we further consider that he seems to be under the impression that statements of one kind can somehow get cancelled out by statements of another kind ('The garbage stinks.' 'Nonsense! That garbage can has been in this family for fifty years!'), it is very tempting to infer that Mr Frye, for all his show of philosophical sophistication, is an unreconstructed old-style rationalist who believes that most of the assertions made in normal critical discourse are merely 'subjective' and hence of little or no consequence. And so to some extent he is, I think, but to stop there would be to let him off too lightly. The fact is that Mr Frye on occasion shows himself perfectly willing to subscribe to normal evaluative utterances on the basis of their truth. For example, when Ezra Pound, 'in the middle of his *Guide to Kulchur*, expresses some disinterested admiration for the lyrical elegies of Thomas Hardy', we learn that 'the effect, in that book, is as though a garrulous drunk had suddenly sobered up, focused his eyes, and begun to talk sense';[7] and it seems reasonable to suppose that Mr Frye would not have spoken of sense and sobriety had the author praised been, by some extraordinary quirk of Pound's mind, Wilhelmina Stitch. This example, it is true, follows immediately after the arresting assertion that 'evaluat[ive] criticism is mainly effective as criticism only when its valuations are favourable', an assertion that arouses a lingering suspicion that Mr Frye's vulgarity in the matter of numbers may be accompanied by a Chamber-of-Commerce vulgarity of the 'Boost, Don't Knock' variety. The simpler conclusion, however, is that Mr Frye has his own literary pantheon quite clear in his mind and that the only critical assertions that can engage his interest, or at least win a patronizing nod, are those that accord with it. And this brings me to a related and more disturbing aspect of Mr Frye's general position.

It seems to me hardly escapable that Mr Frye's show of speaking out boldly on behalf of intellectual liberty is a sham of a rather nasty kind, and probably this lies near the centre of my present quarrel with him. 'The belief that good and bad can be determined as inherent qualities is the belief that inspires censorship', he informs us, 'and the attempt to establish grades and hierarchies in literature itself, to distinguish what is canonical from what is apocryphal, is really an aesthetic form of censorship'. Well, there are forms of censorship that are a good deal more objectionable than the kind that Mr Frye detects here, even if we grant that he is using the term correctly (which in fact we shouldn't; if someone asks you for the names of three or four of the best thriller writers and you say Hammett, Household, Chandler, Hamilton, you're no more playing censor than you are if you tell him where he can get the best Chinese food in town). Mr Frye himself, as I have intimated, is plainly enough of the opinion that some works are in some meaningful sense 'better' than others. He can refer casually to 'the major writers of literature', he appears to feel that Shakespeare, Milton, Joyce, James, and Eliot are among them, and he even (I think) judges that Henry James is superior to Mickey Spillane (though since he is also of the opinion, seven lines later, that 'the difference between good and bad is not something inherent in literary works themselves, but the difference between two ways of using literary experiences', it is hard to see any rational basis for the judgement – or for the assertion that 'it is a writer's merits that make the criticism on him rewarding, as a rule'). Indeed, Mr Frye, when he doesn't stop to think about being Northrop Frye, is as well aware of the literary situation as the rest of us. It is when he *does* stop that the trouble starts, for he thereby gets into an obvious enough quandary, and the only way out of it for him is the not uncommon one of intimating (with the aid of his appeal to 'tradition') that the hierarchies that *he* establishes for himself are not 'his' hierarchies at all, they are somehow objectively and unarguably out there, so that when anyone disagrees with him it is they who are being merely subjective and eccentric. And it seems to me that most of the thrust of his article is towards suppressing such disagreements.

Having remarked that 'criticism, to be useful both to literature and to the public, needs to contain some sense of the progressive or the systematic, some feeling that irrevocable forward steps in understanding are being taken', Mr Frye observes amusedly that 'we notice that all the contributors to *The Pooh Perplex* claim to be supplying the one essential thing needed to provide this sense of progress, though of course none of them does'; and the tenor of the article makes clear that more is intended by that 'of course' than simply that the imagined representative critics in Mr Frederick C. Crews's vulgar little book are dull-witted. Early in the article, Mr Frye announces with seeming modesty that he is unaware of using any particular critical method himself or of having invented a particular school of criticism (though if he really believes the latter claim he must be the only person in English in Canada who does). Mr Frye's modesty seems to me duplicitous, however. The dominant tone of the article is that of someone who believes that he himself *can* provide the requisite 'sense of progress'; and since for Mr Frye there are in fact 'no different "schools" of criticism today, attached to different and irreconcilable metaphysical assumptions', it appears that critics who disagree with Mr Frye are not simply doing different things from Mr Frye, they are, by the very act of presuming to be critics, committed to doing the *same* thing as Mr Frye but are too stupid to realize it and so are doing it less well. It is Mr Frye, we gather, who is triumphantly sane and central and anxiety-free. Other critics, especially those who engage in evaluation, are all too likely to be guilty of 'critical arrogance', or 'critical dandyism', or 'pedantry', or to be critically 'undemocratic', or to be preoccupied with their own 'social position' and have 'a particular hankering to be a gentleman', or to be imprisoned in 'historical variables', or to be indulging in 'critical narcissism' and depriving criticism of its 'content', or, in general, to be in one way or another lost in a 'shadow-battle of anxieties'.

In other words, just as Mr Frye tries to escape from personal judgements by appealing indirectly to statistics to objectify them, so too he attempts to escape the discomforts of propounding a highly idiosyncratic (if eclectically arrived at) critical position by insisting obliquely that he is miraculously not standing in any 'position' at all, he is simply and objectively and *au-dessus de la mêlée* looking at the Truth about literature and criticism. All critics and theorists, of course, like to believe that what they say is true. To my knowledge, however, only Mr Frye has sought to prove that all critical activities that conflict with his own must *a priori* be so wrong as not to be worth paying serious attention to by anybody. Well, to want to put beyond a pale all the people you disagree with is understandable enough, though one recalls what sort of things generally happen when this is done at the socio-political level. It is understandable, too, that a certain kind of teacher should yearn to be able to enter the classroom armed with his certified 'established classics' and 'clear everything out of the way except understanding' and 'submission'. Understandable or not, however, Mr Frye's attitude, for all his genuflexions towards democracy when it suits his purposes, seems to me fundamentally and unpleasantly authoritarian, and to deserve being seen as what it is; '"No sovereignty; – " "Yet he would be King on't."' Even C. S. Lewis, with whom Mr Frye shares certain fallacies,[8] didn't pretend to that; they were *his* opinions that he was advancing, and he was advancing them against other individuals who might, in his estimation, be horribly wrong but whose assertions on that account deserved taking all the more seriously. In this he had a far sounder and saner grasp than Mr Frye of the nature of critical discourse – and so, I suggest, have all the evaluative critics whom Mr Frye so cursorily dismisses.

When I spoke earlier of the relative lack of novelty in certain of Mr Frye's assertions, I had in mind, of course, that we were entering the territory already posted by other theorists with such catch-phrases as 'non-referentiality', 'a rapt intransitive attention', 'the autonomy of the work of art', and so on. It seems to me, however, worth insisting as firmly as possible that the automatic assumption that a work of literature is essentially different from other pieces of discourse has been going around far too long, that it has never been adequately demonstrated, and that the burden of proof, especially when someone makes use of it as casually as Mr Frye does, is still wholly on its proponents. One gets very weary (at least if one happens to agree with I. A. Richards that 'poetry is the *completest* mode of utterance')[9] of having the utterances of Shakespeare and Dostoevsky, Tolstoy and Melville and the Eliot of *Four Quartets* hustled away into a species of linguistic harem; and one grows weary, too, of attempts to convert criticism into the attendant eunuch. I will record furthermore my impression that Mrs Isobel C. Hungerland has demonstrated beyond reasonable question in her *Poetic Discourse* that 'all the modes of meaning, features, and functions of everyday language are found in poetry';[10] and if, taking comfort perhaps from the writings of such professional philosophers as R. G. Collingwood, Mrs Hungerland, and Mr Philip Wheelwright, we happen to regard the arts in general as the area where human existence in all its bewildering complexity gets the most fully confronted, then I submit that the fuller our own response to literature – fuller in the sense that as much of our personality as possible is engaged in depth – the better. And it is precisely through the greatest writers that our perceptions and valuations get the most fully clarified and our demands correspondingly sharpened. When we are very young we may find it hard to imagine anything more enthralling about a desert island than *The Swiss Family Robinson*. By the time we have grown intellectually and emotionally, with the assistance of further reading, to the point where we can appropriate *The Tempest* reasonably fully, we have become different persons, and during the act of appropriating it we are changing further. And our reactions to *The Swiss Family Robinson*, should we happen to return to it subsequently, will inevitably differ from our childhood ones. Mr Frye, as I have indicated, is scornful of the conception of literature as 'a hierarchy of comparative greatness, the summit of which provide[s] the standards for the critics'. But in a sense we don't arrange literature hierarchically at all, it arranges itself, just like most other things in life. (Yeats presumably had something like this in mind when he wrote, 'All good criticism is hieratic, delighting in setting things above one another . . . and not merely side by side.

But it is our instinct and not our intellect that chooses.'[11]) And to
seek to arrest the process and exist in a succession of mentally unrelated encounters with works of literature, even assuming that such
an existence were possible, would be to impoverish the psyche and
diminish the chances of growth, especially the growth that comes
with conscious and purposeful discrimination. These facts, and
most of the other facts that I have been putting forward, seem to me
implicit in the writings of virtually all distinguished critics, even
though those critics would not necessarily have described their activities in such terms. They have not, that is to say, been
approaching literature like judges in a Miss Universe contest concerned with awarding so many points for deportment, so many for
physique, so many for skills, and so on, and then totting things up,
striking averages, presenting prizes, and going home with a pleasurable sense of time well spent. On the contrary they have been
passionate men very deeply involved in existence, who have been
responding vigorously and sensitively to the modes of utterance and
being of other men, and constantly discriminating between various
aspects of them; and in their commitment, their courage, and their
indomitable independence they can assist the growth of such qualities in those of us who will attend to them. Unlike Mr Frye they
minister to self-responsible freedom and maturity.

  I said near the outset that we can get a clearer idea from Mr Frye's
article of why he should be as popular as he is. His own major conclusion and message seems to me to be the following:

The central activity of criticism, which is the understanding of literature, is
essentially one of establishing a context for the works of literature being
studied. This means relating them to other things: to their context in the
writer's life, in the writer's time, in the history of literature, and above all in
the total structure of literature itself, or what I shall call the order of words.

And to this there can scarcely be a 'traditional' academic who
wouldn't say Amen, even though he might be a trifle foggy about
that 'order of words'. It isn't really so paradoxical that Mr Frye, the
ostensibly advanced critic, should have been able to speak so comfortably out of the centre of what for a good while was one of the
most stultifyingly traditionalist English schools on the North
American continent, and it must undoubtedly be very pleasant for a
great many of his readers (or receivers of his reputation) to be reassured that the only respectable function of the literary

commentator is to provide 'contexts' for traditionally approved works. Isn't that, after all, what they themselves have been doing all along? Now they can stop worrying. To borrow from Mr Dooley: '"Northrup Frye – I use him f'r purposes iv definse ... I have niver read him," I says; "he shtands between me an' all evalytive cr-rit'cism," says I; "I've built him up into a kind of break-wather," says I, "an' I set behind it, ca'm an' contint, while Arnold an' Winthers an' Eliot an' Layvis an' Jawnson rages without," says I.'[12] For that matter, should one plume oneself on one's adequacy to the Time of Camp it can be no less gratifying to feel liberated, Caliban-like, from all oppressive notions of natural hierarchies, of sharply varying degrees of intelligence and sensitivity and critical insight, of the rareness of the possibility of being brilliant and the much greater likelihood of being wrong or dull – in sum, from most of the pain and risk of intellectual and emotional selfhood. Some ways of escaping from 'anxieties', however, seem remarkably close to being intellectual lobotomies.

Well, I suppose that in the end each of us chooses the critical stance that accords with his stance towards existence generally. I can only say that in one way or another an evaluative 'noticing of things in the literary work of particular relevance to one's own ex-perience', *pace* Mr Frye, should in my personal but also, I suspect, traditional opinion belong at the very centre of reading and criti-cism. I do not see how we can profitably notice things of particular relevance to other people's experience, and if we are looking for things that aren't relevant to experience at all, then the grounds on which we wish to promote the official teaching of literature would appear extraordinarily shaky. 'Insight criticism', as Mr Frye con-temptuously calls it, will no doubt be 'random' if done by ill-organized minds, but some minds are at once both richly open to experience and very finely organized. Mr Frye seems to me in general to be singularly short on a capacity for opening himself to possibly disturbing encounters with other minds. Though he has borrowed various formulae from other critics (indeed, I suspect that one reason for his ineffable self-assurance may be that for a long time he was the only person at Toronto apart from McLuhan who was reading the newer criticism, and so couldn't be called to account in his dealings with it), he gives no signs of ever having attended closely to their arguments and procedures. And there is no sign, either, that he has ever felt that great literature is a matter not of a 'total structure' but of human utterances, utterances by other individual human beings who may well be his superiors in many ways, who may have experienced and comprehended more things than he has, and from whom he could conceivably learn something about how to live. Instead there is only the overweening satisfaction with being Northrop Frye and the kind of 'tolerant aplomb' that comes about, as he himself half intimates, by resisting the pressure of works of art to stimulate us 'into a response of heightened awareness'. The self-satisfaction appears a long way from being justified.

In the face of the pretensions of Mr Frye and the enthusiasms of his science-minded admirers at Trinity College, Connecticut, and elsewhere, it is tempting to end by simply quoting T. S. Eliot's observation that 'there is no method except to be very intelligent'[13] and letting it go at that. But a little more seems called for in amplification. In one way, of course, to speak of science in connection with literature and criticism is to reveal a radical incomprehension of all three; great and good literature is not a world, it is *investigations* of a world – our world – and while we can meaningfully speak of the philosophy of science it would be meaningless to call for a science of philosophy.[14] Furthermore, to insist that criticism must 'contain some sense of the progressive or the systematic, some feeling that irrevocable forward steps in understanding are being taken', is fatuous if unaccompanied by a recognition that literature is almost as varied as life itself and that intelligent and passionate people progress and organize and understand in a variety of ways. However, it is becoming increasingly plain that critical discourse is liable to *deteriorate* in a variety of ways unless in certain respects there is a shift towards the empiricism that is so admirable an element in the sciences – a determined effort to cease bombinating, in Mr Frye's fashion, about a magical entity called literature, and instead to examine introspectively and scrupulously how language actually functions in our own mental economies and what happens as we move existentially along the road of discourse that leads, without interruption, from a casual 'Good morning!' to *Moby Dick*. In saying this I am not imagining that any mode of investigation will present us with marvellous discoveries that invalidate the explorations of good critics, any more than the revelations of twentieth-century psychology have diminished the stature of good art.[15] Nor am I suggesting that most of us should start doing this sort of thing formally. My point is, rather, that good criticism has always involved the existential self-awareness that prevents the talking of certain kinds of nonsense; that we live in a time, however, when various assumptions about the nature of the mind and 'reality' make it easier to talk critical nonsense; and that any investigators of consciousness who can help to reverse the trend will deserve very well of all of us.[16] Reviewing a study by one of the greatest of Mr Frye's despised evaluative critics, a social psychologist was able to observe:

It is the distinction of this book that it consistently treats poetry as one of the major products of normal human activity, and the making of poetry as being at least as responsible an occupation as, say, scientific research. In fact the quality of the book may be indicated by saying that an intelligent scientist ... could read it without getting exasperated.[17]

The same could not be said of 'Criticism, Visible and Invisible'; and in this, as in other respects, it is representative of Mr Frye's contribution to literary studies.[18]

Swift and the Decay of Letters

As Mr Ricardo Quintana has said, 'It is possible ... to analyse [Swift's] controlling ideas with some accuracy, and yet to miss entirely that quality of the man which sets him apart from all of his contemporaries.' In discussing Swift's satirical treatment of the literary life of his own times in *A Tale of a Tub* and *The Battle of the Books* I shall not, therefore, attempt to deal with his neo-stoicism, his concept of right reason, or his religious beliefs, for it seems to me a mistake to assume that his revulsion from much of the writing that surrounded him stemmed primarily from his holding such relatively public ideas. In any discussion of *A Tale of a Tub* as a whole, of course, they have to be invoked. But in an important sense Swift's rationalism, neo-stoicism, and Christianity were negative beliefs; that is to say, their function for him was primarily to aid in restraining and making harmless the emotions. Underlying his treatment of literature, on the other hand, I think we can discover certain more positive and personal feelings about what qualities were admirable in individuals and in society; and it was because he possessed those feelings that he was able to earn the devotion of a man so different from him in many ways as Yeats. With their aid he resisted a social process involving, among other things, the ascendancy of the crowd over the individual, the substitution of method for invention, the exaltation of the present over the past and the future over the present, and, at bottom, the replacing of strenuous moral endeavour by a spiritual passivity compounded of mere perception and sensation. The essential nature of that process, I believe, was what he symbolized by the spider in *The Battle of the Books*; and what he opposed to it was what he symbolized by the bee. I shall begin by considering briefly the nature of the two opposing concepts of the admirable human life that seem to have been interacting in his mind when he wrote the two works that I am concerned with.

Though science and philosophy in seventeenth-century France and England differed in their development in much the same way as the most distinguished of their originators had differed – Bacon having emphasized the importance of experimentation, while Descartes denied it – at bottom both were alike in that, metaphysically, they tended to reduce man to the status of a ticker-tape machine, a mere receiver and recorder of impulses. For the English apologists for the new science, no less than for Descartes, happiness, and indeed all right thinking, was to reside ultimately in the morally neutral contemplation of the 'real' world of measurable qualities. 'The Experimenter', Thomas Sprat wrote in 1667 in his *History of the Royal Society of London*, 'labors about the plain and undigested objects of his senses, without considering them as they are joyn'd into common Notions'; and elsewhere in the book he contrasted the uneasiness of always pondering theological, social, and human problems with the comfort of contemplating nature, and emphasized the superiority to 'the glorious pomp of Words' of 'the silent, effectual, and unanswerable Arguments of real Productions'. Superficially active and industrious with their barometers, white powders, and dissected dogs, the members of the Royal Society were in reality, according to Sprat, engaged in obtaining the same kind of passive and hedonistic satisfactions that they might otherwise have sought under the aegis of the neo-Epicureanism of the period. 'This course of Study', Sprat wrote,

will not affright us with rigid praecepts or sour looks, or peevish commands, but consists of sensible pleasure, and besides will be most lasting in its satisfactions, and innocent in its remembrance.

What raptures can the most voluptuous men fancy to which these are not equal? Can they relish nothing but the pleasures of their senses? They may here injoy them without guilt or remorse.

And when Sprat triumphantly enumerated the recent discoveries of science, it was in a very different spirit from that in which Elizabethans and Jacobeans had viewed the explorations of their own times. It was now, as it were, the compass that counted, not the sea-discoverers who used it – and counted because, like the other discoveries, it appeared to assure the rapid approach of a time of comfort in which (Sprat again) 'the beautiful Bosom of Nature will be expos'd to our View; we shall enter into its Garden and taste of its Fruits, and satisfy ourselves with its plenty; instead of idle talking and wandering under its fruitless shadows'. It was the pseudo-philosophical web of such an outlook, I suggest, that Swift sensed stretching over much of the cultural life of his contemporaries; and there were reasons why he should have been particularly disturbed by it.

During his formative years as secretary to Sir William Temple, Swift had found at Moor Park a concept of right action and true human creativity that was the antithesis of the foregoing. The moderate Epicureanism of his employer, like his pleasure in gardens and 'old Wood..., old Wine..., old Books..., and old Friends', was only the earned resting place of a man who had lived with considerable strenuousness. In his writings, Temple's admiration of energy was as pronounced as his love of rationality, and it was the former quite as much as the latter that Swift took over and made his own. 'Though it be easier to describe Heroick Virtue, by the Effects and Examples, than by Causes or Definitions', Temple wrote in a well-known passage,

yet it may be said to arise from some great and native Excellency of Temper or Genius transcending the common Race of Mankind, in Wisdom, Goodness and Fortitude. These Ingredients advantaged by Birth, improved by Education, and assisted by Fortune, seem to make that Noble Composition, which gives such a Lustre to those who have possest it, as made them appear to common Eyes, something more than Mortals, and to have been born of some Mixture, between Divine and Human Race; To have been Honoured and Obey'd in their Lives, and after their Deaths Bewailed and Adored.

That Temple, naturally, is not speaking of mere energy of personality, of the kind that Swift himself later took exception to in his scornful references to Perseus and Hercules in *A Tale of a Tub*, is emphasized by what follows. According to Temple, Heroick Virtue, the possession of which he denies to Caesar and Alexander, so conduces to the general good that its 'Character ... seems to be, in short, The Deserving well of Mankind.' It is, in fact, the highest form of wisdom; and between wisdom and wit (that other great manifestation of human energy) Temple makes the connection in his essay 'On Poetry': 'To the first of these are Attributed, the Inventions or Productions of Things generally esteemed the most necessary, useful, or profitable to Human Life, either in private Possessions or publick Institutions: To the other, those Writings or Discourses, which are the most Pleasing or Entertaining to all that read or hear them...' Here, presumably, we have the origin of Swift's remark in 'A Digression concerning Criticks' that 'One Man can Fiddle, and another can make a small Town a great City, and he that cannot do either one or the other, deserves to be kick'd out of the Creation.' And such a yoking of art and practical wisdom is by no means to the disadvantage of the former, as Temple goes on to show in his account of the creative process:

But tho' Invention be the Mother of Poetry, yet this Child, is like all others born naked, and must be Nourished with Care, Cloathed with Exactness and Elegance, Educated with Industry, Instructed with Art, Improved by Application, Corrected with Severity, and Accomplished with Labor and with Time, before it arrives at any great Perfection or Growth. 'Tis certain that no Composition requires so many Ingredients, or several of more different Sorts than this, nor that to excel in any Qualities, there are necessary so many gifts of Nature, and so many Improvements of Learning and of Art. For there must be an universal Genius, of great Compass as well as great Elevation. There must be spritely Imagination or Fancy, fertile in a thousand Productions, ranging over infinite Ground, piercing into every Corner, and by the Light of that true Poetical Fire, discovering a thousand little Bodies or Images in the World, and Similitudes among them, unseen to Common Eyes, and which could not be discovered, without the Rays of that Sun.

Here in Temple's writings, it seems plain, is the basis of Swift's aesthetics and literary morality in *The Battle of the Books* and *A Tale of a Tub*. The qualities that for Temple primarily ennoble both poetry and public action are energy, invention ('the first Attribute and highest Operation of divine Power'), wisdom, self-mastery, and wit (for Swift 'the noblest and most useful gift of human nature'). And for both Swift and Temple these were to be found preeminently in that idealized classical civilization concerning which Christopher Dawson has written:

It is not easy for us to realize the strength of this classical tradition. For three hundred years men had lived a double life. The classical world was the standard of all their thought and conduct. In a sense it was more real to them than their own world, for they had been taught to know the history of Rome better than that of England or modern Rome; to judge their literature by the standard of Quintilian; and to model their thought on Cicero and Seneca.

It was, I believe, with the standards of Moor Park firmly appropriated – the standards that he symbolized by the bee – that Swift contemplated the very different world of contemporary English letters.

In his incursion into the battle of the Ancients and Moderns, Swift superficially had the worst of it. Looking back at the episode from a literary-historical viewpoint, we can only raise our eyebrows at such oddities as his attribution of insanity to William Wotton's methodology, his sustained attack upon Richard Bentley, his obtuseness about Bernard de Fontenelle, his extraordinary lists of adversaries, remarkable no less for their omissions (such as Newton and Locke) than for the placing of some of the inclusions (Thomas Rymer, for instance, who was notoriously on the side of the Ancients). And when we recall the similar battles of the present century, it is difficult not to feel considerable sympathy for a movement, especially one with Fontenelle as its most distinguished spokesman, that was essentially an attempt to break through a kind of historical sound-barrier and endow the present with as much reality and significance as the defenders of the Ancients accorded to the past. Yet, coarse and unjust as his attack in some ways was, I think that Swift was re-sisting a process that seemed to him to work insidiously but undeniably towards the corruption of contemporary writing. For now the average author need no longer feel any obligation to measure himself, consciously or unconsciously, against the classical writers whose greatness had formerly been felt more or less in Temple's terms. Instead, as Swift made explicit in *A Tale of a Tub*, his contemporaries had almost succeeded in destroying the felt power of those writers as individual personalities, either by outright denigration or by busying themselves only with forms and texts, and were now proceeding to address their own works solely to the mental world of the anti-historical present. And the literary climate of the present was of a kind peculiarly to hinder the creation of any new and valid critical standards. The strength of party politics was growing at such a rate that soon almost all of the rapidly multiplying professional writers would be earning their livings in the service of one or more of the main factions; the increasingly influential upper middle classes of London were relatively lacking in a cultural tra-dition of their own and tended to absorb from the aristocracy their less admirable qualities only; and pleasure-seeking women were playing more and more conspicuous roles in fashionable society. Thus, when it was not mere propaganda, literature tended increas-ingly to be thought of as mere entertainment, an undemanding way of killing time; and whichever kind of commodity he was trying to provide, the average writer was drawn almost inevitably into gross flattery of his patrons and a pervasive concern to keep as closely abreast as possible of the rapidly and arbitrarily changing fashions. Consequently, whenever an appeal was made to higher standards than the resulting mêlée of competitiveness and personally motivated criticism provided, it could only be to a posterity whose critical status, logically, would have to be on a par with that of the present reading public. And in dealing with such appeals Swift was justifiably ruthless. Conscious as he was of the body's decay, devouring time was for him as terrifying a reality as it had been for the Elizabethans and Jacobeans, and his evocation of it, in the 'Dedication to Prince Posterity', and of the ephemerality of most contemporary publications is one of the most powerful things in the whole book. In his own eyes, that is to say, there could be no valid escape from the obligation to live and write self-responsibly in the present by the light of respectable standards personally believed in.

If we grant the fundamental soundness of his view of the ordinary reading public, Swift's at first somewhat odd yoking of the Royal Society group, the coffee-house cliques, and the pedants gains considerably in impressiveness when we consider that these, the intelligentsia of the period, not merely did not assist in the preservation or erection of valid standards but actually worked against them. Moreover, the nature of their treason was of a kind peculiarly to exasperate Swift. By continually emphasizing the theme that the Ancients lacked a methodology, the apologists for the Moderns were in fact replacing the standard of individual merit and endeavour by that of collective knowledge, so that now the question was always '*What* did a man (such as Pythagoras) know?' and not 'How did he come to know it?' Admittedly an awareness of the incongruity of anyone's being patronizing about Pythagoras did seep sufficiently into the contemporary consciousness to produce the defensive argument, which even Fontenelle and Wotton felt impelled to counter, that it was actually harder to develop an idea than to originate it (though even then Wotton went on to suggest that of the two activities the former might well be the more useful). But, such minor exceptions aside, a complacent insistence on the paramountcy of method seems to have been pervasive, since it was now perfectly possible for a modern, confronted with the apparent comprehensiveness of Newton's discoveries, to feel that there was very little left to discover about the 'real' world and that what was required now was largely the consolidation and dissemination of knowledge. It was this point of view, as manifested in connection with literature, that Swift attacked so admirably in 'A Digression in the Modern Kind' and 'A Digression in Praise of Digressions'. And his metaphor of the army of learning ravaging the territory it occupies has a painfully modern flavour, as do his comments upon the uses of indexes, compendiums, abstracts, and interpretative systems – 'Authors need to be little consulted, yet Criticks and Commentators and Lexicons carefully must', for example.

The nature of the impetus that all this gave to the further corruption of standards is clear; it was what Bacon had earlier pointed to when he extolled the scientific method for its ability to 'place all Wits and Understandings nearly at a Level'. On the one hand we find Sprat attempting to lure polite gentlemen into the Royal Society by asking, 'Are they affrighted at the difficulties of Knowledge? Here they may meet with a Study that as well fits the most negligent minds as the most industrious.' On the other, with the help of proliferating aids to easy knowledge, the same gentlemen could presumably rapidly acquire the kind of nodding acquaintance with Virgil and 'The Rules' that would confirm them in the self-satisfaction that the authors competing for their attention were engaged in promoting. And the bearings that the fashionable concerns with method had for authors themselves Swift devastatingly indicates at the end of 'A Digression in Praise of Digressions':

By these Methods, in a few Weeks, there starts up many a Writer, capable of managing the profoundest and most universal Subjects. For, what tho' his Head be empty, provided his Common-place-book be full; And if you will hate him but the Circumstances of Method, and Style, and Grammar, and Invention; allow him but the common Privileges of transcribing from others, and digressing from himself, as often as he shall see Occasion; He will desire no more Ingredients towards fitting up a Treatise, that shall make a very comely Figure on a Bookseller's Shelf, there to be preserved neat and clean, for a long Eternity, adorn'd with the Heraldry of its Title, fairly inscribed on a Label; never to be thumb'd or greas'd by Students, nor bound to everlasting Chains of Darkness in a Library: But when the Fulness of Time is come, shall happily undergo the Tryal of Purgatory, in order to ascend the Sky.

Brilliant though Swift was as a diagnostician of literary ills, we would not, of course, go to *The Battle of the Books* or *A Tale of a Tub* for any purely literary criticism of a kind intended seriously towards remedying them. In its way, of course, his description of the ideal critic in 'A Digression concerning Criticks' is clear enough, with its talk of assisting intelligent readers 'to pronounce upon the productions of the Learned, form [their] taste to a true Relish of the Sublime and the Admirable, and divide every beauty of Matter or of Style from the Corruption that Apes it'; and so is the conception of the self-discipline that writing should entail that comes out in 'An Apology', especially in the following:

The Author assures those Gentlemen who have given themselves that trouble with him [of attempting to answer the book] that his Discourse is the Product of the Study, the Observation, and the Invention of several Years, that he often blotted out much more than he left, and if his papers had not been a long time out of his Possession, they must have still undergone more severe Corrections; and do they think such a Building is to be battered with Dirt-Pellets however envenom'd the Mouths may be that discharge them.

But such passages do not really take us very far, and the obvious fact is that Swift's concern with literature in these two books, especially *A Tale of a Tub*, was of another kind from that of a literary critic as described in the Digression. Though he spoke approvingly of the invention and use of critical 'rules', he himself was doing something more complicated, and I think more important.

Swift, as I have tried to indicate, was a man extraordinarily sensitive to the tendencies of certain of the beliefs of his time; and, as he sensed with that poetic intuitiveness not possessed by otherwise more intelligent contemporaries of his, such as Locke and Fontenelle, the ends towards which they were conducing were individual madness and the erection of ideologies having for their supporters the status of religions and leading, sooner or later, to the 'Establishment of New Empires by Conquest'. In *A Tale of a Tub* he was concerned with literature not as a commodity to be marketed and weighed but as something that was symptomatic of the ideas and moral health both of the individuals producing it and of the times in which they lived; and he judged ideas less for the 'correctness' of their arguments than for their power to lead people towards or away from the kinds of virtues that he cherished. I have tried to show how he attacked the essential illiteracy, ignorance, and intellectual self-complacency of his own period for edging the individual towards the spiritual passivity that was then to a considerable extent a philosophical ideal. But he also saw beyond the smooth front of that ideal to the fact that rationalism always produces its own kind of unreason; and it is a mark of his genius that in 'A Digression in the Modern Kind' he linked together the purely rationalistic and the occultist criticism of Homer. Both were unhistorical, both went to the forms of the work rather than to the moral personality of the writer as a living force, both were part of a tendency to find easy ways to knowledge and power, and both, ultimately, conduced to the kind of madness the attack upon which, as Mr Quintana and Dr Miriam Kosh Starkman have shown, forms the centre of *A Tale of a Tub*.[1]

III

Theories and Practices:
the Hammonds' *The Village Labourer*

One of the more disturbing aspects of studying literature is the look of fixity that things can increasingly wear. The more at home we are with individual works, the harder it can become to feel other minds mysteriously at work in them and to imagine ways in which they might have been different; and the longer we contemplate the 'periods' of literary and cultural history, the more we are liable to feel half consciously that what happened in them too was more or less inevitable. Such tricks of the mind are especially ironical in that it is to literature above everything else, presumably, that we go for the richest manifestations of individual consciousnesses and for the translation of abstract forces-of-the-period back into terms of actual living and creative choosing. And those works especially deserve to be cherished that can help arrest this occupational atrophying of the imagination. One such work – and a great one – is *The Village Labourer,* 1760–1832, the first fruits, in 1911, of the distinguished collaboration between the British social historians J. L. and Barbara Hammond.[1] It does not obviously invite the attention of students of literature: its subject – how agricultural enclosures were carried out in the late eighteenth and early nineteenth centuries, the disastrous consequences for the English peasantry, and the abortive revolt of some of them in 1830 – sounds non-literary and undramatic. In fact, however, the book stands with George Sturt's *Change in the Village* (1912) and Lawrence's *Sons and Lovers* (1913) as the culmination of an important pre-1914 socio-literary trend, and while Lawrence's book is the more valuable for adolescents, the Hammonds' seems to me decidedly the greater and more moving. The authors have chosen a major episode in which the workings of a particularly well-liked culture – eighteenth-century upper-class English culture – can be profitably re-examined without distractions by conventional literary associations. They take the reader back dramatically to the actual human conditions behind some of the forces at work during the period; their demonstration of what can happen when such conditions are obscured by received ideas and over-simple theorizings is permanently relevant; and the richness and power of their narrative are such that the epithet 'epic' scarcely seems too strong for it.

In a sense, of course, the whole 'discovery' of the labouring class from the 1880s on involved a disruption of received ideas – Charles Booth's massive *Life and Labour of the People in London* (1891–1902) is an obvious example – but a good deal of the most influential work of this kind was done on rural rather than urban life. There were a number of reasons for this, among them the greater ease with which first-hand observations could be made by the educated, but one of the most important was that here the discrepancies between stereotypes and actualities were becoming increasingly obtrusive. Here, supposedly, was that Merrie England of avuncular squires, jolly farmers, and simple grateful peasants of which the lineaments had been fixed in the much-imitated pages of Washington Irving's *Sketchbook*; in reality a grave agricultural depression, with accompanying labour problems, had lasted almost continuously since the second half of the seventies. Of the various fresh approaches to the problems of rural life the one that was to have the longest influence – it stands directly behind the work of the *Scrutiny* group and such derivatives from it as Richard Hoggart's *The Uses of Literacy* – was the firsthand examination of individual labourers and labouring life that began in 1901 with George Sturt's *The Bettesworth Book*, was continued by Sturt himself and a number of other writers, and was designed to show that the labourer was not the spiritless clodhopper incapable of managing his affairs without direction from above that it suited the well-to-do to see him as. A scarcely less influential approach at the time, however, was the revelation by conventional scholarly means that the contemporary structure of rural society was very far, historically, from being the natural thing that even so acute an observer as Richard Jefferies had taken it to be. Its most important accomplishment was to reveal how immense had been the reshaping of rural life by the enclosures; how far this was from being a commonplace can be gauged from the fact that as late as 1895 a very scholarly history of the English peasantry could still contain virtually no mention of the subject. The Hammonds' contribution to the discussion of enclosure – a discussion that began effectively with W. Hasbach's *History of the English Agricultural Labourer* in 1894 and intensified in the early 1900s as the idea of a fresh redistribution of land was mooted – was to translate economic generalities much more fully into the particularities of individual conduct and experience, and to do so with an especially keen interest in the English class structure.

Though the Hammonds virtually never mention Edwardian England in the book, it is plain how contemporary circumstances sharpened their interest in the events that they were probing, nourished their sense of ironies and injustices, clarified their strategies and led them deep into issues that were central then and are relevant even now. *The Village Labourer* appeared the year after, and was presumably being written during the course of, the battle between the House of Lords and the Liberal Government over Lloyd George's 1909 budget, a battle in which the last-ditch polemics of the Conservatives were the culmination of years of upper-class uneasiness at the social changes that had put the Liberals into power in 1906 with a massive majority and a commitment to heavy social legislation. This was a period, that is to say, in which the hierarchical image of the nation and its history was being put forward – and, up to a point, combated – with unusual vehemence. It was an image that had attained its most memorable form in the eighteenth century, not only in the ideas then current but also in the remodelling of the English countryside through enclosure and the creation of some of the loveliest estates in Europe, heart-stirring embodiments of a combined order and naturalness. Something of the authority it still possessed when the Hammonds were writing and of the energy required to penetrate behind the image can be gathered from the following key passage:

In both societies [the Hammonds are comparing eighteenth-century England and Republican Rome] the aristocracy regarded the poor in much the same spirit, as a problem of discipline and order, and passed on to posterity the same vague suggestion of squalor and turbulence. Thus it comes that most people who think of the poor in the Roman Republic think only of the great corn largesses; and most people who think of the poor in eighteenth-century England think only of the great system of relief from the rates. Mr Warde Fowler has shown how hard it is to find in the Roman writers any records of the poor. So it is with the records of eighteenth-century England. In both societies the obscurity which surrounded the poor in life has settled on their wrongs in history. For one person who knows anything about so immense an event as the disappearance of the old English village society, there are a hundred who know everything about the fashionable scenes of high politics and high play, that formed the exciting world of the upper classes. The silence that shrouds these village revolutions was not quite unbroken, but the cry that disturbed it is like a noise that breaks for a moment in the night, and then dies away, only serving to make the stillness deeper and more solemn.

Something more interesting than a simple undercutting of a traditional view of things, however, goes on in the Hammonds' description of that solemn stillness.

Implicitly and obviously deliberately, the manner of *The Village Labourer* demonstrates that if the authors are attacking certain aspects of upper-class conduct on behalf of the labouring class, it is not because they themselves are gazing uncomprehendingly at upper-class culture from the outside or are writing primarily for culturally deprived readers. On the contrary, the book is addressed to precisely the kind of sophisticated enquirer alluded to in the above quotation, the sort of reader able to appreciate the authors' own very eighteenth-century qualities – their clarity and dry wit, their alertness to a variety of ironies, their juxtaposings of splendid generalities and sharp particulars, their concern with justice, reason, and the public good, their assumption that their readers are decent people to whom the exposed iniquities will appear in the same light as to themselves, their care not to obliterate individual differences with angry generalizations or dehumanize the people whose activities they abhor, and the weight and resonance of their prose on the occasions when it becomes impossible to contain a generous indignation.[2] And these qualities undoubtedly made the book a more valuable weapon for intelligent Liberal and Fabian readers, since they showed how Conservatives had failed to understand some of the very standards they professed to be defending against the barbarians. Yet in some ways the progressives were as much the target of the book's indictment as were the traditionalists. Both groups were imbued with ruling-class attitudes, and as writers like Stephen Reynolds and G. K. Chesterton were pointing out, the former were in fact the more authoritarian in their approach to the lower orders, and now had the power to attempt their 'improvement' officially. Hence it was significant that the Hammonds were not talking about gratuitous and isolated atrocities but were examining the operations of the centre of power and, in theory, wisdom in the nation. The whole process of enclosure took place under the auspices of Parliament, and its consequences involved debate and decision at every stage, which is why the book has a cohesiveness and drama that are lacking from its companion volumes, valuable though the latter are as social history.[3] And the Hammonds expose more than the iniquities possible under an unrestrained aristocracy. They show what can happen when *any* powerful minority forces through large and irreversible changes in a complex social organization in the name of progress.

When the Hammonds were writing it was natural to think of the enclosure movement as a straightforward, even a classic, instance of the advantageous workings of inevitable social and economic forces. In the Hammonds' own words:

the accepted view is that this change marks a great national advance, and that the hardships which incidentally followed could not have been avoided: that it meant a vast increase in the food resources of England in comparison with which the sufferings of individuals counted for little: and that the great estates which then came into existence were rather the gifts of economic forces than the deliberate acquisitions of powerful men.

. . .

The rulers of England took it for granted that the losses of individuals were the gains of the State and that the distresses of the poor were the condition of permanent advance. Modern apologists have adopted the same view.

In their analysis of how enclosures actually came about the authors expose this kind of thinking as the crass and slipshod thing that it is. Pushing beyond the smoke screen of talk about 'forces', they show in abundant detail and with a beautiful precision that particular landowners and legislators did particular things in deplorable ways, that deplorable consequences resulted not only for individuals but for the national community, and that they could have been greatly mitigated, if not avoided altogether, had those responsible acted more intelligently. And they do so in a way that flushes their readers out of the mental security of large loose conceptions and impels them, as in drama or fiction, into an intimate relationship with the actors and events.

The reassuring upper-class version of the mechanics of enclosure is given with studied objectivity at the outset of the brilliant third chapter:

An enclosure, like most Parliamentary operations, began with a petition from a local person or persons, setting forth the inconveniences of the present system and the advantages of such a measure. Parliament, having received the petition, would give leave for a Bill to be introduced. The Bill would be read a first and a second time, and would then be referred to a

Committee, which, after considering such petitions against the enclosure as the House of Commons referred to it, would present its report. The Bill would then be passed, sent to the Lords, and receive the Royal Assent. Finally, the Commissioners named in the Bill would descend on the district and distribute the land. That is, in brief, the history of a successful enclosure agitation.

By the end of the chapter we have not only experienced the maddening injustices and absurdities involved in an ostensibly reasonable process of social amelioration (all the more maddening because perfectly consistent with respectable Parliamentary procedures); we have also been confronted with familiar aspects of the upper-class world in an unaccustomed context. Especially telling in this respect is the culminating account of the forces at work behind a particular Bill in which, after another strategically neutral introduction, the authors take us into the private correspondence of the ordinary, harassed committee chairman. As we read the amplified account of the transactions we are liable to catch ourselves acknowledging how eminently natural the activities of those concerned appeared to them, and even sympathizing with the chairman, George Selwyn, in the difficulties he runs into. And precisely because of this recreation of a familiar and agreeable milieu we are also likely to feel a peculiarly baffled rage as

This glimpse into the operations of the Committee enables us to picture the groups of comrades who sauntered down from Almack's of an afternoon to carve up a manor in Committee of the House of Commons.... We can see Bully's [Lord Bolingbroke's] friends meeting round the table in their solemn character of judges and legislators, to give a score of villages to Bully, and a dozen to Stavordale, much as Artaxerxes gave Magnesia to Themistocles for his bread, Myus for his meat, and Lampsacus for his wine.

As the Hammonds point out,

'Bully has a scheme of enclosure which, if it succeeds, I am told will free him from all his difficulties.' The [Parliamentary] journals may talk of the undrained fertility of Sedgmoor, but we have in this sentence the aspect of the enclosure that interests Selwyn ... and from beginning to end of the proceedings no other aspect ever enters his head. And it interests a great many other people besides Selwyn, for Bully owes money.

But the section reflects back in more than the obvious way on the rebuke to a petitioner by the Speaker of the House on another occasion, in which he observed that 'the House was always competent to give every subject the consideration due to its importance, and could not therefore be truly said to be incapable at any time of discussing any subject gravely, dispassionately, and with strict regard to justice'. The revealed power of received ideas and attitudes suggests that frequently there may have been little or no conscious hypocrisy in such utterances;[4] and we are likely to find ourselves wondering with growing desperation what possible arguments could have been used to the more intelligent fellow parliamentarians of Bully, Selwyn, and their friends to avert the impending representative fate of Sedgmoor. The history of ideas is one thing, the history of people thinking something else.

But though they reanimate the attitudes at work, including the more commendable motives behind enclosure, the Hammonds demolish the slovenly notion that it was simply of the period to believe such and such a theory, as if some kind of compulsion were acting on the minds of all reasonable men that could be reacted to in only one way; and the operation reminds us that stupidity and intelligence are pretty much the same at any time. To be sure, we see how certain theories were indeed very influential for the worse, even on men of the calibre of the younger Pitt. For example,

When we remember that the enterprise of the age was under the spell of the most seductive economic teaching of the time, and that the old peasant society, wearing as it did the look of confusion and weakness, had to fear not only the simplifying appetites of the landlords, but the simplifying philosophy, in England of an Adam Smith, in France of the Physiocrats, we can realise that a ruling class has seldom found so plausible an atmosphere for the free play of its interests and ideas. *Des crimes sont flattés d'être présidés par une vertu.* Bentham himself thought the spectacle of an enclosure one of the most reassuring of all the evidences of improvement and happiness.

But the authors also show convincingly that

of all the remembered writers of the period who had any practical knowledge of agriculture or of the poor, there is not one who did not try to teach the governing class the need for reform, and the dangers of the state into which they were allowing rural society to drift. Parliament was assailed on all sides with criticisms and recommendations, and its refusal to alter its ways was deliberate.

And when they demonstrate how even less excusable was its continuing refusal to do anything after the predicted and atrocious consequences had arrived, there is a special intellectual drama in how they meticulously take up objection after objection against the alleged seriousness of conditions, and disingenuous palliative after disingenuous palliative, and show their unsoundness. As we read we become aware of the pressure of twentieth-century observers likewise disposed to deny that things were all that bad: that the loss of the village commons really mattered so greatly, for example, or that anything much could have been accomplished had Parliament adopted the remedial measures that were proposed. Once change in general has come to be labelled progress, and especially when a particular change is in the direction of largeness and consolidation, is accompanied by energetic theorizing of a familiar kind, and is brought about by orthodox procedures, there is a natural reluctance to grant that seemingly intelligent men can really be comprehensively in error. *The Village Labourer* reminds us that they can indeed; it shows how complete can be the self-assurance of reformers with large neat schemes for making things more efficient, and how devastating the consequences of those schemes. And a little more needs saying about the 'large' ideas involved.

When the book appeared, the short but brilliant section on the Game Laws must have done the most to disrupt the conventional picture of a benevolently ordered, hierarchical community, so shocking was the discrepancy between the Merrie England of gallant gentlemen-sportsmen and the forgotten actualities: e.g., 'Seven peasants exiled for life, nine exiled for fourteen years, and two condemned to the worse exile of all. In that village at any rate there were many homes that had reason to remember the day when the pleasures of the rich became the most sacred thing in England.' What is most interesting here, however, is the Hammonds' culminating reminder, concerning the hideous conditions awaiting transported poachers in Van Diemen's Land, that

this [penal] system was not the invention of some Nero or Caligula; it was the system imposed by men of gentle and refined manners, who talked to each other in the language of Virgil and Lucan, liberty and justice, who admired the sensibility of Euripides and Plutarch, who put down the abominations of the Slave Trade, and allowed Clive and Warren Hastings to be indicted at the bar of public opinion as monsters of inhumanity.[5]

Classical civilization as viewed from a neo-classical viewpoint was an upper-class affair, and the book is a monument to how insubstantial the cottagers and their culture became when viewed in the light of the grandeurs and elegancies of that civilization.[6] Moreover, it is not only the darker side of a classical education that peeps out when we read how 'when Pitt, who had been pestered by Eden to read his book [*The State of the Poor*], handed a volume to Canning, then his secretary, that brilliant young politician spent his time writing a parody on the grotesque names to be found in the Appendix'. Nor is it only the limitations of neo-classicism that are emphasized by the Hammonds' observation that 'all the elements seemed to have conspired against the peasant, for aesthetic taste, which might at other times have restrained, in the eighteenth century encouraged the destruction of the commons and their rough beauty'. The book also sharpens our awareness that all ideas and ideals willy-nilly strengthen or weaken our power to perceive accurately and act intelligently. And it stands with works like Jane Jacobs' *Death and Life of Great American Cities* as a warning about how formalism can abet a perennial tendency to disregard the unaesthetic complexities of human nature in the interests of manipulating people more easily.

This mention of the neo-classical brings me appropriately to the epic quality of the book. Viewed in the light of the upper-class attitudes discussed so far, the idea looks preposterous of course; the only aspect of the labourers' conduct that could be adduced in support of it, presumably, would be their 'revolt', and this spontaneous outbreak of demonstrations in a number of counties was so brief and ineffectual that it went uncelebrated by serious writers until W. H. Hudson, put on its track by conversations with old labourers, described it in 1910 in the best chapter of *A Shepherd's Life*. Yet *The Village Labourer* possesses an epic *gravitas* none the less, and this quality is the crowning aspect of the Hammonds' critique of those attitudes that would deny dignity to the labourers and to what was done to their society. Furthermore, it reminds us that such *gravitas* is not a matter of forms or conventions. We are presented with a conflict between two cultures in an extended episode of tragic significance, and in a way that reaffirms the ultimate importance of the individual. In the course of the destruction of the peasant society there was always the possibility that a forceful display of intelligence and courage by key members of Parliament could have changed the course of events: and when, after an increasingly appalling tightening of the screws, the revolt of the labourers finally came, it had the moral grandeur of a last desperate assertion, against enormous odds, both of individual dignity and of the right to respect as members of a valuable culture. In the trials that followed, as in most major tragedies, crimes and the responses of people to them became the crucible in which the values of all concerned were tested out.

The chief upper-class representatives at those trials were, of course, the judges and prosecutors, and in their conduct we see at their most significant, because now literally a matter of life or death, the attitudes that have been emerging in the course of the book. We witness a forceful acting out of the social philosophy expounded in one of the Hammonds' telling quotations from Burke – a philosophy still with life in it when the Hammonds were writing and perhaps not altogether dead even now:

Good order is the foundation of all good things. To be enabled to acquire, the people, without being servile, must be tractable and obedient. The magistrate must have his reverence, the laws their authority. The body of the people must not find the principles of natural subordination by art rooted out of their minds. They must respect that property of which they cannot partake. They must labour to obtain what by labour can be obtained; and when they find, as they commonly do, the success disproportioned to the endeavour, they must be taught their consolation in the final proportions of eternal justice.

Hardly surprisingly the roll-call of courtroom iniquities – the displays of gross judicial bias, the convictions obtained on the flimsiest evidence, the wildly fluctuating sentences, the almost lunatic disproportion between offences and punishments, and always the outraged sermonizings of the judges about Law and Order – soon comes to oppress us like those figures of the casualties in Flanders that flashed above the stage in Joan Littlewood's *Oh What a Lovely War*. But if we are particularly conscious, because of the Hammonds' masterly quoting, of the individual but representative figures of the judges upon the bench and the prosecutors below them, we are also conscious of the no less real, if less individuated, figures of the accused facing representatively their persecutors. As the Hammonds point out, there was no collective heroism or even dignity, though individuals stand out – Henry Bunce, for instance, who after laying himself open to prosecution by testifying in favour of the accused, 'sprung over the bar into the dock with his former comrades'. Yet, as the names and offences go by, and the living

presences of the accused are evoked, and we learn of the restraint
and good humour that they had displayed during the riots under
conditions in which a bloody revolution would not have been out of
order, we become more and more conscious of the decency and
patience of a whole class confronting and, for those with eyes to see,
putting to shame the insolent mouthers of upper-class platitudes
into whose hands they had been delivered. And by the end we have
been made aware of the anguish of a countryside.

For these riots, apart from the cases of arson [i.e., rick-burning], for which
six men or boys were hung, aristocratic justice exacted three lives, and the
transportation of four hundred and fifty-seven men and boys, in addition to
the imprisonment of about four hundred at home. The shadow of this
vengeance still darkens the minds of old men and women in the villages of
Wiltshire, and eighty years have been too short a time to blot out its train of
desolating memories.

Yet it is not paradoxical that a substantial part of the concluding
chapter is a moving tribute to the strengths of eighteenth-century
upper-class English civilization, and the final stress should be put
where the Hammonds put it with their reflection that 'if moral
courage is the power of combating and defying an enveloping
atmosphere of prejudice, passion, and panic, a generation which
was poor in most of the public virtues was, at least, conspicuously
rich in one'. If the book abounds in instances of injustice and stupidity, it is also rich in examples of intelligence and a passion for justice,
and it reminds us of what it can mean to exercise those qualities in
unglamorous situations. When the Hammonds wind up their
account of the trials with a description of Cobbett's magnificent
self-defence in the sedition trial that the government had rashly
embarked on after their victories over the powerless, our hearts
warm along with the authors'. Yet in some ways it is the defeats of
less gifted men that can speak to us most – of Samuel Whitbread, for
instance, whose 'most notable quality was his vivid and energetic
sympathy' and who 'spent his life in hopeless battles and ... died by
his own hand of public despair'. In their account of Whitbread's
fruitless attempts on two occasions to get a minimum wage bill
passed during the period of greatest distress for the labourers, the
Hammonds make us movingly conscious of what energy and persistence can be required of the perceptive and of how the worst
enemy of all may be the indifference or amused contempt of our

peers. In the words of another parliamentarian, Lord Suffield, fighting in vain to get an intelligent ameliorative bill passed,

The fact is, with the exception of a few individuals, the subject is deemed by the world a bore: every one who touches on it is a bore, and nothing but the strongest conviction of its importance to the country would induce me to subject myself to the indifference that I daily experience when I venture to intrude the matter on the attention of legislators.

Boring or not, however, it was Whitbread and Suffield and a handful of others like them who were right, and the many with the large ideas and the mathematical proofs and the majestic image of Progress on their side who were wrong, in relation to the course of events described so brilliantly and so heartbreakingly in *The Village Labourer*.[7]

George Sturt's Apprenticeship

> The strength of savagery and the vitality of it – these I want,
> but not its harshness.
>
> George Sturt, *Journals* (1891)[1]

For a while in the early sixties, it was difficult to pick up an English
weekly without coming upon some forward-looking academic
alluding scornfully to 'the organic community' or 'the old wheelwright's shop'. It was hard to tell whether Sturt himself was the
target of the sniping or only the use to which others were thought to
have put him. But in any case it is regrettable that he should have
been thought of so exclusively in such terms, and that even
Raymond Williams should have found nothing better to say of him
than that *Change in the Village* and *The Wheelwright's Shop*, 'while
original and valuable in their observations, go back, essentially, to
Cobbett'.[2] Sturt was an intelligent, subtle, and unsentimental man
who considered himself – quite rightly – an artist, and up until the
First World War his artistic energies were directed in an interestingly tendentious manner. Concerned to define creatively for
himself a richness he had sensed in labouring-class minds, he was at
the same time acutely sensitive to how dull-witted, improvident, incapable of self-discipline and self-management, and in general
thoroughly inferior the rural labouring class must appear to even the
enlightened middle-class reader. And in his first four rural books he
was interested at least as much in class as in culture.

Change in the Village (1912) is the best of those books, but he
made his breakthrough in *The Bettesworth Book* (1901). Before it,
no one, not even Richard Jefferies, had presented rural labouring
people with such respectful and convincing immediacy. After it, so
many other writers did so in the pre-war years – among them
Stephen Reynolds, Ford Madox Ford, M. Loane, W. H. Hudson,
and Christopher Holdenby – that we can virtually speak of a school
of Sturt and trace a direct line of influence from it, via F. R. Leavis
and Denys Thompson's *Culture and Environment* and *Scrutiny*, to

the attitudes towards class and culture displayed in Williams' *Culture and Society* and Richard Hoggart's *The Uses of Literacy*. What Sturt did was reveal unsuspectedly interesting aspects of labouring-class minds, in ways that could modify even the procedures of professonal sociologists. (It is instructive in this regard to compare the Charles-Booth-derived method of B. Seebohm Rowntree's *Poverty* in 1901 with that of Rowntree and May Kendall's *How the Labourer Lives* in 1913; twelve years of informal participant observation lay between the two books.) And by way of the pages on the labourers' revolt in W. H. Hudson's *A Shepherd's Life*, a work that would obviously not have been written without his example, Sturt presumably also influenced J. L. and Barbara Hammond in their *The Village Labourer*. In these pages I shall deal with how he became the kind of writer that he did.

Returning to his Surrey cottage from a visit to Sturt near the end of the nineties, his friend Arnold Bennett reported admiringly in his journal that:

I had not been with him an hour before I was compelled to readjust my estimate of the depth of his immerson in literature. Writing occupies all his thoughts in a way I had never suspected. With the most perfect naturalness, he regards everything as 'material', and he assumed that I should do so too. A more literary temperament than his would be difficult to conceive. He doesn't 'search' for stuff; his task probably is to cope with the masses of material which thrust themselves upon his attention. He sits down at his writing-chair and handles note-books and papers with an air of custom and familiarity which I have never seen in a writer before.[3]

Sturt achieved this kind of certitude relatively slowly (he was thirty-five when his first book appeared in 1898), and it is remarkable that he did so at all. During most of the first decade of his manhood he was uncomfortable in his wheelwright's business, hungry for a broader cultural life, possessed of no very obvious aptitude for authorship, and afflicted by temperamental deficiencies that would have crippled a less intelligent man. He had taken over the family business reluctantly in 1884 upon the death of his father, after six years of school-teaching. And when he did commit himself fully to 'playing at authorship', as he drily described it years later in *The Wheelwright's Shop*,[4] it was during the nineties, a decade especially qualified to stultify or pervert such gifts as he had. Yet he won through to peace of mind, literary distinction, and a quiet but significant influence. His development up to 1901, when the first of his books on the rural labouring class appeared, is illuminating in regard to his work, heartening in its display of effective intelligence, and instructive about the nature of a healthy relationship between a man, his art, and his environment.

To judge from a passage in *The Wheelwright's Shop*, Sturt had been writing since his early twenties ('literary exercises – imitations of Thoreau or Emerson or Carlyle'[5]), but what stands out at the start of the journal that he began in 1890 at the age of twenty-seven is his preoccupation with how to live. As he explained a couple of years later, 'I remember a period when I was frequently puzzled by the apparent futility of all activity. Every occupation seemed to be but a means of killing time – a kind of waiting at a station, until the train should arrive to carry us on our journey. And on our journey *whither*? What is life *for*? I would ask myself.' Such speculations were not just abstractly philosophical ones, either.

Quietly in the dark just now [he noted in 1890], I had a sense (only for a soon-gone minute, yet very real) of my own limitations: that in the future, I should find myself even such a man, dreamy, flabby and rather loose-mixed, as at this moment. Why hope for anything in the future *better* than the now, when it would surely be the same self, in whom the greatness would still be wanting?

His health had never been good – almost from birth he had suffered badly from asthma, and the early pages of the journal contain numerous references to colds and to the irksome necessity for always '*being careful*' – but more than bodily health was in question. From the judicious and unegotistical pages of *William Smith, Potter and Farmer* (1919) and the lovely *A Small Boy in the Sixties* (1927) we can piece together a picture of what he was like as a child, and one of his principal characteristics was obviously a low amount of bodily vitality and a psyche that had to do a good deal of excluding of potentially disturbing experiences. He was happiest in the enjoyment of small-scale comforts and pleasures, with every-thing feeling secure and harmonious – the sunshine in Farnham Park; evenings in his grandparents' farmhouse when the curtains had shut out the night and all the objects in the room were fam-iliar and the grown-ups were talking peacefully among themselves; illustrated travel books in which he could lose himself; a luxuriously heated bedroom at Christmas-time. And quite early he was sensitive to anything that threatened to disrupt harmony, such as a group of ugly new brick cottages, in ways that would later bear on his empathy with labouring people in the face of change. By his own account too he was imperfectly aware of other persons as individuals ('a small egotist ... chiefly concerned to shine and be petted all the time'), yet at the same time heavily dependent on them for stimulation because 'in solitude my attention was but sluggish'.[6] Such a constellation of traits, especially when combined with a fair amount of youthful ambition, does not normally make for later success and maturity.

In some ways Sturt was fortunate: almost everything in his growing-up in Farnham seems to have conduced to fortifying his personality rather than fragmenting it. But even so, it is clear that in his late twenties he was still suffering from an imperfect, or at least intermittent, grasp upon reality. 'Have been rather dull and flabby all day'; 'This afternoon feel empty headed'; 'My senses grow numb in these days, and I have little feeling: merely a succession of disconnected impressions'; 'Sick these last few days, with a morbid activity of introspection' – remarks like these make some of the early pages of the journal uncomfortable reading. Unlike many people in his condition, however, he not only saw what was wrong with himself but was doing something about it, in ways recalling Leavis's statement apropos of D. H. Lawrence that intelligence is 'the power of recognizing justly the relation of idea and will to spontaneous life, of using the conscious mind for the attainment of "spontaneous-creative fulness of being"'.[7]

'What is that, which I should have been, under *any* environment?' he had enquired in 1891. 'Could I find and cultivate *it*, there would be fullness of life.' Spontaneity, fullness of being, the outflowing of powers from deep within the psyche (art, he was to write later in *The Ascending Effort* (1910), his book on aesthetics, 'owes its triumphs and subtle influence to the fact that it issues straight from our organic vitality'[8]), and the kind of strength of character that comes therefrom rather than from rigid ideas taken over from others – these were the qualities that at that time he most admired. And the three figures whom he talked of with most respect in his journals, all of them interestingly enough Americans, were Whitman, John Brown (a man, he comments in 1890, whom none of the ordinary standards of measurement will fit at all; '"Good" and "bad" don't apply; you might almost as well try to estimate his "goodness" in

£. s. d.!'), and, above all, Thoreau. ('At this present time', he wrote in the same year, 'there is no man who speaks to me through his books so intimately.') Various entries that year indicate his awareness of what, at a modest but feasible level, the right kind of engagement with reality felt like for himself. We find him noting, for example, in a way that brings to mind Thoreau's marvellous physicality, how 'most of my impressions that are worth anything are met on the surface by my soul coming out to meet and welcome them. So one gets an intensified delight from them: a solid, rather than a plane or *superficial* pleasure'. And a few days later he complains of how, during an unsatisfactory walk,

in myself I felt an insufficiency: could not well enough gather all these impressions together, so as to get the character of the hour. Perhaps a more deliberate observance was needed: a more conscious control of my senses. I stood too far behind my material sight, had not come to the door of my ears to listen, but was still dozing within.

The descriptions that resulted from the observing that he did on his walks were not particularly distinguished, and had we read them and the above passages at the time, we would probably not have predicted much of a future for their author. It is impossible to imagine Richard Jefferies needing to write to himself in such a fashion. But I believe that it was because having and formulating the experiences that he wanted was so difficult for Sturt that his respect for the act of writing was so strong. Knowing what true expression felt like, he was unwilling to accept substitutes, to dilute rather than strengthen his personality. We find him noting in 1890, for example, of 'an itch for writing that keeps me indoors', that

writing for its own sake, the only reasonable activity or art available to me, is rather a thing to be avoided. I prefer letters. In seizing the passing impressions and fixing them in writing, there is a danger of committing oneself; of pushing an idea farther than it will go; and of stereotyping or petrifying the impressions that should be untrammelled and alive.

And in the same month he records his fear of 'writing (in this private book) for publicity at some future time – the after years looking over my shoulder', discusses how to avoid 'that dishonest and conceited thirst for book-production', and reports how 'I find still some distrust of this diary experiment, and doubt my own sincerity . . . It seems as if even ledger and daybook would be less objectionable. Better to be faithful (what *does* that mean?) in that lower and more

barren activity, than to poison a more desirable one by unfaithful-
ness.' It was the same kind of scrupulousness that caused him to ask
near the end of the year, 'I love Thoreau of late more than any other
writer; but while I am reading him, where am *I*?' and to record how
'I read Thoreau's *Summer* with great content; until I found myself
reading at last for the sake of reading, and put it by' (a remark that
V. S. Pritchett would later consider an example of the Victorians'
'intimidating earnestness'[9]). And the scrupulousness had its bearing
on his approach to art and culture in general.

When we read a comment in December 1890 like, 'I thought
today, if I had real positive bodily health, that would be brave living
out of doors always, I could dispense entirely with all books,
pictures, music and the rest of it', it is obvious enough that his
attitude, as he himself immediately acknowledges, is one-sided. But
he is not simply being obtuse. True, even twenty years later, as set
out in *The Ascending Effort*, his aesthetic system had a good many
holes in it, and though he was capable of offering perceptive criticism of particular works, the range of his reading and the number of
works that interested him deeply seem to have been relatively small.
But if in his late twenties he did not have a comprehensive view of
art, he was also unable to accord it the automatic veneration that
serves chiefly to fatten the egos of persons who have committed
themselves to dealings with it. He kept his gaze steadily upon the
quality of the encounter of the individual with the work of art, and
he was alert to possible ironies, such as when 'The other day I read
. . . a piece of poetry by Robert Bridges, on "Snow". Very nice: still,
how absurd, to be *reading* about snow, when, outside was snow in
plenty, and I could have my own impressions at first hand.' And in
the same year, apropos of how 'to a large extent modern taste in art
is born of a timorous purism', he complained that art,

divorced from passion, becomes feeble and anaemic, unattractive and
unreal. Perhaps it was this that made it so distasteful to Carlyle, and that
causes the Philistine to stand aloof. He feels, it may be, that such Art has
nothing to do with life, but is a digression rather. A Culture to be generally
appreciated must be one that will take the whole of Existence and improve
it.

Sturt would eventually provide in *The Ascending Effort*, for all the
serious faults of that book, a surprisingly tenable defence of art
along the lines of that last sentence, just as he succeeded in 1892, in a

quasi-existentialist 'leap', in resolving his questionings about the purpose of living, thereby releasing his energies for more productive thinking and writing. What concerns me here, however, is how he came to write about labouring people in particular.

In 1896, apropos of a pamphlet by Shaw that he had been reading, he observed that 'I can't help thinking that the respectable Philistine, thinking so much less than Shaw and drinking so much more, has the firmer grasp on existence and may be, in his unconsciousness, moving towards something better than thought grown morbidly restless.' He himself was in an unusually favourable position to appreciate the qualities of ordinary people. For all his complaints in the early pages of his journal about the demands that his business made on his limited energies ('a thorough nuisance to me: – nothing but a long disgust', he called it in 1891), he had benefited greatly from it as a social observer. His relations with his men, as *The Wheelwright's Shop* abundantly shows, gave him a rich education in the intricacies of a craft. The work that his business did was unquestionably useful and respected, and was carried on in a still fairly uncommercialized spirit. And he was able to treat with the farmers, tradesmen, and other clients whose needs he got to know personally as a social equal. In other words, for an intellectual involved in the 'real' world, Sturt was in an oasis of calm and decency. He wasn't an underpaid clerk, or a hack journalist, or any of the various other disagreeable things that sensitive contemporaries of his were obliged to be; and he didn't have to live in the London that bore down so hard on people like George Gissing's Edward Reardon and E. M. Forster's archetypically sensitive and ineffectual Leonard Bast. In consequence it was easier for him to look at the doings of unintellectual people around him without in self-defence seeing them simply as embodiments of undesirable social traits. When a couple of his farmer customers tried to beat him down in price, he was able to record how 'The meanness of the men made me angry in thinking of it: and I fancy they would only behave so to one they looked upon as a simpleton... Yet I cannot despise them: men of considerable parts, and a strength of purpose far greater than I can boast... They are not better than I, nor worse; but different.' And in a similar spirit he wrote of a pedlar who had probably been in and out of jail, 'He has learnt his way to live, as I mine. If he likes that way, can I say he is wrong, even though I might endeavour to baulk him if he crossed *my* way?' Neither better nor worse, but different – here, I think, we are very near the centre of his own approach to the labouring class.

The general movement of Sturt's thinking as I have described it was away from rigid divisions, and especially the divisions resulting from claims to superiority based on ostentatious dealings with art and culture – claims that could no doubt have permitted cultured middle-class persons to look down on Sturt himself as a provincial tradesman. 'These highnesses and lownesses are so superficial', he wrote in 1890 of contemporary soulfulness, 'and yet we make so much of them. It would matter less, if we always accepted, and never overlooked, the broad base of common humanity.' And quite early on he was glimpsing in labouring people what, in a different connection, he called 'something with emotional force in it: alive, pushful, quickening to the pulses'.[10] In 1891, for instance, he struck a characteristic note when he said of the family of one of his workmen:

Many little children: two quite small boys being the cheekiest daringest youngsters I ever *did* see: I should suppose, quite unmanageable. Rare stuff – plucky, strong, handy, and self-reliant – in all those boys. Easily got at, too, and developed, if there were any 'enterprise'. But English enterprise looks for wealth in Central Africa, or down in coal mines: and is a black unsatisfactory poverty-stricken enterprise after all.

And his journals soon began to include accounts of his conversations with Freddy Grover (or to give him his literary name, Bettesworth), the old villager who worked in Sturt's garden. Though at first, as he acknowledged in *The Bettesworth Book*, it was the 'quiet humour' and 'unconscious oddity' of the conversations that attracted him,[11] they obviously quickly became charged with more significance for him. His first journal entry in 1890 had begun, 'Those who have read Thoreau's "Walden" will remember his friend the Canadian wood-chopper, – "a Homeric man"', and had gone on to note how 'To the self-conscious Thoreau, taking the mastery of his own life, consciously choosing at every step, this man, Homeric, and as it were at the other end of civilization, affords a strange contrast.'[12] In Bettesworth – a 'common labourer' almost wholly ignorant of current affairs – Sturt himself had discovered someone as interesting and as worthy of his respect as Thoreau's wood-chopper or the heavily dramatized figures of Mulvaney and Co. that Kipling (a recurring name in the journals) was celebrating during those imperialist years. And as his esteem for Bettesworth as a representative labouring man increased, so did his voiced dislike of the condescending attitudes of well-to-do middle-class people, especially 'refined' ones, towards the villagers.

Yet a perception of the common – or uncommon – humanity of particular labouring people, and indignation at the arrogant assumption by the well-to-do of superiority to them and of the right to exploit or 'improve' them, need not by themselves result in a particular kind of literary treatment of labourers, or even any treatment of them at all. Sturt's first book, after all, was a novel, and we know from Bennett that he wrote at least one other. There are clues enough, however, to why he abandoned fiction in favour of the kind of writing to be found in *The Bettesworth Book* and its successors. To say that he had no talent for fiction-writing and that he recognized it would be over-simple. *A Year's Exile* (1898) is a very bad novel, certainly. The prose in which Sturt establishes characters and settings and narrates the quieter portions of the action is painfully thin, and when he tries to intensify the action and deal with stronger feelings, he is capable of iniquities like, 'He thought of Edith's foot; it had once made him think of marrying her!... "The little empty-headed flirt", he muttered, calling the pavement's attention to his sentence on her with a vicious blow.'[13] Yet there is truth in the judgement by the *Academy*'s reviewer (internal evidence suggests it was Bennett) that

in spite of its unobtrusiveness and quietude, this book is, in fact, an ambitious one, in that the author has tried to disclose much more of the baffling subtlety of life than the usual novelist cares to attempt. His success has not been complete ... but it is sufficient and striking enough to arouse a sincere interest in Mr. Bourne's future.[14]

The book is concerned with testing out, by means of rather intelligent plotting, the conflicting claims of fin de siècle aestheticism and the moral life, and shows a considerable awareness of complexities, the issues being, most of them, ones that had been making their appearance in Sturt's journal during the decade and were clearly of deep personal importance to him. Resolving them in the novel must have done a good deal to strengthen his assurance that his own low-keyed mode of life away from the London literary scene was the right one for him. And even the pervasive weakness of the prose, while it drains the book of life and forces the reader's attention too much upon the ideas, could have served, paradoxically, to justify the

Academy reviewer's 'sincere interest in Mr. Bourne's future'. Sturt is so bad even when dealing with a subject that he knows intimately – when he introduces a labouring man, it is a perfectly stock type, a sentimentalized, sermonizing old shepherd who would fit comfortably into any Merrie England book – and so incapable of doing things that his journals show him perfectly able to do, such as describing people's physical appearances effectively, that it is evident that his mind had suffered a kind of cramp from the awareness that he was Writing a Novel. That sort of difficulty can be overcome with experience, and there seems no reason why Sturt could have not become a competent, if very minor, novelist had he really wanted to.

The truth is, however, that he was not really interested in fiction-writing, and for intelligent reasons. In 1899, after *A Year's Exile* had come out, he had this to say in his journal:

In the night I was trying to discover some notion that might be worked up into a novel, when I shall again have time. But none came. All the ideas I could get were variations on the old themes, and all very mechanical. I wondered, 'Shall I ever write another novel?'

Then it occurred to me that I was going to work in a wrong way. I was not – and am habitually not – interested in these conventional motives for a book: the stories of love ending happily or unhappily. In the actual world this sort of thing is seldom observable; and when I am told of an engagement or a marriage, the news never excites me in the smallest degree. And yet the world is interesting – far more so than any book. What is it that I like to watch? That should be the writer's first question: and his second would be, How am I going to show it to the public? How hold it under the reader's nose so that he cannot fail to get the whiff of life?

And a year earlier, when he returned to an entry which he had interrupted the night before to record some fourteen-hundred words of low-keyed conversation between a village youth and a girl in the lane beside his garden, he had given a strong indication of what he himself most liked to watch:

I find it difficult to resume about Farnham Fair.

Not because I could not go on, exactly where I left off last night, and write the next word, and finish the picture: but because, after that conversation above, my observations appear to have been 'from the outside'. I looked at it as in the Zoo one looks at the animals, knowing nothing of the inner life going on. My description at best could be no more than a mere water-colour; and to write that, now, feels like fidding while Rome is burning.

The kind of inner life that he most wanted lay, of course, in those low-keyed conversations with Freddy Bettesworth that he had been recording in his journal with a similar fidelity.

At the start of the decade, Sturt had noted how, while he was reading Thoreau's *Summer*,

In a moment of impatience, [I] found myself turning the leaves towards the end of the book, as if there something more dramatic might be looked for. But in this scattered record of many seasons, the dramatic and affecting and stimulating has no special place: may occur anywhere, as in life: for it is without system.

The free-associational talk of Bettesworth about a broad variety of rural topics both gave Sturt the subject matter for *The Bettesworth Book* and suggested how to present it. Despite his reference to watching, what Sturt was obviously out to recreate was the experience of *listening* to someone – listening with the attentiveness that comes when 'the dramatic and affecting and stimulating ... may occur anywhere'. And the rhetoric of the book was designed to ensure that the reader obtained as much as possible of the whiff of life. The absence of the customary Merrie England information about Sturt's own background, his house and garden, and the village, like his explicit refusal to provide a detailed physical description of Bettesworth, helped to prevent middle-class readers from visualizing the relationship in familiar terms of more or less well-dressed employer and rough-hewn garrulous rustic, rather than of two interacting consciousnesses. The introductory and transitional information that Sturt did provide anticipated some of the other instinctive reactions of middle-class readers and pointed them towards the more novel interest that Bettesworth afforded. And the deceptive casualness of the chapter organization left the reader free over substantial stretches to piece things together on his own with a proprietory sense of discovery. Such books can be unsuspectedly influential.

Modest as *The Bettesworth Book* might look, Sturt had in fact succeeded in capturing in it the vitality and strength that he had spoken of a decade earlier. For the first time a labouring man had been allowed to speak at length for himself about the things that interested him most, instead of being subordinated to the demands of a plot or an economic or political thesis. And the effect was to bring the reader into touch with a vigorous and intelligent mind that

might be very different from his own but which he could not easily
patronize, and which in some respects – its versatility, its curiosity,
its independence, its sense of the livingness of the living things
around it – he might very well envy. As Bennett (I take the anonymous reviewer to be he) remarked, Bettesworth was 'a model whom
in many respects the learned, the superior, the elegant, and the wise
of this world might imitate with advantage'.[15] Six years later, in
Memoirs of a Surrey Labourer, Sturt would deepen and enrich the
relationship as he quoted from his subsequent journals, elaborated
on the quotations, and in a sustained exercise in sincerity felt his
way back into the painful and problematic years of Bettesworth's
decline, increasing dependency, and death. And five years after that,
in *Change in the Village* he would engage much more extensively in
the imaginative self-projection into others' experiences that was one
of his most distinctive strengths as a writer.

'It is so many years before one can believe enough in what one
feels even to know what the feeling is', Sturt's near-coeval W. B.
Yeats – another survivor of the nineties – remarked in 1914 in the
first of his autobiographies.[16] As his journals show, Sturt did indeed
have a strong sense of what he felt. But he was almost forty when
The Bettesworth Book appeared, and it was not until *Change in the
Village* that he reached his full stride. What has interested me in
these pages is how he managed increasingly to externalize his preoccupations so that even when he was talking about matters at a large
remove from the normal interests of literary men, he was still
exploring zones of feeling that concerned him intimately – and was
all the more effective thereby as a social commentator. In this
respect there is one last feature of *The Bettesworth Book* that I
would like to mention, and which obviously derived from his own
experience of craftsmanship as described in *The Wheelwright's
Shop* and from that feeling of his for the craft of writing that so
impressed Bennett. What made *The Bettesworth Book* so influential
where thinking about class was concerned was that Bettesworth was
presented in it as not only an interesting man but a *professional* one,
someone who was totally competent in his work and who could be
most fully and satisfyingly himself by giving himself up to it. It was
this that placed him on a level with the heroic military and civil professionals who were being held up by Kipling to the middle class as
embodiments of its finer aspirations. And the book pointed forward
to the explorations made by Sturt himself in *Change in the Village*,

with its demonstration that there was not one culture that trickled down and civilized people, but various cultures, each with its own satisfactions, skills, and strengths. At the outset of this essay I questioned the assumption that Sturt was essentially a purveyor of rural nostalgia. I suggest that what in fact he was doing in those pre-war years was transposing class problems from economic and political terms into cultural ones, and doing so with a thitherto unmatched concreteness – the concreteness of art.

Atget and the City

Between the 1890s, when he turned to photography for a living, and his death in 1927, Eugène Atget made literally thousands of photographs of Paris and its environs. He was one of the supreme twentieth-century artists in any visual medium, he was one of the most heroic, and the image of him going out year after year under the 'dreadful weight' of his old-fashioned camera, wooden tripod, and glass photographic plates[1] is as compelling to the imagination, and deserves to be as well-known, as those of Van Gogh and Cézanne in the grip of their comparable obsessions with locales. Of the results of his passion, Miss Berenice Abbott, the preserver of many of his pictures, his most helpful commentator, and one of his best editors, has finely said:

The pictures ... are deposited layer upon layer on the consciousness. The final total is similar to the vast range of Balzac's human comedy, where his hundreds of characters move in and out of complicated relations and the specific action or event described is richer because the reader remembers actions and events in which these men and women participated. Only with Atget's photographs, the direct sight is at last seen, in intimate impact with a city, a civilization with its amplifications, an epoch of history.
   Atget's realm of creative effort was not, however, the human comedy or the human tragedy, but the miracle of the city he loved beyond words.[2]

His oeuvre brings to mind Baudelaire's statement, apropos of 'the epic side of modern life', that 'The life of our city is rich in poetic and marvellous subjects. We are enveloped and steeped as though in an atmosphere of the marvellous; but we do not notice it.'[3] And it richly displays certain relationships between 'form' and 'life', especially where the heroic and the pastoral are concerned. In all these respects it is of special interest to the student of literature as well as to the *aficionado* of photography.
   For all the breadth of his subject matter, however, it is plain that Atget was not equally interested in everything – interested creatively, I mean. On the whole his photographs of public buildings

such as churches seem unremarkable aesthetically; so do those of upper-class exteriors and interiors; so do those of unrelievedly squalid scenes without people in them; so do those of towns outside Paris; so do those of architectural details; and so do those of groups of people in the Paris streets taken in candid-camera fashion unawares. They have their own kinds of interest, of course, both as historical documents and as examples of Atget's unselfconscious professionalism in gaining a living from clients who had no interest in photography as an art. Furthermore, Atget took some very distinguished pictures of almost all the subjects mentioned in this essay so far. Nevertheless, when we go by the degree of originality, iconographical richness, and formal brilliance displayed, his finest pictures fall preponderantly into the following main groups: pictures of unpeopled or virtually unpeopled Paris streets, *quais*, and courtyards; pictures of commercial establishments; pictures of stationary vehicles; pictures of the great public gardens and parks; pictures of trees and flowers in close-up; pictures of *petit-bourgeois* interiors; and pictures of working men and women posing for their portraits in the streets in the course of their work. Furthermore, there seem to me to be some definite relationships between those groups. I propose to concentrate on those groups and those relationships with a view to establishing certain cardinal points in Atget's vision of the city.

I

That the less well-to-do areas in the city should have been the more inspiring to Atget seems easily enough explainable: the things in them bore far more marks of human use than those in the better neighbourhoods. Yet if the felt presence of the human is an essential feature in Atget's best urban photographs, it is noteworthy that little or no part is played by actual people in many of those pictures, and I think that this paradox gives us a valuable point of entry into his creative intelligence. To explain that absence on technical grounds alone won't do. As Miss Abbott has emphasized, Atget was a professional, and if he persisted throughout his career in using a camera that was cumbersome, obtrusive, and relatively slow, it was plainly not because he couldn't afford one of the smaller and technically much better ones on the market but because it suited his needs very well. And if he did a good deal of his work in the early morning or at other times when empty streets could easily be found, it wasn't because his camera simply couldn't cope with people in motion. It could cope with them surprisingly well, as a number of his pictures testify. I am aware that, given his subject-matter and the need for relatively long exposures, it was in fact more convenient for him to work when few people were around. My point, however, is that we should assume that Atget did exactly what he wanted to do and that it makes no sense to think of 'this man of violent temper and of absolute ideas [who] had all the patience of a saint with his photographing'[4] as chafing for thirty years against the restrictions of an unsuitable camera. A more persuasive argument, accordingly, would be that his dozen or so years as an actor before he took up photography had affected his way of seeing: his pictures do indeed, as Miss Abbott points out, 'repeatedly suggest the stage setting which one beholds after the curtain goes up',[5] and the sense that people will be using the various entrances and properties is a powerful factor in the humanized quality of the scenes. However, I think that the explanation needs to be more complex. If we are intensely conscious of ordinary lives interpenetrating those temporarily empty streets and squares and rooms, I suggest that this is because we are conscious of being there in an ordinary sort of way ourselves. And I suggest too that if Atget engaged only very marginally in the kind of candid work that can be seen in many photographs from the 1890s and early 1900s, this was because what he was involved in seizing was not directly a peopled city but certain basic aspects of the city as they impinged on someone actually living in it in an ordinary daily way.

More specifically, what Atget seems to me to have been fundamentally concerned with was the city as a place in which we move around, consume things, seek mental refreshment, and rest. And from this point of view the candid approach in which other people are caught in more or less interesting action can be irrelevant, or at least very peripheral, the product of a specialized way of looking (partly journalistic, partly derived from artists like Degas and Toulouse-Lautrec) in which the observer has screwed himself up to an abnormal alertness to other people's movements and expressions. Looking on, in other words, has replaced the kind of seeing that accompanies *doing*, and a sense of distance results. When Atget himself, even, takes a candid photograph of a horse-drawn omnibus at rest with two or three men on top, the conductor fiddling with some mechanism, and a bystander lighting a cigarette, our reaction is likely to be, 'Ah, a bit of bygone Paris ... quaintness ... *la belle époque*!', rather than the immediate kinaesthetic sensation that here is an object that we might at any moment climb aboard ourselves or that, like Alfred Stieglitz's superb Fifth Avenue vehicle in a snow storm, might knock us down if we don't step back onto the sidewalk. Normally, however, it is precisely such a sense of the kin-aesthetic and tactile that Atget gives us with unsurpassed brilliance, and especially with regard to the activities I named at the start of this paragraph. Let me give an example.

It isn't, I judge, accidental that one of Atget's best-known pictures should be of a cheap boot or boot-repair store with several rows of boots displayed on shelves outside it. The picture is one of those characteristically subtle ones of his, of which I shall be giving a number of examples, in which the eye is immediately drawn to one feature ('What a funny lot of shiny boots!') but in which all the features interact as natural symbols or epitomizations. The leather of the boots is supple and highly polished, bringing irresistibly into our consciousness the feet walking in them and the hands shining them. Below them are the worn-looking stones of the sidewalk. Resting on that sidewalk side by side at one end of the shelves and reinforcing the sense of muscular effort with hands and feet are a cumbersome pair of wooden clogs and a battered garbage pail with the lid slightly off. At the other end of the shelves is a chair. And glimpsed through the one small window of the store is what is pre-sumably the white-bearded and capped owner of the store quietly eating his lunch. The subtle evocations of movement and rest are so thoroughly and naturally a part of the objects that to introduce the term 'symbol' here at all, with its by now almost inescapable conno-tations of over-ingeniously imposed abstractions, seems like an act of treachery. But the facts are that Atget does again and again work in terms of the juxtapositions of natural symbols and that the total effect in the boots picture is a simultaneous apprehension of the lives of other people animating those boots and thousands of pairs like them, and of our own shod feet upon the sidewalks.

As I said, it is not accidental that a picture so central to the city ex-perience – and especially to the pre-1914 city experience, as Céline's *Death on the Installment Plan* testifies – should have lodged itself in the minds of admirers of Atget, just as it isn't accidental that for a good while Atget should have been represented so exclusively by his urban pictures in brief samplings from his work, even though some of his nature photographs are as great as any we have, not excluding Edward Weston's. There is something peculiarly compelling about Atget's city streets that seems to place the viewer in them almost physically, and I believe that it is intimately related to his technical means. As I suggested, there is every reason to suppose that Atget used the particular camera that he did because it suited him, faults and all; and the most immediately obvious of those faults are the tilting of the ground plane and exaggerated foreshortening that the lens produced. At times the distortion is quite wild; at others it is almost unnoticeable; but it is there to a greater or lesser extent in many of the street scenes that I have looked at, and it seems to me essential to Atget's way of seeing. What he got with it was the sensation of things advancing, receding, and moving to left and right of us in a way kinaesthetically closer to normal seeing than occurs with the so-called normal lenses that most other major photographers have used. I suspect that he received the impulsion towards it from Van Gogh's work, just as he may also have received from Van Gogh the impulsion to document a whole region in depth, a feeling for the rich significance of the everyday, and a tendency to polarize things into either scenes empty of people yet richly redolent of them, or posed studies of representative individuals. But whatever the cause, the effect is a continual vitalization of the walking areas that he presents – those sombre courtyards diminishing sharply away from us, only to open up again with a doorway or staircase or a tunnel-like archway offering a glimpse of sunlit street beyond; those streets narrowing sharply away after their openings have been punched dramatically in façades viewed more or less at right angles, or shooting up or downhill; those interminable *quais*; and most important of all, in a number of pictures, the cobblestones and flagstones themselves whose lines if projected forwards would pass a foot or two *below* our own feet, and hence subliminally draw our attention to them correctively. Furthermore, the users of the streets, too, get vitalized by the lens in a number of important pictures. In one of the best known, in which an itinerant lampshade-seller is posed in the middle of a sloping cobbled street, the surface of the street seems to flow down to and past us, and one of the vendor's professionally indispensable legs, ending in a slipper whose texture contrasts ironically with the hardness of the cobbles, is also elongated towards us, so that the man seems to be half in motion and at work even while standing still. The same effect of movement occurs with the slightly elongated wheels of most of the parked vehicles – cabs, buses, delivery carts, and so on – that Atget photographed in close-up; and a number of those vehicles get further vitalized by seeming to extend out of the frame towards us.

And the centrality of the city streets and of movement on them, thus dramatized, points us straight towards the centre of Atget's apprehension of the city as a whole. It wasn't, I judge, simply a quest for picturesqueness, or a need for well-lit models, or even a professional empathy, that led him to take in the late 1890s a series of pictures of street vendors in his first year or two as a professional photographer (it is one of his greatest series); and it seems to me fitting that the four that have been the most often reproduced should be those of a bakery woman with her cart, the lampshade-seller, an umbrella merchant, and an organ-grinder and his singer – caterers, respectively, to the need for food, light, shelter, and entertainment. I am suggesting that what drew Atget to the vendors in the first place was an intuitive perception of them as agents and embodiments of vital city processes that he was to go steadily deeper into. Human essentials being made available for consumption, waiting to be handled, chosen, used in the public places provided or carried away through the streets into rooms like those into which his camera penetrated – it is the drama of the city's bounty and plenitude that stands out in Atget's finest work, and it is a drama that is at once physical and spiritual. As Mr Arthur D. Trottenberg has well said, 'the bittersweet nostalgia so obvious in the work of ... Atget is not primarily directed to buildings, streets and parks. It is, rather, concerned with the pulsation of life in a city which once had time to nourish its inhabitants in more meaningful relationships than obtain today.'[6] Let me try to define that pulsation.

II

When we turn to Atget after flipping through the pages of pre-1914 illustrated popular journals like the *Strand Magazine* and *L'Illustration*, we realize how little he was concerned with the 'modern' aspects of city life and how wise he was in this, or at least what kinds of oversimplifications he was thereby avoiding. The genuine drama of mechanical speed and force is brilliantly captured in the handful of pre-1914 photographs by J. H. Lartigue; it is genuine, that is, in the sense that the drama is as much that of the glimpsed racing motorists and motor-cyclists as of their vehicles. But the emptiness of a romantic concern with mechanical speed and force by themselves, as displayed notoriously by the Futurists, needs no underlining here; and the way in which the general speeding-up of city rhythms could work on individuals in a fashion very much the reverse of creative and romantic is recorded unforgettably in *Death on the Installment Plan*, that salutary corrective to idealizing the *belle époque*. Furthermore, as soon as the city becomes conceived of in terms of mechanical force and energy, anyone who attempts to reassert 'human' values is liable to fall into one or both of two inadequate antitheses. Either he opposes the natural, simple, and pastoral to the noisily mechanical; or he opposes the heroic and romantic to the sordidly mercantile; and either way he almost inevitably opposes the past to the present. It seems to me that Atget's astonishing poise, his continual voracious interest, curiosity, wholly unsentimental love and respect for so many different forms of existence, his Rembrandtesque ability to treat in exactly the same spirit the conventionally beautiful and conventionally sordid, issued from the fact that in *his* approach to the energies of the city he was able wholly to avoid these dichotomies. A good starting-point is certain pictures in which he himself took explicit cognizance of what may be called the pastoral and heroic ideals.

A number of his photographs of the great formal gardens in and near Paris could be cited, but there is one that seems to me to epitomize almost all of them and to be one of Atget's most glorious masterpieces. It is of an elaborately carved urn at Versailles, taken from slightly below centre and from so close up that the top curve of the rim and the bottom curve of the base are largely cut off. On the side towards the camera the face of a sun-god in strong bas-relief stares out over our heads, framed by twined and leafy stone branches; his hair flames outwards, light-rays stream out beyond it, the face is superhumanly pure, calmly certain of its strength, slightly contemptuous, unpitying. On the right side of the urn, in profile against a blank sky and somewhat below the god, is the head of a ram or goat, with massive horns curving round in an almost complete circle; its slightly demonic, yet likewise wholly self-assured and calm countenance hangs broodingly over the out-of-focus blacks and whites of a formal walk, a fountain basin, the end of a dense row of trees, all in dazzling sunshine. To the left of the urn is the almost total darkness of undifferentiated foliage. In its tension between Apollonian and Dionysiac energies, its celebration of light and its reminder of no less natural darkness, its seizing on energies made all the stronger through art because embodied in cool and orderly forms, and its juxtaposition of, on the one hand, natural things (the trees, I mean) rearranged by art and then overwhelmed by the natural force of light, and, on the other, the symbolical representations of natural things and forces that, in the crispness of the uneroded carvings, appears almost *super*-real, the picture is one of the most brilliant succinct elucidations that we have of the neoclassical ideal – an aristocratic ideal in which the heroic and the pastoral are almost inseparably intertwined. But more than merely something that is past is involved. The urn, the statuary and fountains and ornamental trees in the other photographs, and the great parks themselves, are available still to the ordinary stroller, and not only testify formally to human yearnings for ordered energies and energized calms but also help to promote such yearnings. And not only that: the transforming and shaping power of the photographs themselves serves to recall that there are other ways in which those yearnings can find expression and dissemination. Let me turn back to Atget's photographs of the city.

Where more or less straightforward, untransposed pastoral and heroic forms (often intermixed) are concerned, there is a plethora of examples in Atget's work: classical faces and figures surmount windows and doorways, flowers intertwine in art-nouveau, rococo, and even gothic ornamentation, horses rear up magnificently above rococo circus façades, a deep military drum looms over the doorway of a restaurant, a puppet-show holds children rapt in the Tuileries gardens, and so on. At times, too, Atget calls our attention to straightforward rural forms persisting in the city (an automobile and motor-cycle emphasize by contrast the low-slung rustic-looking architecture of a courtyard), or dramatizes a rural object in such a way as to lend it heroic proportions (wooden ploughs look like field-guns, a timber-waggon takes on an ominously martial air), or shows more or less straightforward yearnings for the rural in the city (a top-hatted cabby, brass-buttons on his top-coat, trousers falling over incongruously heavy plebeian boots, pauses in front of a flower stall). But interesting as a number of these pictures are as testimonials both to the persistence in the city of older forms and to the cravings of ordinary people for reminders of the rural and for more

dramatic and artistic enlargements of their horizons, they seem to
me among Atget's less memorable ones aesthetically. I suggest that
it was when the forms had become the most thoroughly assimilated
into and marked by ordinary lives that Atget's creative energies were
the most fully aroused. And the resulting pictures, both singly and
juxtaposed, can take us a good deal further into Atget's handling of
the commercial.

III

Let me describe, without comment for a moment, two of his finest
pictures of this kind – or, indeed, of any kind. The first is of a corner
of a *petit-bourgeois* or perhaps even working-class room. A small
neat cooking-stove stands on the left, with a metal pot on it and
other utensils hanging tidily from the front. To the right of it is a fireplace with a large mirror over the thick slab-like mantelpiece and a
curtain hanging down over the grate; and it is this right-hand part of
the picture that chiefly interests me, though obviously it would be
less effective without the black and shiny functionalism of the stove
to contrast with it. In the centre of the mantelpiece stands a massive
ornamental vase with a frieze of fruits running round it, and out of it
is growing a plant whose broad leaves stretch almost to the edges of
the mirror. Five more pots and vases, as well as a lamp and what
looks like a figurine, crown the mantelpiece; three of them are orna-
mented with flowers, the fourth with classical figures in bas-relief.
The wallpaper is covered with a floral design, the curtain over the
fireplace with another, and flowers are painted on an ornamental
pot standing on a ledge to the left of the stove. Four pictures are on
the wall. One is a print of fruit lying beside an earthenware crock;
the other three are elegantly framed photographs of, respectively,
two châteaux and the battlements of a castle. This photograph of
Atget's has been reproduced only twice, so far as I know. The other
– a close-up of the front of a secondhand shop – is much better
known. Two trunks stand on top of each other on the left; on the
right two hampers stand on top of each other on a very large trunk;
cascading down between the two blocks and sprinkled over the
right-hand one are at least thirteen ruined top-hats, probably of the
sort worn by cabbies; and behind them in the window, and hanging
outside too, are riding-boots and livery jackets. Reflected in the
window are a high building with lighted windows, and the branches

of a tree. Both pictures seem to me the product of the same vision; and to bring out more clearly what that vision was, I shall turn for a moment to Atget's nature pictures.

When I spoke earlier of Atget's greatness as a nature photographer, it was a particular group of the nature pictures that I had in mind. To be sure, there is a distinguished lyrical charm to a lot of his pictures of the countryside – lanes, fields, woods, lakes, etc. – but the ones in which his genius is the most apparent are the close-ups or near close-ups of individual trees and plants, and what especially characterizes these is their unmatched evocation of natural *energies*. Exposed roots surge down banks towards us; a couple of blossoms, one above the other, are shot from so close that they become mere blurred white contiguous explosions; from a single base among rocks and water four slender trunks sweep outwards and soar lyrically up and out of sight, echoed by a fence of saplings in the background, blurred by light; the massive triple fork of another tree, bark seething in close-up, fills almost a whole frame, rivalling any Abstract Expressionist analogue in force and daring; and there are other pictures almost as fine. Furthermore, just as it is these wholly unprecedented pictures that most immediately display Atget's completely free vision and effortless formal mastery, so too it is in some of them that we are most aware of light as a creative force in his picture-making – blurring, shaping, infiltrating, vitalizing, in ways that once again bring home to us how essential to him were the technical 'imperfections' of his camera. And when we return to the city scenes by way of the two city photographs that I have described, we can see how it is still fundamentally natural energies and processes that are being celebrated there too.

For Atget, there was no intrinsic opposition between the heroic and pastoral on the one hand and the commercial on the other. In the picture of the beflowered room the stress falls entirely on the loving accumulative energy and orderliness of the room's occupant, rather than on any pathos latent in his or her multiplying of artistic windows opening into unavailable modes of existence, or any irony in those windows being so obviously mass-produced and in questionable taste. Atget never concerns himself with 'taste' at all. He is concerned instead with how things *function*, and the objects here are obviously functioning very well in the psychic economy of their owner. In the top-hat picture, likewise, it isn't commercial sordidness that gets emphasized. The counterbalancing of the urban detritus by the reflected aspiring building and tree interlocks with the quasi-organic form (water over rocks) that the detritus itself has assumed, and, when further reinforced by the associations of the trunks and hampers, places the fact of consumption and wearing out in a context of natural and desirable movement and change. Another picture of a store-front is even clearer in its symbolic juxtapositions. A plethora of trunks and suitcases form two intricately arranged mounds on the sidewalk outside the store, the aisle between them being guarded at the store entrance by two top-hatted, elegantly bewhiskered, and very gentlemanly dummies. The sunshine warms them, just as it warms the four pieces of clothing swinging from hooks on the small awning over them, and picks out casually a couple of groups of hanging trumpets and a drum; but behind them there is darkness. Oblivious to all the invitations to voyaging and masculine gesturing, the aproned store-woman, hardly noticeable at first, sits bent over her sewing in front of the jauntier of the two dummies, while above the awning the second storey is reassuringly firm and domestic in the sunlight.

Journeyings and rest, the placid and the martial, a calm explicitness and an evocative chiaroscuro – these are obvious enough. My chief point, though, is that what the picture as a whole embodies is the drama of commercial distribution and consumption, with the eye-catching variety of goods making possible a variety of important and natural human activities. Viewed in this light, neither the provenance of those goods nor their transmission (however 'humble' the trades-person engaged in it) is ignoble. And the intermingled heroic and pastoral aspects of the commercial are even more apparent in certain pictures in which traditional symbols and icons are absent altogether. At least three of Atget's photographs of foodstuffs on display – respectively vegetables, poultry, and seafood – are characterized by an energy and drama almost as great as in the nature pictures that I have mentioned. And there are a couple of unpeopled café pictures, one interior, one exterior, all radiant with early morning sunshine yet welcoming with coolness too, which in their calm splendour bring to mind alike the more lyrical rural panoramas and the loveliest shots of the great formal gardens. Furthermore, in their structures, materials, and neat rows of identical forms both places are replete with intimations of the new technological forces that have produced them, without being in the least degraded thereby. And the crisp white lettering of the names of

Bass Extra Stout, Dewar's White Label, and other delicacies on the windows of the exterior scene is an important part of the charm, as is the commercial iconography in various other pictures.

All this bears on Atget's handling of people.

IV

Replete with life and promises as a lot of the city locales are, it is obvious how, with a slight shift of vision and emphasis, some of them could become oppressive and anti-human; and some of Atget's pictures of people or their surrogates seem to touch on this possibility. It is especially tempting to take a tip from those haunting images of store mannequins that caught the eyes of the Surrealists and were among the earliest of Atget's works to be reproduced. There is, for instance, the famous single figure displaying work-clothes between cases of cheap shirts and dental items – headless, handless, its sleeves hanging down limply, its feet mere shiny black wood and turned in upon each other in a slightly crippled-looking way, its waist cinched in tight by a very wide leather and canvas belt reminiscent of strait-jackets, its neck circled incongruously by a stiff collar. Or there is the equally well-known one of the better-class store window in which three impeccably dressed male mannequins in the upper half of the picture have been dissolved among the reflections on the window into little more than disturbingly individual faces (hopeful, sly, pensive), while below and in front of them bulk, successively, a much more solid *headless* figure and a row of neatly draped and labelled striped trousers running the width of the picture. Or there are the slightly inane bewigged female faces lost among the shadows and reflections in the windows of a coiffeur, or the menacing row of headless, white-jacketed figures, with a headless waiter in the centre, massed against the spectator, or the rigidly corsetted hour-glass-shaped busts in another well-known picture. In other words, there would seem to be intimations enough in Atget's work of the fact that heroic city formalism and artifice, if they enlarge existence, can also lead to their own kinds of entrapment, constriction, and dehumanization.

And where photographs of actual people are concerned, the ones of prostitutes would seem to contain some especially sharp and ironical juxtapositions. A gleaming handsome house-front, its lower-storey windows all leaded stained-glass squares, its street number enormous between the two upper-storey windows, runs the whole width of a frame, and it is only after a minute or two that the mind registers that the small figure in the doorway to the far left is wearing a thigh-length white dress and little-girl white socks, that she is in fact no little girl at all, and that another woman, presumably the madam, is leaning casually on the balustrade of the window above her. In another picture an elegantly dressed woman sits meditatively on a chair in a corner of a slum courtyard; heavy flagstones are under foot, the doorway to her left in the grimy walls is black and sinister, bars stand in front of the tiny glimpse of sky in the extreme top left corner. In a third, and one of Atget's finest, the juxtaposition of elegance and the tarnished is reversed again. The fifteen feet or so of windowless façade that occupies most of the frame consists of dark, massive, classical wooden panelling, with a portico over the high central doorway; the kerbstones and cobblestones that occupy the rest of the frame are massive too, the overall impression of strength in the *things* in the picture being intensified by the sharp oblique sunlight and a considerable lens distortion; and posed in the middle of the doorway is the only object with soft outlines, the slightly diffident figure of a prostitute in knee-length white dress and worn-looking boots over little-girl socks. Her hair is frizzled, her mouth seems painted askew, her nose (but this may be a distorting effect of the sunlight) looks as if it had been broken and slightly flattened, a worn-looking fox fur hangs round her neck, its strangely animated head resting on her forearms. This is the picture to which Atget gave the expressive title 'Versailles'.

Yet it is still the balancing of forces that must be insisted on. Miss Abbott seems to me quite right when she says that 'the material presentment of life so entranced [Atget] that he did not enter into satire or social criticism. He had a task large enough to re-create the whole visual world of Paris in photographs.'[7] And in his treatment of people Atget is no more a social critic than was Rembrandt. Even in the pictures that I have described there are other elements that must not be overlooked. In the picture of the male mannequins, for instance, the peculiar richness and fascination derive from the dominant sense of *life* in it. If there are solid and rather inhuman-looking trousers at the bottom of the frame, at the top and overlaying the mannequins are the hardly less solid-looking reflections of the sky, a tree, a street front dominated by a neo-classical building; and if two of the faces have the slightly suspect, smiling

painted animation of early-1920s movie heroes, the third, turned
away from them, is sensitive, meditative, wholly natural and individual. Again, in the corset picture a corset on a bust hanging in the
doorway (animated associatively by a blurred garment swinging
free below it that sets the key of the whole picture) opens down-
wards like the bell of a strange flower, while empty corsets in a row
at the bottom of the picture are spread out like seaweed or polyps,
and tightly folded ones in the window to the left of the doorway
seem strange abstract shapes carved in wood or plaster. And in this
world of metamorphoses, its strangeness intensified by the blackness out of which these forms emerge, there is even a sort of dignity
in the poised central bust, while three tiny photographs of fashionable ladies in the window recall that the elegance aspired to is not
necessarily the less real because of the grotesqueness of the means
used to attain it. Again, where the series of prostitutes is concerned,
two more pictures should be mentioned. One is of a couple of figures
posed casually in a doorway, he a youngish soldier in undress
uniform and cap, legs comfortably crossed, hand on hip, face
moustached and good-humoured, she in a short, white, simple
house-dress, the door slightly ajar behind her, a faintly diffident
half-smile on her youngish-looking, unmade-up face. They are completely real and individual beings, posing for the camera in the
course of a normal relationship. So are the three handsome, dark-
haired, middle-aged 'girls' in the second of the two pictures, posed in
a doorway in a comfortably neighbourly fashion like three housewives who have been visiting each other. And even the other
prostitutes and/or madams that I have mentioned have likewise
posed for Atget and been taken in a way that enables them to be
there simply as individuals, not types, viewed without indignation,
contempt, sentimentality, or fuss of any kind.

The same disinterested respect for identities informs Atget's
better-known pictures of individuals in more reputable trades. His
subjects are simply *there*, taken in their professional clothes and for
the most part engaged in the pursuit of their professions, sometimes
smiling, sometimes pensive, occasionally a shade odd (like the little
umbrella-merchant, black-coated and hatted in the hot sunlight) or
even, like one or two of the prostitute/madams, a shade sinister. As
far as the main emphasis goes, these are plainly not people
entrapped and distorted by the city; in Miss Abbott's words,
'human dignity is expressed in each and all' of the pictures.[8] And

two pictures stand out especially in this regard. The first seems to me one of the masterpieces of twentieth-century art, for all its relative simplicity and immediacy of impact. Heavily whiskered, middle-aged, expressionless under a shabby hat, a street musician stares towards the camera from behind a little street-piano. His right hand blurs slightly as he turns the handle, his left hand rests on the other corner of the machine, and against or on that hand rests the hand of his tiny, long-skirted, black-scarved singer, who is gazing upwards, head thrown back, mouth half open as if in song. Their clothes are heavy-looking, redolent of dirt and perspiration; the man is unprepossessing, the woman almost a midget; the positioning of the wheels of the piano emphasizes the travelling they do, the oil-cloth cover on the piano recalls the weathers they face, and the bourgeois façade behind them is not hospitable. Yet the expression of radiant happiness and pride on the woman's face is unequalled by anything that I can recall in art except the closing shot of Marlene Dietrich in Josef von Sternberg's *Scarlet Empress*; and, with the incongruity in ages, yet manifest closeness of the couple, the picture seems to me one of the greatest pictorial images of *love* that we have. The second picture is even more relevant to the essential preoccupations of Atget that I have been trying to trace. A working-girl and a youngish street-vendor or porter are standing talking in a courtyard, taken in profile, he capped and with a basket strapped on his back, another in his hand, she in an ankle-length long-sleeved black dress with a coarse-looking apron over it. (A couple of similarly attired older women look on from the right; it is probably a brief break from work.) The sunlight falls intensely on the scene, blotting out with its brightness most of the lines between the paving stones. The wicker-work of the basket on the man's back and the side of his head are crisp in the light, but shadow hides his eyes and a drooping moustache conceals whatever expression his mouth may have. The girl's brightly lit face is framed against a black doorway in the rear of the courtyard and in contrast with her formal-looking dress is incongruously youthful. The opportunities for irony are obvious, but they are not taken. The two figures stand relaxedly, self-confidently, she a little taller than him but perfectly poised and very feminine, he very masculine, the two of them meeting as individuals and equals – and doing so, obviously, to a considerable extent *because* of the city trades whose ostensibly trammelling insignia they wear. It is appropriate, too, in view of Atget's general emphasis on enlargement, enrichment, and nourishment in the city, that stretching in pleasantly flowery, slightly out-of-focus tall letters across the whole width of the rear wall of the courtyard above the couple's head is the word '*Dégustation*'.

V

Yet distinguished as are Atget's portraits, it is not really paradoxical that his subtlest and richest evocations of individual lives in the city should come by way of studies of the inanimate; I mean, of unpeopled domestic interiors. Such studies are not as common in art as they deserve to be – indeed, there are few of the first order to set beside those of Van Gogh and Bonnard – and a special kind of alertness would seem to be required for them. What has to be sensed by the artist is both the triumph that the domestic mundane can represent, and also a larger cultural dimension. As to the latter, I have touched already, in discussing that much beflowered interior by Atget, on how a room can be simultaneously an expression of its occupants and, by way of the artifacts present in it, a revelation of cultural forces that have helped to make those individuals what they are; and what an alertness to this sort of thing can result in, we have the brilliant photographs of Walker Evans in *The American People*, as well as Atget's own, to remind us. But it is the other aspect that interests me now, the aspect that is missing from that book by Evans.

In Atget's kitchens and bedrooms and dining-rooms, it is the moral beauty and blessedness of *order* that speaks out to us, however humble the objects or incongruous the juxtapositions. The elegant or would-be elegant items inspire us with a sense of their loved meaningfulness and life-enriching qualities for the rooms' inhabitants, the aesthetic incongruities keep before our eyes the individually *made* ideals of domestic harmony and security embodied in those rooms, and the minor untidinesses remind us both of the human tendencies towards chaos that have in fact been held in check here and of the fundamental human activities that the rooms facilitate. And where those activities are concerned, the lovely chiaroscuro effects in a number of pictures are especially charged with significance. In a picture as lovely as a Chardin, light picks out a basket of loaves and groceries in a corner, a dresser-top covered with cooking items, and dishes and folded cloths on a table next to it, in a symbolic juxtaposition of the raw materials, the means of transformation, and the place of consumption. In another, an elegant bed emerges like an island from a darkness that fills almost the whole lower half of the frame and surges part way up the majestically swelling coverlet. In another again, a bourgeois dining-table set for one person blazes out of the semi-darkness and is echoed by a handsome lampshade overhead, embroidered with heroic figures. The whole complex of crisply defined wine-bottles and wicker bread-basket and other 'commonplace' items on the table, awaiting whoever will come through the door in the background, stands there as something which, though transitory and easily disruptible in itself, yet has behind it a whole powerful structure of values and activities making possible civilized decency. And in all of the photographs that I have mentioned in this paragraph is discernible that mingling of heroic and pastoral elements that I have tried to elucidate in this essay. If I am right about Atget's indebtedness to Van Gogh, it is worth remembering that behind the latter stands the whole Low Countries tradition of painting, and that in that painting at its greatest, as in Brueghel and Vermeer and Rembrandt, we see likewise a loving elucidation of the mundane that both brings out its heroic aspects and permits a harmonious fulfilment of the heroic aspirations of the artists. And even if I am wrong about the indebtedness, the parallel still stands.

There is one last picture that I wish to describe, since it can stand as a summation of so much that I have been saying in this essay. It is of the exterior of a rag-picker's shanty on the outskirts of Paris, in one of the poorest of all the areas of the city. The shanty almost certainly consists of only one room and at its peak can be scarcely over eight feet high. Junk leans against one side, the walls are a patchwork of odd-sized planks and bits of canvas, the ground in front, trodden flat, is stony and barren-looking. A folding chair of the sort found in the great public gardens stands in front of the open door, while inside the doorway is discernible a battered, rustic-looking milk can. To judge from the lighting, the square aperture in the front wall of the shanty is the only window, and is probably unglazed. Immediately below that window, however, is a small window-box, and from the front of that box a number of strings run up to the wall above the window. A species of vine climbs up them. Above the level of that window, furthermore, at least twenty toy animals and dolls, salvaged presumably from some nearby dump or collected in the course of the owner's daily scavengings in the city, have been nailed in baroque profusion over the whole façade. Just below the peak of the roof, too, is fastened a large stuffed bird, with one of its spread wings pointing skywards. And on the front edge of the roof itself stand yet more animals, the uppermost one of which likewise gazes skywards. To complete the picture, resting on the surprisingly tidy ground at the corner of the house nearest the camera is a pair of old boots. The picture as a whole is not remarkable formally, but that is beside the point — or rather, in a sense it is very much to the point. The very fact that the dwelling-place itself has been so evolved and organized that no special selecting by the camera is required to bring out its symbolisms makes it an especially valuable — and moving — epitomization of those basic needs and aspirations that, in Atget's vision of it, have gone into the making of the city and in one form or another continue to seek outlets there.[9]

Reflections on the Organic Community

I

At the end of the sixties, my wife and I spent eight months of a sabbatical leave in the much anthropologized community of Tepoztlán, a large village or small town of some five thousand inhabitants in a narrow valley about fifty miles south of Mexico City. There had of course been changes in it since the time of which Stuart Chase was speaking in the passage from *Mexico* (1931) that F. R. Leavis and Denys Thompson quote in *Culture and Environment* ('There is not a bathtub in Tepoztlán, or a telephone, or a radio ... or an electric light, or a spring bed', etc.[1]). A sizeable number of houses now had modern conveniences, in part because of the small colony of outsiders like ourselves, and the village shops were quite well stocked. There were also three or four schools, a modest medical clinic, a football field, half-a-dozen small restaurants, and a rather fancy hotel. (After we left, a municipal auditorium was added, chiefly for showing films in; previously they were projected onto a wall in one of the school-yards, and the audience sat on the ground.) And the city of Cuernavaca was less than an hour away by one of the battered green-and-white buses that shuttled back and forth at frequent intervals, while more comfortable ones left every hour or two for Mexico City. Nevertheless, the village still felt surprisingly close to the account of the 'organic community' given by Leavis and Thompson and to the description of Tepoztlán in Robert Redfield's book of that name (1930) to which they refer their readers.

The village was still agricultural, the only obvious mechanical activities being the frequent tinkering with one or another of the saurian-like buses. The plaza, with its modest municipal building, its formal gardens around a bandstand on one side, its arcade on another, its handful of shops and restaurants, was still the focal point of the village, especially during the bi-weekly market with its eighty or more vendors, some of them laying out their wares in the same spots that Redfield had noted forty years before. The hotel and the more expensive houses, built mainly of local stone, did not obtrude themselves. The other houses were still made of raw or stuccoed adobe, with outdoor cooking areas, and trees in their yards, and fowls and pigs roaming loose. The cobbled and steeply sloping streets, while navigable by patiently manoeuvring delivery trucks, were little frequented by automobiles. The women almost all wore dark dresses and shawls, the men sombreros, sandals, and work clothes. Their staple food was still corn, beans, and chili peppers.

Furthermore, the village structures and festivals were still predominantly as Redfield and, following him in *Life in a Mexican Village* (1951), Oscar Lewis had described them. There were still seven *barrios* or neighbourhoods, each with its chapel and elected *mayordomos* and fiestas. On the nights of Christmas week, there were still ritual processions of women and children three times around each chapel, singing the traditional nativity song with candles in their hands, and asking ritually at the door for admittance in remembrance of the nativity story. (The moment at one of the chapels when, at the third asking, the door slowly opened and the two bells exulted overhead is one of the most moving religious occasions that I can recall.) At the three-day fiesta before Lent, masked and costumed figures still danced for hours in the packed plaza. On the eve of All Saints' Day, families still sat outside their doors at candlelit tables with food for the dead, while bonfires burned smokily in the streets. And there were other public displays of one kind or another: a torchlight procession by primary-school children commemorating the founding of their school; funeral processions, accompanied by the village band, going down to the cemetery near the football ground; wedding processions, with an obsessional discharge of hand-held rockets; football games; a small informal rodeo; a spectacular *barrio* display of fireworks on elaborately constructed open-work towers thirty or forty feet high; and no doubt others that we missed.

Undoubtedly I was predisposed to find the village interesting, quite apart from its associations with *Culture and Environment*. The North American city in which I live is one in which it is still safe to walk for exercise, and my neighbourhood has its visual charms, but I can walk for a couple of miles in it without seeing anyone whom I recognize, let alone know to talk to, and without observing anyone engaged visibly in work, or any indications of what individuals live in the houses that I pass. Hence I responded with particular pleasure not only to what I have described but to the topographical richness of Tepoztlán, the variousness of the houses and yards, the constant evidence of work – women in their outdoor kitchens or going to or from the plaza, little girls carrying little pails of ground maize, men with machetes, wandering livestock, and so on – to all the things that made the village feel much larger than the approximately one-and-a-half square miles that it occupied. As George Sturt remarked of the Farnham of the 1860s, 'there was always something going on, something to be noticed'.[2] But it was not merely picturesqueness that made being there so satisfying, and in fact Tepoztlán was not a conventionally ingratiating place. With its Aztec temple twelve hundred feet above it on the spectacular northern wall of the valley, it felt closer in some ways to the sixteenth century than to the twentieth. The people were unsmiling and undemonstrative, even at the fiestas. We heard, convincingly, of several recent killings and attempted killings, among them a paid-for murder by the village milk-seller, a handsome man now back on his horseback rounds after being bought out of prison by his sponsors. And I have no reason to doubt that the village answered to George M. Foster's characterization of peasant communities in general in *Tzintzuntzan: Mexican Peasants in a Changing World* (1967): 'Life in these communities is described [by observers] as marked by suspicion and distrust, inability to co-operate in many kinds of activities, sensitivity to the fear of shame, proneness to criticize and gossip, and a general view of people and the world as potentially dangerous'[3] – features intensified in Tepoztlán by the Mexican tradition of *machismo* analysed so well by Octavio Paz in *The Labyrinth of Solitude* (1950, revised edition 1959).

But the point is that the village manifestly still *was* a community, with its own pace and its own tough identity. And, like the pre-enclosure community sketched by Sturt in *Change in the Village* (1912), it was one in which the stimuli that I have been describing were available to almost everyone. As in most mediaeval European cities, the plaza was no more than ten or fifteen minutes walk from anywhere in the community, and even for someone with only a few centavos to spend on chili peppers, or a couple of pesos for beer, the way to and from it was replete with information-bearing objects and activities: the state of the fruit trees, the coming along of the livestock, the outdoor cooking, the washing, the street-corner loungers, the children. Moreover, while some of the *barrios* were more prosperous than others, even the poorest villagers were not secluded in ghettos of one kind or another, physical or psychological. The structures of their houses and yards were basically the same as those of most of their better-off neighbours; their clothing was the same as most people's; and except at weekends, when there were sometimes noisy influxes of middle-class excursionists from Mexico City, they could feel part of a common culture imposing its own decorum on everyone. Some of the men obviously drank heavily, particularly during the dry season when there was no work in the fields. But I never observed children yelling, fighting, or bullying, or adolescents aggressively affirming their cultural uniqueness, or adults noisily making fools of themselves; and one of the charms of the place was the little girls of the village, gravely walking together in their shawls and obviously relishing the sensation of comporting themselves like their mothers and grandmothers. It was, so far as I could see, a functioning organic community.

II

Nevertheless, I have felt curiously uneasy about giving the account of Tepoztlán that I have, and the reason is more than merely my consciousness of my limitations as a social observer, even when assisted at the time by the works by Redfield and Lewis that I have mentioned, or, later on, by Foster's *Tzintzuntzan* and Erich Fromm and Michael Maccoby's *Social Change in a Mexican Village* (1970), which deals with a community near Tepoztlán. Like the Milton controversy, also so inseparably associated with Leavis, the concept of the organic community is obviously a crux, an area of major value-conflicts. As the reactions to Leavis's *Two Cultures?* (1962) demonstrated, to urge the claims of the organic is to lay oneself open to charges of amateurism and impressionism, of mere subjectivity, of profitless nostalgia, of a major and reactionary misreading of cultural history. And over the years there have been numerous sarcastic allusions to the organic community. It seems worth enquiring into the reasons for these attitudes.

Leavis's own references to the organic community are very few, and no impression can reasonably be derived from his work, let alone from *Scrutiny*, of any belief in a Golden Age of freedom from pain and tragedy and want, or any country-house elitism. On the contrary, the hostility that he aroused over the years was obviously partly due to his forcing readers away from the pleasures of self-forgetfulness in effort-free ideal structures, whether the imagined Edenic bliss that so enchanted C. S. Lewis in *Paradise Lost*, or the idyllic classical world that figures in a good deal of other poetry, or the idealized rural England of the Georgians. And his 'puritanical' promotion of Bunyan and George Eliot and the Lawrence of *The Rainbow* was a challenge to the myth-making efforts of the over-class to pre-empt rural culture for itself after defining culture in its own terms. Nor does the work of Sturt leave us in any doubt as to the harshness of rural life and work, present or past. There is plenty about that harshness in the first third of *Change in the Village*, for example, and *Memoirs of a Surrey Labourer* (1907) is a detailed and painful chronicling of the passage of a particular old labouring man towards death. Furthermore, in his pre-1914 works as a whole Sturt was thoroughly *engagé*, attacking the cultural stereotypes that permitted the over-class a comfortable sense of moral superiority to the under-class and a complacent belief in their mission to improve the under-class by replacing its cultural patterns with their own. His pioneering use of participant observation and its related rhetoric, and his concern with labouring-class culture *as* a culture, were almost certainly known to Redfield – who later described *Change in the Village* respectfully in *The Little Community* (1955) – when he made what a confrère called his 'epoch-making' study of Tepoztlán. And Redfield has been a key figure in recent sociological thinking about the peasantry, concerning which the editors of *Peasant Society: a Reader* (1967) observe: 'The formal study of peasants in a nonhistorical, noneconomic context is very recent, going back scarcely twenty years.'[4]

Nevertheless, it is not really hard to see how the weekend-review oversimplifications came about. *Culture and Environment* was avowedly a work of counterpropaganda, one of the most influential such works of our time. Its authors were concerned to counter the insistence of advertising men, industrial magnates, and press lords (assisted by primitive behavioural psychologists) that post-1918 capitalism was a cornucopia that would shower down happiness on all if they would only enlarge their wants, increase their consumption, and applaud an all-out market-place competitiveness. And in their effort to define the gratifications of a very different mode and vision of life, the use that Leavis and Thompson made of Sturt was brilliantly selective.

If my own experience is anything to go by, reading the passages that they quoted, and reading Sturt himself in the light of those passages (with an almost inevitable filtering-out of the less glamorous two-thirds of *Change in the Village*), could cast something very like a spell. Sturt's references to 'the zest and fascination of living ... with the senses alert, the tastes awake, and manifold sights and sounds appealing to [one's] happy recognition', or to 'that satisfaction which of old – until machinery made drudges of them – streamed into their [i.e. his wheelwrights'] muscles all day long from close contact with iron, timber, clay, wind and wave, horse-strength', or the fact that 'it is doubtful if the working hours afford, to nine out of ten modern and even "educated" men, such a constant refreshment of acceptable incidents as Turner's hours bring to him'[5] – passages like these impressed themselves indelibly on the young imagination, for fairly obvious reasons. To be able to lose oneself completely in one's work and be all the more sensorily alive thereby; to engage daily in activities that were never routine, the hours never divided up into mechanical reiterations; to live in an environment that was known and secure, but always informed by small and interesting variations; to experience no sharp distinctions between what one did under compulsion and what one did for pleasure; not to be separated from other people by absolute gulfs, especially those of social superiors and inferiors; to be able to acquire unhurriedly and surely the skills needed for successful adulthood, free of the goadings of competition, and to be in an essentially collaborative relationship with one's peers – what was all this but an enviable continuation of childhood well-being and contentment into adult working life? And the spell was all the more powerful because the states of mind described were located not in a semi-classical landscape but in particular working men and women less than forty miles from London.

On the face of things, therefore, the anti-organic scepticism and sniping might appear to be simply the consequences of maturity, of the kind of adult common sense displayed by Yvor Winters when he observes tartly about the final stanza of Yeats' 'Among School Children': 'The term *labour* seems to mean fruitful labor or ideal labor, and a labor which costs no effort. But where does this labor exist, except, perhaps, in the life of a tree?'[6] Lovely as Marvell's garden may be, it must be forsaken in the end for 'the busie company of men'; Lawrence's Cossethay may be a warm centre of life for the growing Brangwens, but Ursula must willy-nilly leave it for the larger world; and, as Raymond Williams lets us know in *The Country and the City* (1973), the *laudator temporis acti* should recognize that there have always been praisers of times past and that the conditions that he thinks of as traditional were themselves the results of ongoing social changes. Such corrective admonitions will be all the stronger if underlain by the assumption that communities like Tepoztlán will inevitably go the way of Sturt's pre-enclosure community and other 'primitive' forms of social organization. And insofar as nostalgic responses work against the will to action desiderated by Williams in his closing chapter, they undoubtedly deserve to be scrutinized. However, I think that more complex factors than a straightforward concern with social amelioration may be involved in the recoil from them.

III

At bottom, what gives Sturt's works their unique emotional authority is Sturt's own consciousness – the consciousness of a writer on rural England who, unlike Richard Jefferies, or Lawrence, or George Eliot, remained all his life in one place, and who in his writings was continually trying to recapture and interpret the experience of being there and the ways in which it moulded consciousness, his own and others'. He was not talking about Auburn, or Arcady, or Napoleonic England, or even of mid- or late-nineteenth-century England in general. He was writing specifically of The Bourne, in Surrey, where his cottage and garden still stand – or did, at least, in 1962, when my wife and I visited them – and of Farnham, including the Farnham described in *A Small Boy in the Sixties* (1927), with its bands, its street entertainers, its social clubs in procession, its marching soldiers, its police with their prisoners, its travelling vendors, its town-crier, its livestock being taken to market, and all its other sights and sounds. And as presented in that book, it was his own growing consciousness that was enriched by its continuous exposure to a community in which town and country, home-life and work-life (in the behaviour of his own family) were inseparably interwoven. The organicism of which Sturt speaks was not something set in a remote past. It was something which he himself had experienced in the quiet-paced economy of Farnham and its mid-Victorian rural environs; and had he not had that childhood experience, as well as the intelligence and sensitivity to see it later for what it was, he would not have been able to project himself imaginatively beyond the gardening talk of Bettesworth, and the casual overheard conversations of other villagers, to the lost experiences of an unenclosed community.

But the subject of childhood environments has its emotional pitfalls. There is an obvious fascination about the enriched childhoods that are observable in works like *The Mill on the Floss, Huckleberry Finn, Bevis, To the Lighthouse,* Joyce Cary's *House of Children,* and the children's books of E. Nesbit and Arthur Ransome. The catch, however, as Philip Larkin's 'I Remember, I Remember' testifies ('Nothing, like something, happens anywhere') is that our own childhoods may look increasingly impoverished in comparison. And the more those other childhoods take on the air of being the result not of uniquely favoured circumstances but of more general social conditions, as they do in Sturt, the more we are likely to feel culturally damaged in comparison with our predecessors.

I myself, for example, grew up in the thirties in a suburb on the northern rim of London, and in some ways I was fortunate. Originally a village (there was still a mediaeval parish church, with a pre-Victorian house or two nearby), the suburb had not become fully connected to London until after the First World War, and it was still not entirely overrun. There were two parks, one of them the enchantingly landscaped grounds of a former private house; there was a brook bordering a golf course; there were fields and a Home of Rest for Horses on the far side of the golf course; there were ponds and one or two genuine villages within cycling distance beyond; there was an Express Dairy farm inside the suburb, in which one could watch cows being milked; there were coal-cart horses in their stables down by the station who could be visited on Sundays and fed with sugar lumps. Nevertheless, the suburb was simply not a community in the way in which Sturt's Farnham was. Some of the shops along the main street had their charms – the roasting coffee-beans in the grocer's, the intimate organic odours of the seed shop, the white-tiled coolness of the Express Dairy shop, the Atget-like abundance of the greengrocer's, the sweet–sour pungencies of the wine-merchant's, and so forth. But there was no focal point and no natural meeting spot, and I knew nothing about the people who worked in the shops, and never saw any of them outside the shops. There was no market-place, no square, no free secular assembly building of any kind, nor were there any passing entertainments to bring people together: to see a Punch and Judy show, even, one had to go to Hampstead Heath, and the occasional joyless street musicians were objects of pity to be hurried past rather than gathered round. There were pleasurable activities available to children, of course – tennis, miniature golf, and rough cricket in the larger of the two parks; scrambles and pursuits along the brook; roller-skating in an indoor rink; swimming in the excellent outdoor municipal swimming pool; bicycle rides – and from time to time there were entertaining or improving excursions to town. But increasingly, outside the life of school, it was the three or four cinemas in the area that came to figure for me as the place where the intensest inspectable living by other people was going on.

And now that I look back on it, what strikes me most about the general pattern that I have described is that it was one in which the network of acquaintances and interesting places was almost wholly that of childhood. My parents had a number of friends and acquaintances dispersed around London. But when I think back to our first house I can bring to mind only four other households into which I ever entered in our own street; in our second, three; and altogether I can recall barely a dozen houses which I frequented from time to time in the area, the majority through acquaintances made at school. Even then the visiting was largely only among the children, and I remained ignorant, except in the vaguest terms, of the work done by the commuting fathers, whom in any case I rarely saw. I had almost no experience of a structure of adult relationships, working or social, so that it was to the cinema, and the radio, and boys' weeklies, and *Punch*, and thrillers that I turned for knowledge of adults in action beyond the confines of the unextended family and the brief exchanges of the shops. The only more or less local males with whom I conversed substantially were schoolmasters and my father. (In point of fact, even my school was in another suburb.) And I have no doubt at all that my growing-up, despite the media offerings and the relative nearness of central London, was less rich, less conducive to a stable personality, less able to compensate for dispositional defects, and less furnished with a variety of reasonable patterns for emulation, than that of Sturt. Obviously there were other suburbs worse than the one that I have described. As I said, in

some ways I was fortunate, and my childhood, even though notice-
ably different in my own eyes at the time from those enjoyed by
the Bastables, or the Swallows and Amazons, or even the slightly
off-putting William, was certainly not unhappy. But when I
first read *Culture and Environment* and Sturt, at a time when I
myself was about to enter the working world, I felt its limitations
keenly.

That kind of perception is not only uncomfortable to live with
because of what it suggests about oneself; it also makes for certain
larger problems of social interpretation. Clearly it is simply false
that *plus ça change, plus c'est la même chose*. If complaints about
social changes have always been made, it is because changes have in
fact occurred; and the changes producing the kind of suburban community that I have described were immense. There is nothing
sentimental about pointing out that less than a quarter of Britain's
population lived in urban areas at the start of the nineteenth century
and that three quarters did by the end of it, or that London quad-
rupled in population during that period. And the process of
urbanization, or suburbanization, will obviously continue. At the
same time, however, it is natural not to wish to give way to a neo-
Spenglerian vision of inevitable and irreversible decline in the
quality of consciousness. There is a long tradition of counter arguments on behalf of urban virtues and variousness, and testimony
enough in works like *Madame Bovary, Jude the Obscure, The
House with the Green Shutters*, and *Main Street* to the narrowness
and boredom of rural or small-town life. When Ursula Brangwen
leaves the nest for the broader opportunities elsewhere, we applaud;
and I imagine that most of us understand what Nick Carraway is
talking about in *The Great Gatsby* when he says that 'The city seen
from the Queensboro Bridge is always the city seen for the first time,
in its first wild promise of all the mystery and the beauty of the
world.' It is difficult too, at least for someone of my generation, not
to suspect that urban children today have a good deal more available to them in the way of enriching experiences than was available
forty years ago. And accordingly it can be tempting to assume in a
large, loose way that in the long run every loss has its counterbalancing gain, even if we don't see exactly how, and that it really doesn't
matter whether a community is 'organic' or not. It seems to me desirable, therefore, to be as clear as one can about what one intends
by that term.

IV

The term is indeed susceptible of abuse, just as are ones like 'organic unity' and 'dissociation of sensibility'. The latter terms can seem to point at times not just to the words on the page but to absolute states of consciousness, so that critical reading can come to be a quest for tokens as to whether or not the mind of the artist was in a particular state of grace when the words were set down. And the danger is that once an absolute either/or has been postulated, the analytical mind tends to over-react when things don't fit the pattern and to deny that there are really any sharp differences between anything. But there need be no question of any absolute breaks and divisions. The fact that seemingly formless works like *Women in Love* and *Moby Dick* possess a good deal of *sui generis* order is demonstrable, as is the fact that Shakespeare's and Donne's and Jonson's *oeuvres* are different in a number of definable ways from those of Waller and Dryden and Swift. And so is the fact that communities like Sturt's Farnham or Tepoztlán are very different from that in which I myself grew up. The term 'organic community' as used by Leavis and Thompson seems to me quite adequately defined by the examples of various modes of social behaviour given throughout *Culture and Environment*. And the cultural continuity from generation to generation, the common structure of values, the centrality of unmediated talk, the intimate functional relationships with the surrounding country-side, the craft skills, the largely subsistence economy, the absence of any strong competitiveness and ostentatious acquisitiveness, the lack of sharp class divisions – what are all these but features of what Redfield calls the Little Community, 'the very predominant form of human living throughout the history of mankind'?[7] To say that is not to postulate any state of prelapsarian bliss, nor is it to set up any mystical either/or in which, as with virginity, a community is either organic or it isn't. There is obviously a considerable distance between, say, Tepoztlán, Sturt's Farnham, and the Hindu village described in G. Morris Carstair's *The Twice-Born* (1961) on the one hand, and communities like those explored in E. E. Evans-Pritchard's *The Nuer* (1940), George Grinnell's *The Cheyenne Indians* (1923), Richard A. Gould's *Yiwara: Foragers of the Australian Desert* (1969), and Elizabeth Marshall Thomas's beautiful book on the Bushmen, *The Harmless People* (1969), on the other.

And to concern oneself in a *Culture and Environment* fashion with rural communities need not be in the least sentimental, or involve any stultifying contrasting of Edenic ideals and barren actualities. On the contrary, such a concern can be empirical in ways directly relevant to social action. It often seems to be assumed by spokesmen for 'progress' that the relationships between the industrial and the pre-industrial periods is similar to that between historical and pre-historical periods, the latter much larger quantitatively but qualitatively so thin as to be irrelevant. (It is almost as if the future already massively existed, authenticating present changes.) But the structures of villages and small towns everywhere until the nineteenth century were the result of thousands of years of evolution and, in a sense, experimentation in social living, and well over half the population of the world still lives in such communities. Moreover, until the nineteenth century the structures of the great majority of cities were organically related to those of the smaller communities in their regions, being larger and denser but not essentially different in kind. And small communities, when pondered rightly in relation to larger ones, can assist us to define certain patterns of enrichment and test the latter in relation to them. As Leavis and Thompson observe, 'It is important to insist on what has been lost lest it should be forgotten; for the memory of the old order must be the chief incitement towards a new, if ever we are to have one.'[8]

V

Let me turn for illustration to a less exotic community than Tepoztlán. In 1964 and 1966, my wife and I spent the three summer months in a hill village of about four hundred inhabitants, some twenty-five miles from Aix-en-Provence and forty from Marseilles. The sides of the hill and the fields in the surrounding valley were planted with grape vines, olive trees, and fruit trees, with space on the top of the hill behind the village for threshing, the grazing of tethered animals, the growing of small crops, and a lovingly tended walled cemetery dominated by several magnificent cypresses. The fields were unenclosed, and in our landlord's apartment in Aix a framed map showed his family property scattered around like the holdings in those diagrams of the pre-enclosure English village that I used to draw in school. There were no priests, no big farmers, no gentry. There was an elected village council and a mayor; the village

winery was operated collectively; the village café was owned by a
social club called Le Cercle des Ouvriers; and the only paper available in the tobacco shop was the *Marseillaise*, the regional Leftist
paper. There was a well-stocked general store and a small butcher's,
with weekly visits by a fish-merchant and a vegetable merchant, and
periodic visits by sellers of clothing, household utensils, fabrics, and
so on, who set up their stalls in the village square. Housewives who
had other needs, or who wanted variety, could take the small bus
run by the village entrepreneur and go to the nearby town of about
twenty-five hundred inhabitants, which had more shops and in
which twice a week there was a substantial market under the plane
trees. During the two summers that we were there, the village was
also visited by a couple of circuses, one of them prosperous enough
to be able to set up a tent on the hilltop, the other a family affair of
father, mother, two acrobatic children, and some performing dogs
and goats, who put on their show in the village square. In the
autumn, there was a village fête, with dancing, *boule* competitions,
and the like. There were no obvious signs of poverty in the village,
and no displays of wealth; our next-door neighbour, for example,
composedly drove a thirty-year-old car, one of the few cars in the
village.

I remained to the end largely ignorant of matters like family relationships, demographic patterns, the status-and-power structures
of the village, the village feuds, and such less tangible things as the
operative value-system, the modes of socializing the young, and the
degree of nonconformity that could be indulged in without risk. But
the house that we occupied in the village square belonged to a son of
the village, now high up in the regional judiciary but proud of his
village and generously concerned that we should be happy there,
who introduced us to several neighbours; so that it was easier to
chat with people than it might otherwise have been. And when a few
years later I read Laurence Wylie's classic *Village in the Vaucluse*
(1957, revised edition 1964), with its obviously sensitive and
thorough examination of a village less than sixty miles from ours, I
found abundant professional corroboration of what I had glimpsed
and sensed. There were no doubt tensions, antagonisms, rivalries,
exclusions, and unhappinesses of various kinds. The Italian couple
who managed the café during our first year there, for example, were
apparently treated rather badly and forced to leave. But the kinds of
friction that Wylie uncovered in his own village were no more than

could be expected in any reasonably complex social structure involving strongly individuated personalities. And the ways in which, in his account, conflicts were conducted and resolved were clearly a part of the whole system of sober pressures, adaptations, compromises, and general common sense and civilized decency that were also at work in the upbringing and education of children. It is probable that our village was more turbulent during the grape harvesting, when there was a large influx of migrant Spanish workers hired for the occasion. (The year after we left, for example, a Spaniard committed one of the village's extremely rare murders, a crime of passion.) But my point is not that it was normally characterized by an Edenic beatitude, a smiling love-in fraternalism. Rather, it is that the village was probably as near to providing a stable, ordered, decent, interesting, and civilized way of life for the great majority of its inhabitants as it seems reasonable to hope for of any community.

Set on its hilltop, the village had its own clear shape and sheltering identity, away from any worry of traffic, but with the kind of overview of its surroundings that enabled people to feel in touch with things several miles away – on one side the market town and national highway, on another the scrub-covered hills in which the wild boars were hunted in winter by the village hunting club, on another the route to the northeast, deeper into the interior among the observed valleys and receding hills. The physical structure of the village was varied, falling into at least three main areas, each with its own character. For the men, as in Sturt's postulated community, the day's work, done mostly on land of their own and at their own pace, was in a humanized landscape that was always changing with the seasons and always there to be noted on their journeyings up and down and around the hill, each part of the landscape with its own function and charged with human meanings. And back in the village there were available to them the various kinds of socializing and co-operation of the winery, the café, the hunting club, and, for some of them, village politics. For the women, there were the opportunities for informal daily meetings provided by the local stores, the visiting merchants, the bus trips. For adolescents, outside of their school life and the daily bus trip to the secondary school (the primary school was in the village square), there was the square for *boule*, the cinema in the market town, the television set in the café, and at times, presumably, the amenities of Aix. In addition the village was linked

with the surrounding region. It was not only this village that had
its annual fête, for example. The other villages had theirs too, as did
the market town (we went to three or four in the area during our
first summer), and they were staggered so as to permit attendance
from the other communities. And no doubt there were other activities. Our village entrepreneur ran periodic bus excursions to the sea,
for instance.

What I have been describing is a fairly conservative structure, a
characteristic structure of the France that achieved zero population
growth in the 1930s, the France of the relative economic domination of the old over the young. And there is obviously a question
as to its stability in relation to the newer, economically expansive,
media-permeated France that gave Paris its high-rises and tore down
Les Halles – a France, moreover, in which Provence has to absorb
enormous numbers of summer holidaymakers (ourselves among
them), and in which Parisians buying summer properties have
increasingly moved inland from the coast. Moreover, the village's
prosperity partly depended on the improved market for low-quality
wine from the region; and its economic base could presumably be
undermined. Not having revisited the village, I cannot report on
how it has fared, though given its co-operative sturdiness and the
power of the French peasant tradition – the sobriety, the hard work,
the scepticism towards large, vague, glittering schemes, the anti-
capitalist bias, the healthy distrust of the government, and the
general unwillingness to be mucked about with – I would think that
its chances were reasonable. But in any event it is the advantages of
its pattern of life that interest me here, and I will briefly sketch a few
more of them.

The intimate relationship between the villagers and their environment made it easier for there to be meaningful conversation and a
sensible self-projection into other psyches because of the common
problems posed by the crops, the weather, and the like. There was a
relatively sophisticated structuring of village life – economic, social,
political – so that the young, growing up there, could observe a
variety of attitudes in action, attitudes embodied in particular individuals instead of existing solely in the abstractions of the media.
There was a considerable – and healthy – density of character.
'Enlightened' people often speak as if the individuation of country-
men, their stubbornness, their ability to carry grudges for years,
their gossiping, were lamentable defects which ought to be

smoothed out; but it seems clear that these usually make life more interesting, giving a content to thought and conversation, a charge of meaning to daily encounters, or to the avoidance of encounters, of a sort impossible to all but a few of the inhabitants of the London suburb that I described. And there were other kinds of rewards in the village. Not only were there the significant repetitions and variations – the seasonal changes in the landscape and in the work done in it, the seasonal entertainments, the various visits of the merchants. There were also important options open to people. Those who wished to live quietly and reservedly could do so, going about their own business, buying their domestic supplies largely in the village, and taking full advantage of the simplified economic transactions of the winery; and those who wished to travel further afield could also do so, having within easy reach the centres of progressively higher energies and variousness represented by the market town, Aix, and Marseilles. But even someone who moved around very little need not be cut off altogether from 'modernity'. There was television in the café (and probably by now in a number of houses), and the cinema in the market town, and the radio; there were the latest dances at the fêtes; there were refrigerators and other electrical appliances in a number of the homes; there was even, albeit unrelated to the village, an excellent annual music festival in the market town, with accompanying cultural doings, such as the admirable free performance of Molière by a touring company that we saw in the town square.

The point is, however, that all these things were available without being intrusive; they were not harsh invading presences, arrogant agents of the new imperial technology and urbanism. And what I have been talking about was not just a single village with sane relationships between energy and quietude, stability and change, the traditional and the new. Growing up in the village, a person was also a part of a coherent region, and the region, while having a healthy tradition of independence going back to the *ancien régime*, was not in the least provincial in the sense of being remote from the advantages of city life or from the possibility of decent educational facilities. No doubt some or even most of the young would eventually leave the village for larger communities, in what is after all a traditional pattern of migration for those for whom there is no land available or who prefer a larger scope for their activities. (Conrad A. Arensberg's *The Irish Countryman* (1937) is of interest in this connection.) But by that time the values of the community and the region would have been internalized in them, and the physical structures themselves would still be there, to be returned to for visits or retained in the memory as models of possibilities and satisfactions. Whether their children and grandchildren would enjoy comparable advantages and view society with a comparable understanding is another matter, of course. And it is here that the attitudes of intellectuals are so important.

VI

What count most, obviously, are the attitudes of people with power, the people who do the economic and social planning and give or withhold permission to make large-scale changes. But an understanding of the qualities making for psychological enrichment or impoverishment in a community is not something that is easy to arrive at, and when intellectuals lose it or fail to acquire it, and cast doubt upon its significance, it is likely that people with power will too. When I look back on my own childhood, for example, I am gratefully aware of circumstances contributing to my own interest, amateur as it is, in a topic like the present one: childhood visits to grandparents living in a Wiltshire village (my grandfather had been the doctor there) in three Tudor cottages on the village square connected together into a house that was a marvel of flow and variety; a father in love with Roman Britain, and historic London, and the great country houses; three years in Oxford. But I misread my own experiences even so, and would almost certainly have continued to do so had I not come finally to *Culture and Environment*; and without that book and the further reading it led me to, I would not have spent two years in Israel in the early fifties and had for the first time the experience of living in a country in which politics, economics, history, and religion were all intelligibly connected with each other and visibly embodied in the landscapes and cityscapes – a country, moreover, that in those days was paying a good deal more than lip service to the idea of becoming a just society. Furthermore, I can easily imagine an urban or suburban childhood for myself without the fortunate circumstances that I have mentioned, one that would have left me uncomprehendingly blank or hostile in the face of *Culture and Environment* and *Two Cultures?*, whatever touristic enjoyment I might have had from picturesque small communities visited for their holiday sun and food. And I can imagine myself feeling that it was inevitable and natural that rural communities should be swept from end to end by the tides of modernity, and that we were entering an age of new and entirely different human needs. In all of this I would, I judge, have been not only philistine but impractical.

For it is not just the rural that is at issue, of course. To ignore the satisfactions available to rural people, and the cultural and psychological patterns that enable them to have those satisfactions, not only facilitates the subversion and demoralization of rural communities in the fashion analysed so well by Fromm and Maccoby — the entailed denials also make it harder to be sensitive to the comparable urban satisfactions. The features of the Little Community do not all immediately vanish in the city, even though misguided city planners can hasten their vanishing or make their extension harder. In *The Death and Life of Great American Cities* (1961), for example, Jane Jacobs brilliantly shows how the communal satisfactions that I have been talking about can exist in some of the ostensibly least rural areas of cities, often without a patch of grass in sight; and Janet Abu-Lughod very interestingly discusses what she calls 'the continual ruralization of the cities' in Egypt, a process that she sees as occurring in 'many other newly awakening nations as well'.[9] But a prerequisite for the preservation, extension, and reproduction of such areas is the ability to grasp experientially where life *is* — to be able to recognize and take pleasure in a decent stability, a sufficiency of natural meeting points, a human scale, a wholesome, functional diversification of activities, a life-enriching variousness wherever they may be, whether in Tepoztlán, or Greenwich Village, or Venice, or Oxford, or successful *kibbutzim*, or French villages like the one I have described. Otherwise the same supposed realism and unsentimentality that ignores human needs in the country will ignore them in the city too. And there may even be at times a positive welcoming of the destruction of the known and loved, a craving for awfulness *because* it is awful, because it is the really 'real' present. Thus New York is more 'real' than Paris, and other cities increase in reality as they move towards the condition of New York, just as Dostoevsky is more 'true' than Tolstoy as an explorer of the nature and needs of the psyche.

It seems to me more important than ever, therefore, to hold on to the concept of the organic community, and to do so in the conviction that there is nothing sentimental or politically quiescent about being concerned with psychological enrichment and impoverishment, and with the complex testimony of the experiencing psyche, including the testimonies of writers like Lawrence, Jean Giono, George Eliot, Traven, Tolstoy, Gabriel Garcia Márquez, and, of course, Sturt. The structurally healthy community not only satisfies the great majority of the people living in it, but does so because it is a model of a well psyche; the most conscious kinds of persons living in it with relative contentment can feel that there are no parts of it that do not in some measure answer to real needs of their own at various ages and in various frames of mind. But equally a community or parts of a community can be structurally insane and make for madness. The appalling Landsend section of Hubert Selby Jr's *Last Exit to Brooklyn* makes that abundantly clear, as do, more professionally, the demonstrations of the relationships between physical structures and criminality by Oscar Newman in *Defensible Space* (1972) and Jane Jacobs in the seminal work I referred to above. The organic community was not, and is not, a myth, and to the extent that we move away from its psychological structures and patterns, we will have an increase of emptiness, anomie, and violence, because the psyche has been denied satisfactions that it cannot live without.

Notes

Introduction

1 F. Scott Fitzgerald, letter in 1925, quoted by Matthew J. Bruccoli, *Scott and Ernest; the Authority of Failure and the Authority of Success* (N.Y., Random House, 1978), p. 29.

2 Sergio Aragones, *Mad Marginals* (N.Y., Warner, 1974), unpaginated.

3 Walter Kendrick, 'What is this Thing Called Hermeneutics?', *Village Voice Literary Supplement*, no. 18 (7 June 1983), p. 7.

4 Theodore Spencer, 'How to Criticize a Poem (in the Manner of Certain Contemporary Critics)', *New Republic* (6 December 1943); reprinted in Theodore Spencer, *Selected Essays*, ed. Alan C. Purves (New Brunswick, N.J., Rutgers University Press, 1966), pp. 352–5. The article was admirably complemented by Mary McCarthy's 'Settling the Colonel's Hash', *Harper's* (February 1954), reprinted in her *On the Contrary* (N.Y., Farrar, Straus and Cudahy, 1961), pp. 225–41.

5 Jacques Leenhardt, 'Toward a Sociology of Reading', in Susan R. Suleiman and Inge Crosman, eds., *The Reader in the Text: Essays on Audience and Interpretation* (Princeton University Press, 1980), p. 210.

6 Georges Poulet, 'Criticism and the Experience of Interiority', in Richard Macksey and Eugenio Donato, eds., *The Structuralist Controversy: the Languages of Criticism and the Sciences of Man* (Baltimore, Johns Hopkins University Press, 1972), p. 60.

7 Like others of my generation, I was greatly indebted to the criticism of F. R. Leavis, and especially to *The Common Pursuit* and such at that time uncollected essays as '"Thought" and Emotional Quality in Poetry', with their constant pouncing on slack formulations, arbitrary categories, and untenable dichotomies, faults from which I do not suppose the present volume to be free. If post-structuralist criticism, when I finally came to it, did not exactly make me feel like Saul on the road to Damascus, this was largely because of that prior reading. That Leavis was philosophically sophisticated is becoming more recognized these days, particularly since that difficult work *The Living Principle*; and as Glenn W. Most's respectful if ultimately mistaken review-essay on it in *Diacritics* (June 1979) reminds us, he had natural affinities with hermeneutic critics like Heidegger and Gadamer. But he seems to me to have been more complex and more philosophically sophisticated than either of them in his dealings with literature, not only in the much greater range and specificity of the issues that he dealt with, including

the central one of evaluation, but in the subtlety of his procedures. And apropos of rhetorical analyses and the masks of reason, it should be recalled that his 'The Irony of Swift' appeared over half a century ago.

8 Roland Barthes, 'The Two Criticisms', *Critical Essays*, trans. Richard Howard (Evanston, Northwestern University Press, 1972).

9 John Fraser, 'Stretches and Languages: a Contribution to Critical Theory', *College English*, XXXII (1971), p. 398.

10 H. G. Schenk, quoted by Gerald Graff, 'Deconstruction as Dogma, or "Come Back to the Raft Ag'in, Strether Honey!"', *Georgia Review* (Summer 1980), p. 408.

11 'Never explain, never apologize' is no doubt shrewd advice, but a word of caution seems in order here. As a friendly reviewer of *America and the Patterns of Chivalry*, Earl Rovit, noted, the book proceeds dialectically, which seems to have exasperated some of his fellow reviewers beyond measure. Unfortunately, at one point the rhetoric of the book is unintentionally misleading. Not only were seven lines of type mysteriously transposed from near the top of page 27 to the bottom of the previous page. On page 27 it looks as if, having offered a hypothetical and oversimplified indictment of certain things, I go on to provide my own supportive amplification of it. But in fact the hypothetical indictment continues to the end of the chapter.

Prospero's Book: *The Tempest* Revisited (1968)

1 Leo Marx, 'Shakespeare's American Fable', *Massachusetts Review*, II (Autumn 1960), pp. 40–71. Reprinted, with revisions, as the second chapter of his *The Machine in the Garden: Technology and the Pastoral Ideal in America* (N.Y., Oxford University Press, 1964). All but one of my references are to the book.

2 Jan Kott, *Shakespeare Our Contemporary*, trans. Boleslaw Taborski, pref. Peter Brook, 2nd rev. edn (London, Methuen, 1967), p. 240.

3 *Ibid.*, p. 242.

4 *Ibid.*, p. 258.

5 Marx, 'Shakespeare's American Fable', pp. 66–7.

6 Kott, *Shakespeare Our Contemporary*, p. 266.

7 Marx, 'Shakespeare's American Fable', p. 67.

8 Kott, *Shakespeare Our Contemporary*, p. 238.

9 Caliban's contrite remarks near the end, which are made in ignorance of the impending departure of the gentry, appear to be no more than a prudent bowing to *force majeure*. The next well-dressed drifter who turns up on the island with a bagful of books and a pretty daughter will obviously be in for a pretty rough time of it.

10 Derek Traversi, *Shakespeare: The Last Phase* (N.Y., Harcourt Brace, n.d.), p. 200.

11 Derek Traversi, *An Approach to Shakespeare*, 2nd edn, rev. and enl. (Garden City, N.Y., Doubleday (Anchor Books), 1956), p. 215.

12 Kott, *Shakespeare Our Contemporary*, p. 245.
13 Friedrich Nietzsche, *Twilight of the Idols*, in *The Portable Nietzsche*, sel., trans., and introd. Walter Kaufman (N.Y., Viking, 1954), p. 518.
14 Marx, 'Shakespeare's American Fable', pp. 56–7.

Dust and Dreams and *The Great Gatsby* (1965)

1 F. Scott Fitzgerald, *The Great Gatsby* (N.Y., Scribner's, 1925).
2 Arthur Mizener, *F. Scott Fitzgerald* (London, Eyre & Spottiswoode, 1958), p. 177.
3 W. M. Frohock, 'Morals, Manners, and Scott Fitzgerald', *Southwest Review*, XL (Summer 1955), p. 227.
4 Mizener, *F. Scott Fitzgerald*, p. 177.
5 Marius Bewley, *The Eccentric Design* (London, Chatto & Windus, 1959), p. 287.
6 Lionel Trilling, 'F. Scott Fitzgerald', *The Liberal Imagination* (Garden City, N.Y., Doubleday (Anchor Books), 1953), p. 242.

In Defence of Culture: *Huckleberry Finn* (1967)

1 Mark Twain, *Adventures of Huckleberry Finn*, ed. and introd. Henry Nash Smith (Boston, Houghton Mifflin, 1958).
2 Lionel Trilling, *The Liberal Imagination* (Garden City, N.Y., Doubleday (Anchor Books), 1953), p. 108.
3 Leslie A. Fiedler, *An End to Innocence* (Boston, Beacon Press, 1955), p. 146.
4 Leslie A. Fiedler, *Love and Death in the American Novel* (N.Y., Criterion Books, 1960), p. 589.
5 Trilling, *Liberal Imagination*, p. 108.
6 Martin Green, *Re-appraisals: Some Commonsense Readings in American Literature* (London, Hugh-Evelyn, 1963), p. 139.
7 Fiedler, *Love and Death*, p. 589.
8 John Erskine, *The Delight of Great Books* (Indianapolis, Bobbs-Merrill, 1928), p. 264.
9 Carson Gibb, 'The Best Authorities', *College English*, XXII (December 1960), p. 179.
10 Leo Marx, 'Mr Eliot, Mr Trilling, and *Huckleberry Finn*', *American Scholar*, XXII (Autumn 1953), p. 432.
11 Smith, introd. to *Huckleberry Finn*, p. xi
12 Richard Chase, *The American Novel and Its Tradition* (Garden City, N.Y., Doubleday (Anchor Books), 1957), p. 146.
13 James M. Cox, 'Remarks on the Sad Initiation of Huckleberry Finn', *Sewanee Review*, LXII (1954), pp. 396, 405, 401.
14 Sydney J. Krause, 'Twain and Scott: Experience Versus Adventure', *Modern Philology*, LXII (February 1965), pp. 227–36.

15 Tony Tanner, *The Reign of Wonder; Naivety and Reality in American Literature* (Cambridge University Press, 1965), pp. 156, 158, 166.
16 Krause, 'Twain and Scott', p. 230.
17 Kenneth S. Lynn, *Mark Twain and Southwestern Humor* (Boston, Little, Brown, 1959), p. 226.
18 In view of the cursory treatment often accorded them, it seems worth recalling here that the Duke and King occupy over a third of the book. R. W. Stallman may not really be exaggerating wildly when he claims that 'without the Duke and Dauphin, *Huckleberry Finn* isn't worth our attempts to save it' as a great novel ('Huck Finn Again', *College English*, XVIII (May 1957), p. 426).
19 T. S. Eliot, I have since noted with pleasure, remarks in passing of the Duke and King that their 'fancies about themselves are akin to the kind of fancy that Tom Sawyer enjoys' (Introduction to *The Adventures of Huckleberry Finn* (London, Cresset Press, 1950), pp. ix–x).
20 Marx, 'Mr Eliot, Mr Trilling, and *Huckleberry Finn*', p. 432.
21 V. S. Pritchett, '*Huckleberry Finn* and the Cruelty of American Humour', *New Statesman* (8 August 1941), p. 113.
22 Richard P. Adams, 'The Unity and Coherence of *Huckleberry Finn*', *Tulane Studies in English*, VI (1956), p. 96; Smith, introd., p. xv.
23 Alexander Cowie, *The Rise of the American Novel* (N.Y., American Book Co., 1948), p. 614.
24 Henry Nash Smith, *Mark Twain; the Development of a Writer* (Cambridge, Mass., Belknap Press of Harvard University Press, 1962), p. 136.
25 As Mr Fiedler has pointed out, 'having grown up on the edge of civilization, [Huck] has always known, even before his brief indoctrination by Miss Watson, the ethical precepts of her world. No more free-thinker than savage, he not only knows, but, in an abstract way, believes in these codes' (*Love and Death* p. 575).

Othello and Honour (1965)

1 Helen Gardner, 'The Noble Moor', in Ann Ridler, ed. and introd., *Shakespeare Criticism, 1935–1960* (London, Oxford University Press, 1963), pp. 352, 358, 360.
2 *Ibid.*, p. 355
3 *Ibid.*, pp. 354, 362.
4 F. R. Leavis, 'Diabolic Intellect and the Noble Hero', *The Common Pursuit* (London, Chatto & Windus, 1952), p. 147.
5 Gardner, 'The Noble Moor', p. 367.
6 Laurence Lerner, 'The Machiavel and the Moor', *Essays in Criticism*, IX (October 1959), pp. 339–60.
7 Gardner, 'The Noble Moor', p. 351.
8 Leavis, 'Diabolic Intellect and the Noble Hero', p. 150.

The Name of Action: Nelly Dean and *Wuthering Heights* (1965)

1 Emily Brontë, *Wuthering Heights*, ed. and introd. V. S. Pritchett (Boston, Houghton Mifflin, 1956).

2 James-Hafley, 'The Villain in *Wuthering Heights*', *Nineteenth Century Fiction*, XIII (1958), pp. 199–215. See also John K. Mathison, 'Nelly Dean and the Power of *Wuthering Heights*', *Nineteenth Century Fiction* XI (1956), pp. 106–29, on Nelly's limitations.

3 Henry James to H. G. Wells about the governess in *The Turn of the Screw*, 9 December 1898, *Henry James and H. G. Wells*, ed. Leon Edel and Gordon N. Ray (London, Hart-Davis, 1958), p. 56.

4 I will add that I find Alexander E. Jones's commentary on *The Turn of the Screw* and the controversy about it almost wholly convincing ('Point of View in *The Turn of the Screw*', *PMLA*, LXXXIV (1959), 112–22) and that I believe that the governess is sane and truthful, that the ghosts are there, and that they are harmful. The whole notion of the governess's madness, cruelty, and 'shocking obtrusion of the idea of grossness and guilt on ... small helpless creature[s]' (to use the words of the story itself) is merely an amplification of her own references to possibilities that she had been all too painfully aware of herself. And when Oscar Cargill informs us sternly that the governess is in general 'a demonstrable, pathological liar, a pitiful but dangerous person, with an unhinged fancy' ('*The Turn of the Screw* and Alice James', *PMLA*, LXXVIII (June 1963), p. 241), it is plain that far more work would be needed than he has felt obliged to put in to square the postulated intense derangement with the poised and far from self-flattering intelligence of her whole memoir and the intensely analytical wide-awakeness of her revealed mental processes while at Bly.

5 The point about Edgar seems worth making since even so perceptive a critic as Derek Traversi can comment primly, apropos of the dreadful scene that Cathy contrives between Edgar and Heathcliff in the locked room, 'It is no accident that the man who, as a child, had been protected by bull-dogs from the intrusion into the family property of two harmless children calls upon his servants after attempting to retire himself, to eject his hated rival from his house' ('The Brontë Sisters and *Wuthering Heights*', in Boris Ford, ed., *From Dickens to Hardy*, Pelican Guide to English Literature, vol. VI (Harmondsworth, Middlesex, Penguin, 1958)). To which it can be retorted that, though greatly overmatched, Edgar in fact gave Heathcliff a very hard blow on the throat; that he not merely attempted to retire, he did retire – at a walking pace; and that one wonders what Mr Traversi thinks he *should* have done – stayed and let Heathcliff beat him up?

6 Baruch Spinoza, *Ethics*, III, vii, in *Philosophy of Benedict de Spinoza*, trans. R. H. M. Elwes (N.Y., Tudor Publishing Co., n.d.), p. 136.

7 That there may be *some* risk here to Cathy has been indicated, of course, by Doctor Kenneth's advice about the inadvisability of

'crossing' her too much (though it isn't clear how recently before the present crisis he has been giving it). But as Paul Tillich points out in *Love, Power, and Justice* (N.Y., Oxford University Press, 1954, p. 56), 'In every act of justice daring is necessary and risk unavoidable.' Moreover, the fact that a person has been gravely ill nearly four years before and may (though described by the doctor at the time of the present crisis as 'a stout, hearty lass') become so again does not seem to me to entitle her automatically to a perpetual, unlimited imposition of her will on others.

Crime and Forgiveness: *The Red Badge of Courage* in Time of War (1967)

1 Frederic Manning, prefatory note to *The Middle Parts of Fortune: Somme and Ancre, 1916* (London, Peter Davies, 1929).
2 Richard Chase, ed., quoting Charles Child Walcutt (Boston, Houghton Mifflin, 1960), p. xv.
3 William B. Dillingham, 'Insensibility in *The Red Badge of Courage*', *College English*, xxv (December 1963), 194; Mordecai Marcus, 'The Unity of *The Red Badge of Courage*', in Richard Lettis and others, eds., *Stephen Crane's 'The Red Badge of Courage': Text and Criticism* (N.Y., Harcourt Brace, 1960), p. 191.
4 Charles Child Walcutt, *American Literary Naturalism: a Divided Stream* (University of Minnesota Press, 1956), p. 79.
5 See in this connection D. W. Harding's 'The Poetry of Isaac Rosenberg', *Scrutiny*, iii (March 1935), pp. 358–69, with its development of the thesis that 'What most distinguishes ... Rosenberg from other English poets who wrote of the [1914–18] war is the intense significance he saw in the kind of living effort that the war called out, and the way in which his technique enabled him to present both this and the suffering and the waste as inseparable aspects of life in war. Further, there is in his work, without the least touch of coldness, nevertheless a certain impersonality: he tried to feel in the war a significance for life as such, rather than seeing only its convulsion of the human life he knew.' It seems significant that the best poetry to come out of that war was Rosenberg's and the best novel Manning's *The Middle Parts of Fortune*, and that the latter likewise was not a work of 'protest'. An important American equivalent is David Douglas Duncan's superb *This is War! A Photonarrative in Three Parts* (N.Y., Harper, 1951) from the Korean war.
6 Chase, introduction, p. xiv.
7 That the change in Henry would be likely to be a lasting one seems suggested by the striking resemblances between it and what William James describes in *Varieties of Religious Experience* as 'conversion'.
8 Afternote (1966). There are resemblances between what I have talked about in this essay and what seems to me to go on in *The Turn of the Screw*; and the peculiarly *American* nature of the governess's

consciousness and conduct probably helps explain why James's novel has been so much more fascinating for American readers than for British ones.

In one sense, of course, *The Turn of the Screw* is very English indeed in its effortless fitting into the English ghost-story tradition and its almost hypnotically elegant evocation of a hierarchical scheme of things. But if Bly is glamorously the big house, if Miles and Flora are living reminders of all the upper-class pressures working to transform raw children into little ladies and gentlemen, and if the supernatural elements seem peculiarly to invite the conventional religious schematizing indulged in by one or two critics, nevertheless, how the governess herself responds to the situation at Bly is not hierarchically oriented at all. She is as little touched by conventional class feeling as Isabel Archer would have been and, when her trials begin, as little disposed to regret the absence of the traditional helmsman of the estate or to seek help from the traditional local authority on spiritual matters; and she assumes the most awesome spiritual responsibilities without a flicker of a thought – in the face of appalling demonic threats to the souls of her precious charges – about God and the assistance of prayer.

Given the emphasis on the narrowness of her vicarage upbringing and its persistence into her Bly experiences, these omissions are from a realistic point of view inexplicable. From a more poetic one, however, we surely have here yet another of James's brilliant renderings of the kind of nineteenth-century post-Protestant American consciousness that was totally without formal Christian beliefs but still very powerfully influenced by Christian modes of thought and energized by a sense of immense ethical responsibilities. The resemblances here to the problems, consciousness, and conduct of Laura Wing in 'A London Life' (1888) are especially striking, and a major reason for the disparity between *The Turn of the Screw* and its author's avowed intentions was almost certainly that James was working in a region that he had already masterfully explored in the earlier story. I suggest that *The Turn of the Screw* demonstrates a major conflict possible inside such a consciousness and a largely successful resolution of it; and I shall concentrate on the effects on the governess of the strange and crucial encounter she has with Miss Jessel in the schoolroom at the end of chapter 15.

When at the start of that chapter the governess turns away from the church and makes her lonely way back to Bly, she has manifestly come almost to her breaking point, the distance that she has travelled from her initial clarity and certitude being especially sharply revealed in her reflection that if she were now to desert her post no one would blame her. After the encounter, however, her energy and self-assurance are not merely restored, they are much stronger and more purposeful than they have been before. Instead of the mounting and exasperating over-scrupulousness, the inappropriate deviousness, the sheer inability to come to grips with the problems and *act*, we now see in her an almost

jaunty forthrightness and decisiveness that result very quickly in the
sending away of Flora and the saving of Miles. Now, there are various
other striking instances in late-nineteenth and early-twentieth-century
fiction of abrupt and major changes coming about in someone without
any orderly and explored progression from one intellectual position to
another. Isabel Archer's final desperate flight from Caspar Goodwood
in *The Portrait of a Lady* is one, so is Clara Hopgood's decision not to
marry Baruch Cohen in Mark Rutherford's *Clara Hopgood*, so is
Ursula Brangwen's submissive return to Rupert Birkin at the parked car
in *Women in Love* after her flaming rejection of him. The closest
parallel to the change in the governess, however, seems to me to be that
in Henry Fleming after he receives his own 'red badge' from the swung
rifle of the fleeing soldier and rejoins his regiment. In both cases the
increase in self-coherence and the power to act is great; in both the
cause is something that we would normally expect to be harmful; and in
both the change seems to be essentially *right* in a way that testifies to
deep-flowing currents in the psyche that could almost certainly not
have been redirected by ordinary ratiocinative means. Such changes
invite us to consider the nature of those currents.

I suggest that between the first sighting of Miss Jessel at the lakeside
and the schoolroom encounter with her, the governess is being harried
towards breakdown by two irreconcilable attitudes that have a substantial history in the American consciousness and that are being
increasingly vivified for her by the conduct of the children. On the one
hand, an unqualified acknowledgement of the immense power of evil in
the universe is apparent in her whole attitude towards the spectres at
the outset – her immediate intuiting of their diabolical natures, her
unhesitating explications of their malevolent intentions, her unflinching acceptance of the atrociousness of their activities while alive, her
belief in the possibility of total depravity. On the other hand, everything
in the appearance of the children serves to fortify a sense of the possible
immense goodness of human nature when placed – as the children, the
spectres aside, *are* placed at Bly – in near-idyllic conditions where it can
develop without warping by external pressures. Thus the deepest strain
for her is not the threat of the spectres themselves (she is able gallantly
to face Quint down when he invades the house) but the immense disparity between the children's appearance and the actuality that all the
circumstances seem to be demanding that she attribute to them. 'Evil'
for her at the outset of her trials is something hideous, absolute, and, in
a sense, impenetrable; to believe fully in the children's duplicity would
seem to entail putting them irrevocably into the same category as Quint
and Miss Jessel; and this, when she is actually in their company, she
cannot bring herself to do. Hence her impasse. I suggest that what
happens in the schoolroom scene is that her conception of the nature of
evil gets decisively modified and that as a result she can come to terms
with the facts of the children's natures and conduct.

Miss Jessel's impact on her seems to me to be this. Whereas before she has been viewing the spectres merely as malignant and atrocious presences altogether beyond the pale, she is now abruptly confronted with an acutely suffering woman whose loneliness and desperation are no doubt of much the same kind as afflicted her during the later stages of her infatuated and degrading relationship with Quint while she was still alive. And when we enquire how it is that the governess should be assailed by the sensation that it is she herself who is the intruder in this scene, the answer would seem to be that the sufferings and entrapment that have caused her in her turn only a few minutes before to sink down hopelessly on the stairs in exactly the same position as Miss Jessel have brought her also to the point where the difference between them is per- ceptibly only one of degree, not of kind, and where the sheer intensity of the other's sufferings can acquire authority and demand respect. In one sense, of course, there isn't any question of the governess's 'forgiving' the 'terrible, miserable woman' that she drives out of the room with her desperate cry; her situation is more than ever that of another trapped intervener, Nelly Dean, in which what matters primarily is what certain figures are *doing* to others and what steps must be taken to stop them. The new element of dialogue between her and Miss Jessel is striking nevertheless, especially in that climactic point a little later at the lakeside when, as she reports, 'no moment of my monstrous time was perhaps so extraordinary as that in which I consciously threw out to her – with the sense that, pale and ravenous demon as she was, she would catch and understand it – an inarticulate message of gratitude'. I suggest that evil has ceased to be for the governess a grotesque unnatu- ral intrusion into a human existence that might otherwise be almost angelic, and has become instead simply an aspect of purely human conduct characterizable in terms of a spectrum.

Hence, it seems to me, come the greatly increased vigour, directness, and effectiveness with which she now acts towards the children. That Flora may really be, like Quint, thoroughly estranged and unreachable is a fact that she can now confront with something very like equani- mity; the child is no longer for her a slightly unreal illustration of a theory but, instead, a substantial, wily, and exasperating *person* who cannot be 'saved' – not by her, anyway – and must simply be quaran- tined in a practical spirit. More importantly, Miles too has become for her a full and separate individual, and a considerably more complex one than that represented by the image of an incomprehensibly and homogeneously wicked little presence peeping through the eye-holes of a mask of equally homogeneous and scarcely less incomprehensible virtuousness. She has recognized, in other words, that Miles in his wickedness is much closer to Miss Jessel and to herself than she has imagined and that some of the virtues that he displays, far from being simply a mask, are integral parts of his consciousness and are to be cherished precisely *because* of the complex totality of that consciousness; they are the manifestations, that is to say, of deliberate choices made by someone richly aware of other ways in which he could behave if he cared to. The beauty of the relationship between her and Miles during the closing act of the drama is that she has abandoned the somewhat blank ideal roles that she has tried to make the two of them conform to (her giving up of the ambition to be that mere total absence of trouble that her employer egoistically wants her to be is particularly significant) and instead is treating with the boy on equal terms, as one obligated, free, and troubled individual confronting another. It is hardly too much to say, I think, that now for the first time, as Miles himself virtually points out, she is acting towards him with disinterested love. I suggest that this, when coupled with the demonstration that the consciousness of a 'good' person can include complexities of the same order as those to be found in more ostensibly perceptive and glamorous wicked ones, gives her at last an authority for Miles equal to and finally transcending that of Quint, and that hence she is able to save him by enabling him to return voluntarily from his heart-hardening isolation.

If my account is substantially correct, there is no problem about why James chose to include the story with 'The Liar' in the New York edition. In both works the centre of interest is the consciousness of someone endeavouring in the face of appearances, and with errors along the way, to pin down the fact of more or less reprehensible conduct by others and respond to it properly. *The Turn of the Screw* is considerably the more complex of the two, however, and I am inclined to say that those who have been the most thoroughly 'caught' by it are the readers who have made it an occasion to be simple-mindedly self-righteous at the governess's expense.

Rereading Traven's *The Death Ship* (1973)

1 F. R. Leavis, *D. H. Lawrence: Novelist* (London, Chatto & Windus, 1955), p. 14.
2 John Fraser, 'Splendour in Darkness: B. Traven's *The Death Ship*', *Dalhousie Review*, XLIV (Spring 1964), pp. 35–43.
3 Bernard Smith, 'Speaking of Books: B(ashful). Traven', *New York Times Book Review* (22 November 1970), pp. 2, 56–7.
4 Primo Levi, *If This is a Man*, trans. Stuart Woolf (London, New English Library, 1969), p. 17.
5 B. Traven, *The Death Ship; the Story of an American Sailor* (N.Y., Knopf, 1934).
6 *Tales of Grimm and Andersen*, sel. Frederick Jacobi, introd. W. H. Auden (N.Y., Modern Library, 1953), p. 76.
7 F. R. Leavis, *Revaluation* (London, Chatto & Windus, 1936), p. 164.

A Dangerous Book?: *The Story of O* (1966)

1 Northrop Frye, 'Criticism, Visible and Invisible', *College English*, XXVI (October 1964), p. 5.
2 R. P. Blackmur, 'A Good Reminder', *Nation* (14 June 1947), p. 718.
3 Pauline Réage, *Histoire d'O*, préf. Jean Paulhan (Sceaux, J-J. Pauvert, 1954). The text referred to in this essay is *The Story of O*, with an essay by Jean Paulhan ('A Slave's Revolt'), Traveller's Companion Series (Paris, Olympia Press, 1959).
4 *Time* (9 February 1963), p. 30.
5 See especially Louis Perceau's descriptive *Bibliographie du Roman Erotique au XIXe Siècle*, 2 vols. (Paris, Georges Fourdrinier, 1930).
6 In the essay on Richard Henry Dana's *Two Years before the Mast* in *Studies in Classic American Literature*.
7 Afternote. Two years after this article appeared I supplemented it with 'The Erotic and Censorship' in the *Oxford Review* (1968), the arguments of which, *mutatis mutandis*, seem to me still sound.

Yvor Winters: the Perils of Mind (1970)

1 Howard Kaye, 'Yvor Winters: 1900–1968', *New Republic* (2 March 1968), p. 31.
2 Eda Lou Walton, 'Two Poets', *Nation* (17 December 1930), p. 679.
3 *Yvor Winters Reads from His Own Works*, Yale Series of Recorded Poets (Decca).
4 Allen Tate, 'Clarity, Elegance, and Power', *New Republic* (2 March 1953), p. 18.
5 F. R. Leavis, *The Common Pursuit* (London, Chatto & Windus, 1952), p. 285.
6 Afternote. The present essay, which is reprinted virtually unchanged, had its genesis in 1968 when I was asked to review Winters' *Forms of Discovery*. The review appeared in the *Southern Review* (1969) as 'Winters' *Summa*', and doing it also led me to write five essays on Winters and F. R. Leavis, in the following order: 'Leavis and Winters: a Question of Reputation', *Western Humanities Review* (1972), 'Leavis and Winters: Professional Manners', *Cambridge Quarterly* (1970), 'Leavis, Winters, and "Tradition"', *Southern Review* (1971), 'Leavis, Winters, and Poetry', *Southern Review* (Adelaide; 1972), and 'Leavis, Winters, and "Concreteness"', *Far-Western Forum* (1974). The best of them seem to me the second and the fourth. Subsequently (I mention it in the interests of symmetry) I published a review-essay on Garry Watson's *The Leavises, the 'Social', and the Left* in that too-short-lived Canadian journal the *Compass* (1978).

Mr Fry and Evaluation (1967)

1 As in, for instance, the curiously schoolmarmish pronouncement of Mr Lionel Trilling that 'There can be no two opinions about the tone in which Dr Leavis deals with Sir Charles. It is a bad tone, an impermissible tone' ('The Leavis–Snow Controversy', *Beyond Culture* (N.Y., Viking, 1965) p. 150).

2 Paul Smith, 'Criticism and the Curriculum: Part I', *College English*, XXVI (October 1964), p. 29.

3 Northrop Frye, 'Criticism, Visible and Invisible', *College English*, XXVI (October 1964), pp. 3–12.

4 E.g., the assertion that 'Knowledge about things [in contrast to knowledge *of* things] preserves the split between subject and object *which is the first fact in ordinary consciousness.* "I" learn "that"; what I learn is an objective body of facts set over against me and essentially unrelated to me' (italics mine); or the irony of its being Mr Frye who asserts that 'all methods of criticism and teaching are bad if they encourage the persistent separation of student and literary work: all methods are good if they try to overcome it'; or the implications of the seemingly favourable assertion that 'It was natural for an eighteenth-century poet to think of poetic images as reflecting "general ideas of excellence"; it is natural for a twentieth-century critic to think of them as reflecting the same images in other poems'; or the *Through the Looking Glass* effect of Mr Frye's remarking apropos of Leavis that 'an insistence on the "thereness" or separation of critic and literary work forces one [i.e., a critic like Leavis], for all one's concern, to go on playing the same "aesthetic" game' – and later contending, immediately after a defence of his own critical practice, that 'the end of criticism and teaching ... is not an aesthetic but an ethical and participating end'; or the casual impudence – three decades after *Culture and Environment* – of Mr Frye's suggesting as if it were an interesting new idea that schoolteachers ought to be doing something to equip their pupils against 'the assaults of advertising and propaganda'.

5 I must emphasize that I am concerned at this point not with what Mr Frye himself takes literature to be but with the conduct he seems to be desiderating of anyone deciding to study and comment on it. And in this regard there are not two problems of selection but one, if we take Mr Frye's prescriptions at their face value. There is no essential difference between circling a number of pieces of discourse and saying, 'These are literature', and describing further circles inside the main one to indicate degrees of increasing importance. Both operations entail comparisons and contrasts, discrimination, and the implicit assertion, 'If you want to have such and such an experience, you should study this and not that.'

6 Yvor Winters, *The Function of Criticism: Problems and Exercises* (Denver, Alan Swallow, 1957), p. 37.

7 In point of fact, Pound says nothing whatever in that work about 'the

lyrical elegies' of Hardy. He simply talks, in very general terms, about
Hardy's 'poetry' and 'poems'.

8 S. L. Goldberg's masterly 'C. S. Lewis and the Study of English', *Melbourne Critical Review*, v (1962), pp. 119–27, can be recommended at this point.

9 I. A. Richards, *Coleridge on Imagination* (London, Routledge & Kegan Paul, 1934), p. 163; italics mine.

10 Isobel C. Hungerland, *Poetic Discourse* (Berkeley, University of California Press, 1958), p. 43.

11 W. B. Yeats, *Essays and Introductions* (N.Y., Macmillan, 1961), p. 289.

12 The original passage by Finley Peter Dunne is quoted by Jacques Barzun in *Teacher in America*, chapter 11.

13 T. S. Eliot, *The Sacred Wood* (London, Methuen, 1920), p. 11.

14 One agreeable way of getting Mr Frye's ambitions into perspective is to reflect on what the reactions would have been if Mr Frye, following up his theological bent perhaps, had gone into a different discipline and favoured the intellectual world with an *Anatomy of Philosophy*.

15 It is surely high time that somebody pointed out how almost Wittgensteinian a sophistication Leavis in particular has always exhibited about what are and are not valid and profitable moves to make in the handling of language and 'ideas'.

16 Gilbert Ryle's *The Concept of Mind*, for instance, seems to me a far better aid to intelligent talk about literature than most works of literary theory.

17 D. W. Harding reviewing *New Bearings in English Poetry* in *Scrutiny*, 1 (1932), p. 87.

18 Afternote. Three other articles of mine are related to this one, namely 'Evaluation and English Studies', *College English*, xxxv (1973), 'Stretches and Languages: a Contribution to Critical Theory', *College English*, xxxii (1971), pp. 381–98, and 'Modern Poetics: Twentieth-Century American and British', in Alex Preminger and others, eds., *Encyclopedia of Poetry and Poetics* (Princeton University Press, 1965), the latter of which I wrote in 1957 in my second year as a Ph.D. student at the University of Minnesota. Minnesota was a good place to be in those days. It was, I suppose, what might be described as a hotbed of the New Criticism: Allen Tate, Leonard Unger, William Van O'Connor, and Murray Krieger were there (though I never took classes from them), and Robert Penn Warren had left a year or two before I arrived. But it did not *feel* like a hotbed. There was an atmosphere of critical openness, thanks in part to the continuing presence of Joseph Warren Beach; and doing a minor in what was at that time a distinguished Philosophy Department helped some of us become clearer as to our reservations about the Brooks-and-Warren-and-Wimsatt sort of thing, as well as increasing our scepticism about the philosophical gesturings and wisdom-mongerings of persons in English who had done no philosophy. Among the results was the quarterly journal the

Graduate Student of English, which a few of us founded and edited from 1957 to 1960 and which was livelier, brighter, and more ambitious than its title (we intended it half-humorously in contrast to ones like *Howl*) may suggest.

Swift and the Decay of Letters (1956)

1 Afternote. This essay, which was written a good while ago, is published here for the first time, virtually without revisions. It has continued to interest me over the years because of the kinds of connections that I was able to make in it; and I was confirmed in my desire to include it by reading A. C. Elias, Jr's recent learned and ingenious *Swift at Moor Park: Problems in Biography and Criticism* (University of Philadelphia Press, 1982). At this distance from the subject, I shall not put my hand on my heart and swear that the Swift whom I offer with such assurance is in all respects 'the' Swift. But I am quite sure that 'my' Swift is a more credible one than the low-keyed, petty, and academic ironist with whom Mr Elias emerges from his dismantling of the standard account of Swift's attitude to Temple by writers like Irvin Ehrenpreis. 'Whatever his areas of philosophical agreement with the great man', Mr Elias informs us, 'Swift's most cherished function in life was to smile at solemn human pretence, which all too often it was Temple's unhappy fate – despite his best intentions – to embody.' In such a curiously old-fashioned formula, as in the book at large, we lose altogether the Swift of heroic pride and aspiration, the Swift who later so relished feeling near the centre of power during Harley and St John's ministry, and whose subsequent comportment during his lifelong exile in the provinces is one of the most remarkable and poignant episodes in British literary history. To judge from his book, Mr Elias, with his evident and I suspect nowadays representative distaste for Temple's fondness for the heroic, seems unacquainted with the possibility that, as Yeats well knew, to aspire may be in some degree to become; and I am reminded of a colleague's remark apropos of the whole school of ironical academic revisionists, 'They seem to think that reality must always be scandalous' (to which I added, 'Or banal'). But to me, at least, it is obvious that just as it was possible for Temple to aspire to dignity and wisdom as a writer without thereby being hypocritical, so it was possible for Swift to be aware of flaws in Temple but at the same time admire the virtues to which Temple aspired. Mr Elias's Swift, compulsively pulling down Temple and his heroic virtues while going through the motions of praise, seems to me a writer incapable of passion, generosity, and greatness. I prefer the Swift who, in a complex transposition of Renaissance values, would later fight heroically for Ireland and of whom in 'Swift's Epitaph' Yeats wrote:

> Imitate him if you dare,
> World-besotted traveller; he
> Served human liberty.

Theories and Practices: the Hammonds' *The Village Labourer* (1967)

1 J. L. and Barbara Hammond, *The Village Labourer, 1760–1832; a Study in the Government of England before the Reform Bill* (London, Longmans, Green, 1911).

2 The book, of course, demonstrates brilliantly that a concern for precision and an awareness of complexities, especially of people's complex motivations, need not compel the student of society to refrain from making moral judgements.

3 J. L. and Barbara Hammond, *The Town Labourer, 1760–1832; the New Civilization* (1917) and *The Skilled Labourer, 1760–1832* (1919). An excellent placing by a historian of the Hammonds' role in the twentieth-century controversy about the Industrial Revolution and its consequences occurs in chapter 6 of E. P. Thompson's *The Making of the English Working Class* (1963). Thompson's own authoritative account of rural affairs during the period covered in *The Village Labourer* corroborates the Hammonds' in virtually every important respect.

4 In this connection see also the illuminating eleventh and twelfth chapters ('The Mind of the Rich' and 'The Conscience of the Rich') of *The Town Labourer*.

5 This quotation is taken from the Guild Books edition, 2 vols. (London, Longmans, Green, 1948), since it both makes better sense and brings out more clearly for the present-day reader what the authors were getting at. The 1911 edition reads, 'who talked to each other in Virgil and Lucan of liberty and justice, who would have died without a murmur to save a French princess from an hour's pain or shame, who put down the abominations', etc.

6 One of the more interesting developments during the period in which the Hammonds were writing was the growing sense that in certain respects the history of England was not one of the imposition of civilization upon barbarians by invaders and their descendants but, rather, of the imperfect domination of one culture by another and the persistence through the centuries of a genuine village civilization that carried on independently of the activities of the upper class until finally ruined by the enclosures.

7 Afternote. In my remarks about the book's intellectual context there is a curious omission, namely the account of the dispossession of the British peasantry in chapters 26–8 of *Capital*, a work that I did not read until two or three years after this essay appeared. At the end of the fifties I had spent some time trying to familiarize myself with late-nineteenth- and early-twentieth-century discussions of English rural history, but evidently the name of Marx was more or less invisible in them. With its indignation ('the history of this, their appropriation, is written in the annals of mankind in letters of blood and fire'), its precision, and its irony, *Capital* was obviously familiar to the Hammonds, however. And if the irony that I speak of in the previous Afternote is an

4 Jack M. Potter and others, eds., *Peasant Society; a Reader* (Boston, Little, Brown, 1967), p. v.

5 George Sturt, quoted by F. R. Leavis and Denys Thompson, *Culture and Environment; the Training of Critical Awareness* (London, Chatto & Windus, 1933), pp. 71, 90, 70–1.

6 Yvor Winters, *Forms of Discovery* (n.p., Swallow, 1967), p. 220.

7 Robert Redfield, *The Little Communite; Viewpoints for the Study of a Human Whole* (University of Chicago Press, 1955), p. 3.

8 Leavis and Thompson, *Culture and Environment*, pp. 96–7.

9 Janet Abu-Lughod, 'Migrant Adjustment to City Life: the Egyptian Case', in Potter, *Peasant Society*, p. 385. In *The Preindustrial City, Past and Present* (Glencoe, Ill., Free Press, 1960, Gideon Sjoberg suggests that 'An industrial-urban system could, theoretically, be superimposed upon a feudal [i.e., pre-industrial] order without necessarily obliterating the latter; both could function concurrently. France and Italy have displayed this pattern for decades' (p. 337).